The Digital Economy and the European Labour Market

With a focus on the European labour market, this book seeks to understand how digital transformation affects changes in employee-employer relations. These consequences include shifts in job security and job flexibility as well as alternative work arrangements in the digital economy. This phenomenon has both positive and negative implications for employees and employers.

The book presents a theoretical, conceptual and empirical analysis of employment relations in the digital economy, which are manifested, among others, in flexible or non-standard forms of employment, contract work and a radical shift from position-based to skill-based work.

The approach taken in the book provides researchers and students of economics, business and other social sciences with an overview of interdisciplinary theoretical and conceptual perspectives and frameworks on labour market and employment relations. In particular, it presents a comprehensive range of research on flexible forms of employment in the digital economy. The range of issues covered is also tailored to business practitioners who wish to understand the ongoing changes in employment relations and the emergence of new forms of work as a result of digital transformation. It will also be of value to representatives of labour market institutions involved in implementing new forms of work and employer-employee relationships in Industry 4.0.

Maria Urbaniec is an Associate Professor and Head of the Department of Entrepreneurship and Innovation at Cracow University of Economics, Cracow, Poland.

Routledge Studies in Labour Economics

Mediterranean Migration and the Labour Markets
Policies for Growth and Social Development in the Mediterranean Area
Edited by Salvatore Capasso and Eugenia Ferragina

The Digital Transformation of Labor
Automation, the Gig Economy and Welfare
Edited by Anthony Larsson and Robin Teigland

Labour Market Institutions and Productivity
Labour Utilisation in Central and Eastern Europe
Edited by Beata Woźniak-Jęchorek and Michał Pilc

Economic and Social Perspectives on European Migration
Edited by Francesca Fauri, Debora Mantovani, and Donatella Strangio

Foundations of Modern Slavery
Profiles of Unfree and Coerced Labor Through the Ages
Caf Dowlah

Universities and the Labour Market
Graduate Transitions from Education to Employment
Magdalena Jelonek

The Dynamics of Marginalized Youth
Not in Education, Employment, or Training Around the World
Edited by Mark Levels, Christian Brzinsky-Fay, Craig Holmes, Janine Jongbloed and Hirofumi Taki

The Digital Economy and the European Labour Market
Edited by Maria Urbaniec

For a full list of titles in this series, please visit: www.routledge.com/Routledge-Studies-in-Labour-Economics/book-series/RSLE

The Digital Economy and the European Labour Market

Edited by
Maria Urbaniec

Routledge
Taylor & Francis Group
LONDON AND NEW YORK

First published 2023
by Routledge
4 Park Square, Milton Park, Abingdon, Oxon OX14 4RN

and by Routledge
605 Third Avenue, New York, NY 10158

Routledge is an imprint of the Taylor & Francis Group, an informa business

British Library Cataloguing-in-Publication Data
A catalogue record for this book is available from the British Library

Library of Congress Cataloging-in-Publication Data
Names: Urbaniec, Maria (Economist), editor.
Title: The digital economy and the European labour market / edited by Maria Urbaniec.
Description: Abingdon, Oxon ; New York, NY : Routledge, 2023. | Series: Routledge studies in labour economics | Includes bibliographical references and index.
Identifiers: LCCN 2022005276 (print) | LCCN 2022005277 (ebook) | ISBN 9781032184586 (hardback) | ISBN 9781032184616 (paperback) | ISBN 9781003254638 (ebook)
Subjects: LCSH: Labor market—Europe. | Information technology—Economic aspects—Europe. | Employees—Effect of technological innovations on—Europe. | Industrial relations—Europe. | Europe—Economic conditions—21st century.
Classification: LCC HD5764.A6 .D55 2023 (print) | LCC HD5764.A6 (ebook) | DDC 331.12094—dc23/eng/20220207
LC record available at https://lccn.loc.gov/2022005276
LC ebook record available at https://lccn.loc.gov/2022005277

ISBN: 978-1-032-18458-6 (hbk)
ISBN: 978-1-032-18461-6 (pbk)
ISBN: 978-1-003-25463-8 (ebk)

DOI: 10.4324/9781003254638

Typeset in Bembo
by codeMantra

Contents

Figures

Tables

Appendix

Contributors

Víctor F. Climent, PhD, is Associate Professor in the Department of Sociology, University of Alicante (Spain). He is also Deputy Director of the General Foundation of the University of Alicante. He coordinates an ERASMUS+ project on creating research centres in Latin-American Higher Education Institutions in the field of informal work and workers' transition from informal to formal work status. His research interests include methodology for social sciences, sociology of work and labour relations.

Ondřej Dvouletý, PhD, is Associate Professor in the Department of Entrepreneurship, Prague University of Economics and Business (Czechia). He is a member of the scientific and programme committee and editor of the annual Innovation Management, Entrepreneurship and Sustainability (IMES) conference. He is Associate Editor of the *Journal of Small Business Management* and the *Journal of Entrepreneurship in Emerging Economies*. His research interests include entrepreneurial activity, self-employment, public entrepreneurship and entrepreneurial economics.

Michał Głuszak, PhD, is Associate Professor in the Department of Real Estate and Investment Economics, Cracow University of Economics (Poland). He is a member of the Editorial Board of *Entrepreneurial Business and Economics*, and Editor-in-Chief of the *World of Real Estate Journal*. His research interests include urban economics, public economics, real estate economics and green technologies.

Iwona Kubica, PhD, is Teaching and Research Assistant at University College London (UCL) (UK) and the L&D Manager of Women in Tech Club. She has taught, lectured and researched extensively in the UK, Poland, the US, Italy and Switzerland. Her research interests include adaptation to international work environments and relations between technology, society and behaviours.

Joanna Kudełko, PhD, is Associate Professor in the Department of Economic Policy and Development Programming, Cracow University of Economics (Poland). She is the author of many scientific publications and a contractor in national and international research projects. Her research interests include economic policy, social policy, regional economy, European integration, European Union cohesion policy and regional and local development policy.

Agnieszka Małkowska, PhD, is Assistant Professor in the Department of Real Estate and Investment Economics, Cracow University of Economics (Poland). She is the author and co-author of numerous scientific publications, both in Polish and international peer-reviewed journals. Her research interests include public policy, real estate economy, professional ethics and job satisfaction in real estate, and digital economy.

Richard Pettinger, PhD, is Professor of Management Education at the University College London (UCL) (UK). He has written over 50 books and numerous articles on all aspects of management practice and the development of managerial expertise in response to economic, social and technological transformations. He is a regular contributor to conferences as a keynote and expert speaker. His research interests include staff management, employee relations and non-standard patterns of work in relation to the changing economy.

Agnieszka Postepska, PhD, is Assistant Professor in the Department of Economics, Econometrics and Finance, University of Groningen (The Netherlands). She is Research Affiliate at the Institute of Labour Economics and Fellow at Global Labour Organization. She received her PhD in Economics from Georgetown University. Before joining the University of Groningen, she worked at the World Bank as a short-term consultant. Her research interests include labour economics, economics of education, development economics.

Maria Urbaniec, PhD, is Associate Professor and Head of the Department of Entrepreneurship and Innovation, Cracow University of Economics (Poland). She completed her PhD in Economics at the International Graduate School Zittau of the Technische Universität Dresden, Germany. She is author or co-author of over 150 scientific papers in academic journals and monographs. Her research interests include entrepreneurship, innovation, sustainable development, labour market and digital economy.

Dariusz Żmija, PhD, is Associate Professor in the Department of Economic Policy and Development Programming, Cracow University of Economics (Poland). He is an expert in interdisciplinary research networks. He has experience in national and international scientific research projects. His research interests include social and economic policy, regional policy, agricultural policy and rural development, innovations and digital transformation.

Agnieszka Żur, PhD, is Assistant Professor in the Department of Entrepreneurship and Innovation, Cracow University of Economics and the Director of the Executive MBA Programme at the Cracow School of Business (Poland). She is a MOOC developer and the co-author of an award-winning MOOC on Intrapreneurship. She is a member of the Editorial Board of *Social Entrepreneurship Review*. Her research interests include corporate entrepreneurship and social entrepreneurship.

Introduction

Maria Urbaniec

Labour market challenges in the era of digital transformation

Digital transformation is a multi-faceted concept, variously defined both in the literature and in practice. Gong and Ribiere (2021) based on an extensive scientific review and analysis of 134 published definitions developed a unified definition of digital transformation, which differs significantly from other related terms in the literature. They define digital transformation as "A fundamental change process, enabled by the innovative use of digital technologies accompanied by the strategic leverage of key resources and capabilities, aiming to radically improve an entity and redefine its value proposition for its stakeholders" (Gong, & Ribbe, 2021, p. 12). Digital transformation processes are managed at national, regional and sectoral levels through the concept of the digital economy (Ershova, Hohlov & Shaposhnik, 2018).

The development of the digital economy can be seen as the next stage of development of the information society, the network society and the knowledge society. Digital information, which is available in increasing quantities and can be exploited with increasingly sophisticated tools, is an economic resource of great strategic importance. The current trends in on-demand manufacturing and networked industrial capabilities at a global level, which underpin the manufacturing model of smart industry (Industry 4.0), are reinforced and accelerated by the new opportunities. The process by which technological innovations are adopted by companies is complex and long-term, consisting of such interacting factors as economic profit, work organisation and skills management. The relationship between computerisation and jobs is therefore complex and resistant to reductive analysis (Valenduc & Vendramin, 2016).

In general, a variety of different terms are used in the literature to describe digital economic activities. These terms are often used interchangeably without a common understanding of their scope or their relationship to each other. For instance, Industry 4.0 is the name given to the current trend of automation and data exchange in production technologies. It covers cyber-physical systems, the internet of things, cloud computing and cognitive computing

DOI: 10.4324/9781003254638-1

and is commonly referred to as the Fourth Industrial Revolution. According to Schwab & Davis (2018), this concept is helping to blur the distinctions between the physical, digital and biological dimensions. Major technological advances are having a profound impact on economies, businesses and personal lives around the world. Some of the technological drivers of this transformation are related to the development of big data, algorithmic management, 3D printing, quantum computing, intelligent robots, artificial intelligence (AI), the internet of things, nanotechnology, biotechnology, nanotechnology and alternative forms of energy technology. These transformational activities are now referred to as the digitalisation of the economy. They affect many aspects of social life: how labour is exchanged on digital platforms, how consumers become producers (so-called prosumers), how companies revise their decisions about where to produce in the face of robotisation, to name three. While the study of innovation cycles and the transformation of markets has a long tradition, the social sciences are today trying to come to terms with the broader implications of the digitalisation of the economy. The growth of the digital economy also changes approaches to economic development and the future of work, as digitalisation fosters radically new business models, such as two-sided markets using online platforms or goods and services with near-zero marginal production costs (Valenduc & Vendramin, 2016).

As a result of ongoing technological development, socio-economic changes are taking place at the economic, sector and company levels. Digital technologies are reshaping work arrangements in both time and space, reducing barriers of entry to the labour market and lowering transaction costs in the talent acquisition process. The implications of increasing automation and digitalisation have not yet been fully explored. Some studies suggest that nearly half of jobs are at risk of being transformed or disappearing (Frey & Osborne, 2013) and 60% of occupations could be automated with the technologies available today (Chui, Manyika & Miremadi, 2016). On the other hand, the Organisation for Economic Co-operation and Development (OECD) has done careful calculations which find that in 21 OECD countries; on average, only 9% of all jobs can be automated – 6% in Korea and as much as 12% in Austria and Germany (Arntz, Gregory & Zierahn, 2016). Atkinson (2018) argues that the question and concern about the quality of jobs is misplaced because job creation will be based on consumption patterns, and some of these trends will create high-quality jobs, such as in education and service sector, as well as lower-quality jobs in personal services, or 'servant' jobs.

Although studies vary depending on the method used (an occupational or task-based approach) and additional factors considered in the analysis (workplace organisation, investment in technology and education), there is a wide expert consensus on which occupations are most vulnerable to automation (Adams, 2018; Georgieff & Milanez, 2021). They include those that require relatively low skills and focus on routine and repetitive activities. According to forecasts, technological change will have a significant impact on office and administrative work, sales and trading, production and processing, sales assistance and accounting, and call centre work. Significant change will also take place in the automotive, energy and mining industries (Arntz et al., 2016; Kergroach, 2017; Neufeind, O'Reilly, & Ranft, 2018).

Another OECD study looks at what has happened to jobs at risk of automation in 21 countries over the past decade (Georgieff & Milanez, 2021). This study found that all countries have experienced employment growth over the past decade. However, within individual countries, growth was much lower in jobs at high risk of automation (6%) than in jobs at low risk (18%). Low-educated workers are even more concentrated in high-risk occupations now than in 2012. Again, automation risk will increasingly affect low-educated workers in the future, and the COVID-19 crisis may accelerate automation as companies reduce their reliance on human labour and contact between workers or move some production overseas.

Current technological change and digitalisation are also transforming the European Union's economy and labour markets. Almost one third of jobs in the European Union (EU) are described as highly computerised (Eurofound, 2021). Digitalisation processes that affect employment and working conditions and social dialogue are related to automation, robotisation and platforms. Although standard employment (generally full-time and permanent) remains the dominant form of employment throughout the EU, new forms of employment are increasingly appearing on European labour markets (Eurofound, 2021). They involve new formal employment relationships or working patterns related to the workplace, working time and the use of ICTs. New flexible forms of work are related to such concepts as the gig economy, the sharing economy, collaborative economy, on-demand economy and platform economy. These concepts define the modern economy based on the realisation of tasks and projects executed on digital platforms, and not by people engaged in full-time jobs.

Flexible work arrangements are offered by firms to support employees in balancing their work and personal lives as well as to improve the performance of the company itself (Richardson & McKenna, 2014). While there is an extensive literature exploring the antecedents and consequences of flexible work arrangements at the employee and firm level (De Menezes & Kelliher, 2017; Kröll & Nüesch, 2019), less attention has been paid to how to deal with the challenges arising from this increased flexibility. By definition, flexible work arrangements mean that employees work at different times and in different places than may have traditionally been the case, but they perform the same activities and have the same responsibilities and requirements. Unfortunately, there is little understanding of the different aspects of workplace flexibility that would enable a critique-based framework for flexibility research (Bal & Izak, 2021). More research is therefore needed to better understand the dynamic nature of the term workplace flexibility in the business and management literature as well as in practice. Further research should seek to clarify why, when and how flexible forms of employment can be disadvantageous to the employer or employee (Putnam, Myers, & Gailliard, 2014). In general, this phenomenon has both positive and negative implications for employees and employers.

This book contributes to the discussion on the impact of digital economy on the labour market. The main purpose of this book is twofold: (1) to contribute to a better understanding of current trends in employment relations in the digital economy, changing work organisation and introducing new forms of work and (2) to provide a comprehensive overview on various quantitative and qualitative studies in this area. This book presents a theoretical, conceptual and empirical analysis of employment relations in the digital economy, which are manifested, among others, in flexible or non-standard forms of employment, and a radical shift from position-based to skill-based work. The research focuses on challenges for the labour market in the digital economy with a particular emphasis on flexible forms of employment in selected European countries. The following ***research questions*** will be answered:

- what changes in labour market are observed in European Union countries in the digital economy?
- what factors determine the development of flexible employer-employee relations in light of different theoretical paradigms?
- what are the benefits and consequences of flexible forms of employment in the digital economy?

With these research objectives and questions in mind, contributors to this volume, who bring a wide range of international expertise, examine various theoretical and empirical aspects to assess the current challenges that arise from the transformation of work in the digital age.

The structure of the book

Contributions to this book are structured around three parts and 18 chapters. In Part I, contributors examine developments in the labour market in the age of digital transformation from a theoretical and empirical perspective. The volume opens with Maria Urbaniec situating current problems of labour market dualism in the context of the emergence of the digital economy and the related Fourth Industrial Revolution. Her chapter examines the impact of the digital economy on labour market dualism and assesses how technological progress towards a knowledge economy leads to more and better jobs. She emphasises that the transition to the digital economy is a complex process, and that successful adaptation to the digital economy depends on a number of factors, including labour market flexibility and institutional frameworks that provide workers with the upskilling or retraining needed to change jobs. She also explains that workers in the digital economy need to be highly skilled, flexible and adaptable. These characteristics are crucial for successful adaptation and thus for reducing labour market inequalities in the long term.

In Chapter 2, Michal Głuszak highlights that introducing digital technologies into business operations presents various opportunities and challenges. Drawing on a systematic literature review and previous economic and business research, he provides a synthesis of current evidence on the impact of digital transformation on businesses across a range of industries. He also examines how digital transformation is disrupting traditional business models and how innovative business opportunities are affecting the labour market.

In Chapter 3, Joanna Kudełko analyses labour market resources across the countries of the EU from the perspective of how well the countries are adjusting to the challenges of the contemporary labour market. She uses selected statistical indicators, including the structure of employment, level of education, digital skills and their practical applications, and the degree of use of digital technologies in the business sector. Then she analyses the internal differentiation of the EU countries from the perspective of selected analysed variables and presents a synthetic measure for assessing the labour market resources in individual countries, which ultimately allows for them to be ranked. She also examines whether the quality of a country's labour resources affects its economic development.

In Part II, contributors focus on the labour market and employment relations in the digital economy from various theoretical perspectives, considering institutional economics, behavioural economics, innovation theory and agency theory, among others. In Chapter 4, Maria Urbaniec discusses labour market segmentation theory. She analyses how the digital economy affects labour market segmentation and what factors influence the development of flexible employer-employee relations. She indicates that the segmentation of the labour market is treated as an effect of the increasingly widespread use of non-traditional forms of employment and work organisation. This has significantly reduced professional stability, the protection of employee interests and promotion opportunities, among other things. She further stresses that the creation of an inclusive digital economy with quality jobs can be supported by workplace innovation.

In the next chapter, Michał Głuszak analyses labour relations from the perspective of new institutional economics. He reviews the economic literature and analyses the role of implicit institutions in the labour market transformation driven by the digital economy. He identifies the main labour market issues recently addressed by the new institutional economics, such as workplace representation, job security, uncertainty and information asymmetry, bargaining power, strategic behaviour, transaction costs, property rights and organisational arrangements. He also highlights the strengths and limitations of new institutional economics as a tool to explain the hierarchical, interrelated consequences of digital transformation in the labour market.

In Chapter 6, Agnieszka Małkowska examines how behavioural economics responds to the challenges of the digital labour economy. She presents the main assumptions and concepts of behavioural economics and describes the links between behavioural economics, labour economics and the challenges posed by the digital economy. On this basis, she explains how the limiting characteristics of human nature, such as bounded rationality, limited self-interest and limited willpower shape behaviour and relationships in the labour market and in organisations. In particular, she focuses on nudging as a behavioural toolkit and then includes a critical look at the applicability of behavioural economics to labour market transformation.

In Chapter 7, Dariusz Żmija shows how innovations can affect the labour market and employment relations in the digital economy. Based on a literature review, he explains that the approach to innovation has changed in recent years, as well as the ways in which it is created and implemented in companies. He highlights the complex links between the digital economy, innovation and the labour market. Innovation not only destroys but also creates employment in the economy, influences the state and structure of employment, affects the employment relations and contributes to the emergence of new forms of employment.

In Chapter 8, Agnieszka Żur analyses new labour relations in the high-tech sector through the lens of agency theory. Drawing on the assumptions and logic of agency theory, she looks at new labour relations in high-tech industries to understand their contractual nature in the digital economy. To understand potential adjustment and mismatch in agency contracts, she examines two important variables of agency theory-risk and agency control. She then assesses the usefulness of agency theory in explaining contemporary agency problems, discussing its limitations and proposing promising new research directions.

In Chapter 9, Joanna Kudełko analyses the importance of regional resilience in explaining changes in regional labour markets. She shows how regional resilience affects the labour market, especially the size and structure of employment and the forms of employment. She then identifies factors that determine these changes and their positive impact on the labour market, including: modern economic structures, the diversification of regional economic activity, human capital, technological advancement and innovation in enterprises and the availability of financial resources. Finally, she concludes with recommendations for regional policymakers seeking to improve labour markets, and examines the applications and limitations of the concept of regional resilience in explaining changes in the labour market.

Part III outlines flexible forms of employment in the digital economy from an exploratory perspective. It illustrates the diversity of theoretical and practical experiences related to flexible forms of work in selected EU countries. It also identifies the extent of these new forms and underlines the main opportunities and risks associated with each of them. Flexible forms of employment are non-standard forms of employment characterised by: flexibility in terms of the place and time one works, the form of employment relationship, form of employee-employer relationship, remuneration and scope of work. Flexibility is defined as the ability to adapt to new conditions in a dynamically changing market and the ability to adapt to emerging new technological progress.

In Chapter 10, Agnieszka Postepska provides a comprehensive review of non-standard forms of employment in the digital economy in the European Union. Based on the classification used by the International Labour Organization (ILO) and the latest Eurostat data, she presents the use of non-standard forms of employment in the EU countries. She also examines trends in workplace development across the European Union, taking into account the advantages and disadvantages of non-standard employment for both employees and employers.

In Chapter 11, Ondřej Dvouletý and Agnieszka Postepska, based on Eurostat data, show that the proportion of the highly skilled self-employed in EU countries increased significantly between 2011 and 2020. Methodologically, the study uses multiple regression analyses to investigate the determinants of freelancing among European countries. The main results show that freelancing is positively related to the spread of internet users. Freelancing is also to a large extent linked to a country's tax and social security policies.

In Chapter 12, Michał Głuszak and Agnieszka Małkowska analyse the impact of digital technologies on the platform economy and platform work, especially in food delivery and personal transport, as well as in IT services. The authors synthesise available statistical data on platform work in Europe. In order to gain more in-depth insight into the activities of work platforms, they employ a case study approach that considers three categories of work platforms operating in Europe: global, multinational and single-country. They highlight both the benefits of low barriers to entry and the detrimental impact of platform work on skills development and the "trapping" effect for low-skilled and younger workers.

In Chapter 13, Joanna Kudełko and Dariusz Żmija analyse casual work as one of the flexible forms of employment that are gaining popularity in the digital economy. They highlight the benefits and risks associated with this form of employment from the perspective of both employers and employees. Their empirical research is based on the case of a Polish temporary work agency employing casual workers, mainly for German courier companies.

In Chapter 14, Michał Głuszak and Agnieszka Małkowska focus on remote work as a flexible form of work. The concept of remote work is very broad and includes various forms of remote work. The ability to work off-site, anytime and anywhere is undeniably related to the digital economy and the opportunities created by technological progress. The study was based on a survey of managers of medium-sized companies in Poland. The authors identified pandemic benefits and challenges associated with remote working. Despite these unusual conditions, the evaluation of the benefits is positive, and possible barriers and challenges do not seem to be a significant problem. The authors emphasise that remote working offers a number of benefits for both employers and employees.

In Chapter 15, Joanna Kudełko and Dariusz Żmija analyse another flexible form of employment: job sharing, or the sharing a full-time job between several people working part-time and taking mutual responsibility for the implementation of tasks associated with this position. On the basis of a literature review they present the importance of job sharing and then the results of their own research, which show that job sharing is the form of employment least frequently offered by surveyed employers in Poland. In contrast to European countries, in Poland job sharing is offered primarily by companies from the private sector.

In Chapter 16, Maria Urbaniec focuses on the use of interim management for temporary employment of highly qualified and experienced top managers. She stresses that interim management may be in various companies strategically more beneficial and financially more profitable than using other flexible forms of employment. This chapter presents the results of a qualitative study conducted among interim managers in Poland and identifies the impact of technological advances on the activities of interim managers. It also shows that the employment of an interim manager most often results from a company's need to meet specific goals that it is unable to achieve on its own. Creating such positions brings measurable benefits as well as some risks.

In Chapter 17, Iwona Kubica and Richard Pettinger evaluate various non-standard zero-hour work patterns, such as gig economies, portfolio occupations and careers, flexible attendance hours and patterns, and performance payments while working in remote locations. The authors highlight the effectiveness of labour relations, as well as the organisational identity and practices of British workers both from a positive and negative point of view. They then present the employee engagement issues that are required to make these work models sustainable, workable and valuable to all concerned.

In the last chapter, Víctor F. Climent presents an empirical approach to the impact of blockages introduced during the COVID-19 pandemic in Spain on digital workers. His research focuses not only on quantifying the actual movement of workers to teleworking environments but also on identifying structural inequalities and linking them to different profiles of digital workers. These findings are interpreted as the result of historical imbalances in industry and the social structure, confirming that the emergence of teleworking environments in Spain is conditioned and slowed down by industrial typology and social structure. He also points out that the profiles of digital workers are closely correlated with the weak demand for digital environments and teleworking and the low development of digital culture management.

To conclude, the book systematises the current state of the art and identifies, describes and analyses new phenomena, relationships and regularities in the field of alternative forms of work from a contemporary perspective. This can be used to support the optimal exploitation of the opportunities that the digital economy generates for individuals, organisations, sectors (industries) and markets. The current changes on the labour market take place against the background of much broader processes and phenomena, including globalisation and the transformation and integration of economies. Without looking at this wider context accompanying the organisation of work, it is impossible to consider changes in current industrial relations.

The approach taken in the book provides researchers and students of economics, business and other social sciences with an overview of interdisciplinary theoretical and conceptual perspectives and frameworks on labour market and employment relations. In particular, it presents a comprehensive range of research on flexible forms of employment in the digital economy. The range of issues covered is also tailored to business practitioners who wish to understand the ongoing changes in employment relations and the emergence of new forms of work as a result of digital transformation. It can also be of value to representatives of labour market institutions involved in implementing new forms of work and employer-employee relationships. This publication does not exhaust all the issues related to the increased flexibility of the labour market and the emergence of alternative forms of work. Nevertheless, I hope it inspires further research and discussion among both theoreticians and business practitioners.

Note

The monograph is part of a project financed by the Ministry of Education and Science within the "Regional Initiative of Excellence" Programme for 2019–2022. Project no.: 021/RID/2018/19. Total financing: 11,897,131.40 PLN.

References

Adams, A. (2018). Technology and the labour market: The assessment. *Oxford Review of Economic Policy, 34*(3), 349–361. doi:10.1093/oxrep/gry010

Arntz, M., Gregory, T., & Zierahn, U. (2016). *The risk of automation for jobs in OECD countries: A comparative analysis* (Vol. 189). Paris: OECD.

Atkinson, R.D. (2018). Shaping structural change in an era of new technology. In M. Neufeind, J. O'Reilly, & F. Ranft (Eds.), *Work in the digital age* (Vol. 103, pp. 275–284). London: Rowman & Littlefield International.

Bal, P.M., & Izak, M. (2021). Paradigms of flexibility: A systematic review of research on workplace flexibility. *European Management Review, 18*(1), 37–50. https://doi.org/10.1111/emre.12423

Chui, M., Manyika, J., & Miremadi, M. (2016). Where machines could replace humans-and where they can't (yet). *McKinsey Quarterly, July.*

De Menezes, L.M., & Kelliher, C. (2017). Flexible working, individual performance, and employee attitudes: Comparing formal and informal arrangements. *Human Resource Management, 56*(6), 1051–1070.

Ershova, T.V., Hohlov, Y.E., & Shaposhnik, S.B. (2018). Methodology for digital economy development assessment as a tool for managing the digital transformation processes. *2018 Eleventh International Conference "Management of large-scale system development" (MLSD*, 2018, pp. 1–3). doi:10.1109/MLSD.2018.8551846.

Eurofound. (2021). *The digital age: Implications of automation, digitisation and platforms for work and employment*. Luxembourg: Publications Office of the European Union.

Frey, C.B., & Osborne, M. (2013). *The future of employment*. Oxford: Oxford Martin Programme on Technology and Employment, University of Oxford.

Georgieff, A., & Milanez, A. (2021). *What happened to jobs at high risk of automation?* Paris: OECD Publishing.

Gong, C., & Ribiere, V. (2021). Developing a unified definition of digital transformation. *Technovation, 102*, 102217. doi:10.1016/j.technovation.2020.102217

Kergroach, S. (2017). Industry 4.0: New challenges and opportunities for the labour market. *Foresight and Sti Governance, 11*(4), 6–8. doi:10.17323/2500-2597.2017.4.6.8

Kröll, C., & Nüesch, S. (2019). The effects of flexible work practices on employee attitudes: Evidence from a large-scale panel study in Germany. *The International Journal of Human Resource Management, 30*(9), 1505–1525.

Neufeind, M., O'Reilly, J., & Ranft, F. (Eds.). (2018). *Work in the digital age: Challenges of the fourth industrial revolution*. London: Rowman & Littlefield International Ltd.

Putnam, L.L., Myers, K.K., & Gailliard, B.M. (2014). Examining the tensions in workplace flexibility and exploring options for new directions. *Human Relations, 67*(4), 413–440.

Richardson, J., & McKenna, S. (2014). Reordering spatial and social relations: A case study of professional and managerial flexworkers. *British Journal of Management, 25*(4), 724–736.

Schwab, K., & Davis, N. (2018). *Shaping the future of the fourth industrial revolution*. Geneva: World Economic Forum.

Valenduc, G., & Vendramin, P. (2016). *Work in the digital economy: Sorting the old from the new*. Available at: https://www.etui.org/Publications2/Working-Papers/Work-in-the-digital-economy-sorting-the-old-from-the-new (accessed 4 September 2021).

Part I

The labour market in the digital economy

1 Labour market dualism in the digital economy

Maria Urbaniec

Introduction

The European labour market is undergoing a profound transformation, caused by the processes of globalisation and deindustrialisation, and the development of both a service-based and a knowledge-based economy (Imdorf, Helbling, & Inui, 2017; Morel, 2015). One of the current challenges for the labour market and for companies and institutions in almost every business sector is digital transformation (Matt, Hess, & Benlian, 2015). It has given rise to new concepts including the gig economy, sharing economy, collaborative economy, on-demand economy and platform economy (Laß & Wooden, 2020). The current integration of markets, both in economic, social and cultural terms, is changing the shape of the labour market. Employment uncertainty and the popularisation of "flexible" forms of employment cause growing insecurity among some social groups in the labour market. Improving the quality of the workforce is becoming a necessity to ensure elementary, potential accessibility to the labour market in the era of digital transformation (Eltamimi, 2020).

The digital economy also has implications for labour market dualism and job polarisation, leading to a new form of class division and a widening gap between winners and losers in the knowledge-based economy. The literature on labour market polarisation points to the rise of low-paying, so-called unskilled or unproductive occupations. These are interpersonal, face-to-face jobs whose growth is partly linked to intermediary platforms, in areas such as logistics (e.g. Amazon, Deliveroo), transport (e.g. Uber), restaurant, hospitality (e.g. Booking.com, TripAdvisor), domestic help and personal services (e.g. Yoopala, TaskRabbit). These jobs are associated with low pay, bogus self-employment, short-term contracts, part-time work and poor social protection (Palier, 2019).

The economic literature on labour market polarisation does not dispute that these are bad jobs because they are considered low-productivity jobs occupied by low-skilled individuals. One indication of low-productivity jobs is that they are low-paying. Growing disparities in income and job quality are evident in knowledge-based occupations emerging in the digital economy.

DOI: 10.4324/9781003254638-3

The proliferation of digital platforms is leading to new types of both high- and low-quality jobs and business opportunities. There are many positive and pessimistic scenarios about the increasingly fragmented, digital and flexible transformation of work around the world. As expected, this transformation will accelerate economic growth, raise productivity levels and create a new vision of inclusion for all in the digital economy.

In the era of increasing digitalisation, the concept of labour market dualism needs to be redefined in terms of labour market flexibility to reduce the uncertainty of workers' employment in primary or secondary markets. Current development trends are forcing organisations to change strategy. Today's hyperdynamic environment requires openness to innovations and flexibility on the labour market. This is demonstrated by the global Deloitte Human Capital Trends study, carried out with a sample of over 3 600 executives from 96 countries (Deloitte, 2021). Organisations need a new approach to workforce development that recognises both the dynamic nature of work and the equally dynamic potential of employees to reinvent themselves. COVID-19 taught organisations that employees are even more important to thrive amidst constant disruption than they may have previously thought. The literature on labour market changes as a result of digital economy is growing rapidly, but there remain more questions than answers about what we are observing.

The aim of this chapter is to examine the impact of the digital economy on labour market dualism and to assess how technological progress toward a knowledge-based economy leads to more and better jobs. The chapter attempts to answer the question: what determines labour market development in the era of digital transformation? Therefore, the importance of the digital economy for the labour market is first presented, followed by the main assumptions of labour market dualism. The concept of labour market flexibility in meeting the challenges of digital transformation is then described. The final chapter contains the main conclusions and potential directions for future research.

The digital economy and digital labour

The digital economy is a complex concept. Early definitions (Lane, 1999; Tapscott, 1996) focus specifically on the internet, reflecting its emergence as a mainstream technology in the 1990s. The term was popularised at the turn of the millennium with the spread of the Internet. Later definitions have tacked on new technologies including mobile and sensor networks, as well as cloud computing and big data, or, more generally, digital technologies. Tapscott (1996), for example, argued that the digital economy involved two generations of economic activity. The first was informational and consisted of basic tasks such as posting static information on websites, but the second related to communication, reflecting the more interactive activities enabled by the Internet.

Another definition, from the German Federal Ministry for Economic Affairs and Energy (2014), describes the digital economy within the German industrial classification system "Wirtschaftszweig" (WZ), consisting of both the traditional information and communication technologies (ICTs) sector and the internet economy. According to the House of Commons (2016), digital economy refers to both the digital access of goods and services, and the use of digital technology to help businesses. Bukht and Heeks (2017) define the digital economy as the part of economic production derived exclusively or primarily from digital technologies with a business model based on digital goods or services. This definition has fuzzy boundaries but is also flexible enough to accommodate innovations in digital technologies and digital business models over time. It covers the core digital sector as well as a wider range of extensive digital activities, without claiming that all digital activity is part of the digital economy.

One of the challenges with these recent definitions is the wide range of economic activities associated with digital technology. This has led some to follow the example of Kling and Lamb (1999), who divided the field into smaller parts. For example, "doing something digital" can be distinguished from actually "being digital": simply using digital technologies vs. putting them at the centre of all business processes (Asen & Blechschmidt, 2016; Bahl, 2016). As with previous definitions, however, the dividing line remains subjective.

A more precise description of the digital economy has been provided by the OECD (2020), which looked at a number of definitions and came up with a general, binding definition of the digital economy: "all economic activity reliant on, or significantly enhanced by the use of digital inputs, including digital technologies, digital infrastructure, digital services and data. It refers to all producers and consumers, including government, that are utilising these digital inputs in their economic activities" (OECD, 2020, p. 5). These definitions show that the digital sector (IT/ICT) is the core of the digital economy, but the scope of the digital economy is considered to extend beyond this to include a set of emerging digital business models. These models have found widespread economic and social application over the past decade. New business models (e-business, e-commerce, e-banking, etc.) are primarily Internet-based, radically changing their effectiveness in reducing costs, including transaction costs, based on business-to-business, business-to-customer, business-employee, etc. (Turcan, Gribincea, & Birca, 2014).

International organisations including the OECD and the EU are undertaking various digital economy initiatives. The OECD (2014) publishes a wide range of reports, including "Digital Economy Papers" and "Digital Economy Outlooks" and the report "Measuring the digital economy," which includes a comprehensive set of indicators for cross-country comparisons. These reports include indicators primarily on infrastructure, societal adoption and investment in ICTs. However, research on ICT adoption began decades ago, with efforts to measure the "digital divide" within and between nations (Czaja & Urbaniec, 2019; Mueller et al., 2017; Selwyn, 2004).

At the EU level, efforts are focused on measuring the broader digital economy through the Digital Economy and Society Index (DESI). Meanwhile, the European Commission has been monitoring the EU's level of digital advancement since 2014. The annual analysis of Eurostat data allows the identification of priority areas of the digital economy in the Member States that require specific actions and investments. DESI includes 34 indicators relating to five main categories: Connectivity; Human capital; Use of online services; Digital inclusion; and Digital public services (Małkowska, Urbaniec, & Kosała, 2021).

The digital economy is an emerging research area that supports rapid economic development, raises living standards and business stability, promotes efficient use of resources and strengthens environmental protection. This means that it supports the sustainable development of the economy and society (Song, Zheng, & Wang, 2021). The digital economy also demonstrates a developmental advantage that has contributed to reducing the risk of supply chain disruption and has shown great resilience by developing during the pandemic (Chase, 2019; Turcan et al., 2014). Measuring the digital economy faces challenges of blurred boundaries, poor data quality, valuation issues and the invisibility of different digital activities. Given the many caveats, the overall measures reveal significant inequalities: the global North has had a significant share of the digital economy to date, but growth rates are fastest in the global South (Bukht & Heeks, 2017).

Overall, the digital economy is characterised by four specific features: the irrelevance of geography, the key role of platforms, the importance of network effects and the use of big data. These features distinguish it from the traditional economy, in particular due to the value chain transformations related to it (Valenduc & Vendramin, 2016). Bukht and Heeks (2017) indicate that the digital economy is (1) unevenly distributed, (2) growing faster than the overall economy, especially in the Global South and (3) a major contributor to employment growth.

The digital economy is represented at three levels: (1) markets and industries, (2) information platforms and technologies, and (3) the environment for its development. Therefore, the ongoing development of the digital economy significantly affects the labour market, which adapts to the changing needs of society. Numerous studies show that a significant number of professions we know today will be rendered obsolete by the latest generation of robots and their new ability to perform tasks such as printing 3D objects, translating documents, drafting insurance policies, caring for the elderly in their homes, to name just a few. The term 'work' itself may also become obsolete and be replaced by an ever-changing portfolio of tasks and projects delivered through online platforms, including the "uberisation" of work (Valenduc & Vendramin, 2016). Trends reinforced by the digital economy include the emergence of a wide range of flexible and non-standard forms of work, as digital technologies will continue to facilitate and accelerate flexible working arrangements.

A concept that has arisen in the context of the digital economy is that of digital labour. The term 'digital labour' has defined a theoretical proposition that draws on the Marxist tradition to critique the emerging digital economy (Dyer-Witheford, 2010; Fuchs, 2014; Fuchs & Sevignani, 2013). From this perspective, digital labour refers to the unpaid work that web users do through their activity, which contributes to the profits of online businesses and which should be rewarded accordingly.

Over time, the term 'digital labour' has been linked to a much broader set of phenomena that relate to the relationships between work and digital technology. Forms of digital labour can include unpaid online user activity on social media platforms (Gandini, 2020; Postigo, 2016), datafication processes and profiling for advertising purposes (Manzerolle, 2010) and emerging forms of paid on-demand labour mediated (or enabled) by a digital platform, also known as "platform work" (Van Doorn, 2017) or the "gig economy" (Woodcock & Graham, 2019). Although digital labour is associated with a form of digital work, the phrase has grown into a generic umbrella term. The term 'digital labour' points to a new stage in the evolution of the relationship between labour and digital technology, in which the two concepts – digital and labour – are becoming increasingly inseparable. The development of digitisation has an impact on the dual labour market.

Labour market dualism

The dual labour market concept is a theoretical construct that distinguishes between two significantly different areas of the labour market – the primary and secondary markets (Wachter, Gordon, Piore, & Hall, 1974). The dual labour market and the related concepts of primary and secondary labour markets were first introduced by the American institutional economist, M.J. Piore in 1969 (Piore, 1969), and later clarified in a joint study with P.B. Doeringer (Doeringer & Piore, 1971, 1975). The basic hypothesis of the dual labour market is that the labour market is divided into two parts, characterised by different and recognisable features, and in which workers and employers operate according to different rules of conduct. The labour market is not homogeneous; on the contrary, it is a collection of different submarkets, each with different structure and characteristics. These markets are segmented by a distinct system of rules, job behaviour requirements and different skills. This concept further distinguishes between so-called "good" jobs, assigned to the primary sector (core) of the economy, and "bad" jobs, associated with the secondary sector (Eurofound, 2021; Lommerud, Sandvik, & Straume, 2004).

The primary segment offers jobs in large companies, which are largely subject to union supervision and influence. Employment and remuneration mechanisms are determined by the legal system. Employees in this sector are protected from employer arbitrariness, have high job security, promotion prospects, incentives and opportunities to expand their professional knowledge and stable working conditions (Cruz Gómez et al., 2019). Jobs offered in this sector are sought after by the general workforce, are better-paid and enjoy higher social prestige. Employees in the primary market strongly identify with their workplace, trade unions and profession. This is a result of both relatively high wages and the expenditures they make on acquiring appropriate professional qualifications. Employers are also interested in the stability of employment, as they incur certain costs on employee training. Moreover, employers are interested in creating certain attitudes of employees, expected from the point of view of company image. Access to jobs in the primary market is restricted by strict hiring criteria, and a defined path of career advancement through the evaluation and dismissal procedure. Entry into the primary labour market occurs on a strict selection basis to avoid hiring individuals who are unable to properly perform their jobs in a manner considered appropriate.

Jobs in the secondary market are not very attractive (Eichhorst & Kendzia, 2016). The salaries offered in this segment are relatively low, working conditions are modest or even poor, there are no opportunities to upgrade qualifications, little chance for career advancement and high employment instability (Garz, 2013). The secondary labour market is defined as the market for lower-skilled, lower-wage workers in which employers can operate an "open-air" business (Morgan, 1997). Such jobs require little capital investment in the form of training and education (usually short-term job training). Workers are at risk of being laid off depending on fluctuations in the business cycle, following the "hire and fire" principle. This type of workforce provides a "buffer" that allows the organisation to increase production during good economic times and decrease it during downturns. At the same time, the operational core and core workforce remain within the business organisation and do not fluctuate.

With the existence of these two distinct categories of employees, the organisation exhibits greater control over its internal and external environment than would be possible without them. The existence of a "primary workforce" in a business increases the predictability of the organisation's internal operations. In turn, the existence of a secondary, "subordinate" workforce facilitates overall adaptability. This measure of control leads to a differentiated system of status and privilege within the organisation, parallel to and sustaining broader social divisions outside the organisation. This means that the poorest segments of society, from which the secondary labour force is drawn, are most affected by rapid cyclical fluctuations (Epicoco, 2020), especially certain specific groups such as women, ethnic minorities, the disabled and some young people (especially the poorly educated). They all represent a large part of the labour market. In addition, there are various forms of under-utilisation of workers' potential in the secondary market. This occurs in the absence of representation of workers' interests. The unattractiveness of jobs results in high employee turnover. That part of the workforce that has less bargaining power and little chance of entering the primary market ends up in the secondary labour market. This includes immigrants, minorities, young people, some women and other groups labelled as "disadvantaged" or "discriminated against." They are usually employed under worse conditions.

Each market, both primary and secondary, is further segmented. Both markets are divided into different segments based on divisions within occupational groups, industries and unions. Many of these divisions are highly arbitrary, as they are conditioned by institutional and legal barriers that allow only those with proven skills or formal qualifications to enter the market (Boeri, 2011). In the dual labour market concept (Esteban-Pretel & Kitao, 2021), one of the barriers to entry is also the "selective" behaviour of employers who are guided in the selection and evaluation of workers by non-substantive characteristics of candidates such as gender, age, nationality, race. This makes it difficult for some categories of the workforce to enter the primary labour market because they are unable to prove their suitability. If they do enter it, it is only in the lower, "underprivileged" areas of the segment. Adapted only to a short period of employment, secondary sector workers often become unstable workers against their will and expectations. Secondary sector workers' unstable attitudes toward their occupation also result from a lack of motivation and productivity, largely due to a lack of career advancement opportunities and low income. Over time, they lose the willingness and ability to acquire new skills and thus the ability to adapt to changing labour market conditions. On the employees' side, it is often the inability or unwillingness to adopt desired work attitudes, while on the employers' side it is a tendency to cut recruitment costs, to use strategies that eliminate activities for which demand is unstable, and thus reduce stable employment.

These different types of work come under control. With the increasing sophistication of bureaucratic and computerised control, many primary labour market workers are increasingly subject to the strict scrutiny that originally served the detailed supervision of secondary market workers. Managers and many clerical workers are increasingly constrained by strict job descriptions, management by objectives and performance appraisals, making them merely subordinate functionaries in a broader system of tasks (Morgan, 1997, 2011).

The fundamental principle of any segmentation, from the perspective of organisational effectiveness, is the principle of control (Kalleberg, 2000; Rubbers, 2020). To increase the predictability of internal operations, organisations have been increasingly careful to define precisely the characteristics of different types of work and the qualifications needed to perform them, creating different patterns of work for different segments of the population. The actions of occupational groups (especially in the liberal professions) and unions, as well as management policies, have contributed in varying degrees to the causes that divide the labour market into submarkets. Different occupational groups argue their interests by emphasising distinctiveness and exposing what makes them different from others. Working through various lobbies and trade unions, professional groups create artificial barriers to access to different types of work and create patterns of hierarchy within which they rank their members in order of importance (Blanchflower, Bryson, & Green, 2021). Beginning in the 1930s, corporations allowed trade unions and professional groups to influence the definition of occupations (Yamaguchi, 2018), their classification and the determination of the set of qualifications appropriate to them.

Contemporary organisations have standardised work, making specialised qualifications unnecessary. This plays an important role in the creation and perpetuation of "secondary" occupations. Unfortunately, such actions often sanction inequality and even institutionalise discrimination. By creating and reinforcing a labour market system, they reinforce a power structure that favours individuals with certain characteristics and disadvantages others. By developing and applying different patterns of control to workers in different market sectors, organisations create patterns of advantage and privilege that symbolise and simultaneously reinforce underlying socioeconomic divisions.

Dual labour market theory enables the analysis of a wide range of issues. Some examples include barriers to meeting structural labour demand by women and adolescents, the availability of unstable and low-productivity jobs in developed economies, the employment of immigrants in jobs that are unattractive to local workers, barriers to the promotion of unattractive jobs by market mechanisms such as wage increases and the acceptance of unattractive jobs by vulnerable groups (Klimczuk & Klimczuk-Kochańska, 2016; Kogan, 2007). Labour markets differ in terms of the availability of jobs for jobseekers, the remuneration received and offered, the level of job stability and professional development opportunities. Furthermore, the dual labour market theory is one of the key factors behind the gender pay gap. Gender inequality and stereotypes lead to the employment of men and women in different segments of the labour market and to occupational segregation on the basis of gender (Yamaguchi, 2018). These differences result in an overrepresentation of women in low-paid and low-status occupations.

To conclude, there are several reasons for labour market dualism and barriers to mobility between the market's segments (Doeringer & Piore, 1971; Klimczuk & Klimczuk-Kochańska, 2016). One is that the dualism is fostered by enterprises strategising to maximise profits with little scope for mobility between segments. Another reason may be that working in a particular sector provides individuals with histories, attitudes, levels of aspiration, expectations and occupational orientations that distinguish them from workers in other markets. In addition, there are various forms of labour supply, such as flexible working arrangements and part-time work, which can sustain employment in secondary labour markets by prioritising childcare, education or other non-work activities. Labour market dualism is subject to changes resulting from the ongoing digital transformation.

Adaptation to digital transformation through labour market flexibility

In order to meet the challenges of the digital economy and fully exploit the potential of human capital in the dual labour market, labour market flexibility will play an important role. While there are several taxonomies of labour market flexibility, they all address three interrelated issues. First, macroeconomic flexibility, which concerns the response of a country's overall wage level to an increase in unemployment. This was one of the first aspects of labour market flexibility to be studied when unemployment rates began to rise. Second, there is mobility, understood as the movement of workers between occupations, industries and geographical regions. The argument here is that mobility alleviates structural economic adjustment problems. Third, there is flexibility of firms that includes many dimensions: (1) wage flexibility, (2) the absence of hiring and firing rules, (3) the variability of working hours and their distribution over the week and year, (4) the definition of work rules and (5) the mobility of workers between different tasks within the firm – in short, every aspect of a firm's access to and use of labour (Teague & Grahl, 1998).

Flexibility can be considered from a number of perspectives. Some authors have analysed it as a form of employment strategy (Atkinson, 1984; Hunter, McGregor, Maclnnes, & Sproull, 1993). Others have examined the social consequences and impact on employees (Heery & Salmon, 2000) or the relationship between a firm's resources and capabilities (as inputs) and innovation (as outputs) (Storey et al., 2002). In contrast, Raghuram, London and Larsen (2001) reflect on the cultural issue and point out that differences between national flexible working practices in European countries can be attributed to cultural differences.

Flexibility defined in terms of the level of analysis (employee, organisation or contract) can be considered a feature of work or employment, such as flexibility at work, flexible employment or a flexible career (Bal & Izak, 2021; Davidescu, Apostu, Paul, & Casuneanu, 2020). As the term flexibility is found across disciplines, there are potentially conflicting or incompatible views about what flexibility means for individuals, organisations and society. Flexibility can be analysed from two perspectives: employee flexibility and flexibility for the employee. Employee flexibility refers to the individual's flexibility in having options for adaptive actions, thus making them instrumental for the organisation. In contrast, flexibility for employees can provide flexibility to organisations, as flexible employees can provide organisations with a competitive advantage.

Flexible employment brings both benefits and challenges for employees and organisations. Flexible employment is often seen as beneficial because companies need to respond more quickly to changing consumer needs in order to meet competitive challenges. Flexible employment enables companies not only to adapt more easily to consumers by increasing or decreasing the size of their workforce, but also to adapt the skills of their employees.

In addition, the increasing specialisation of firms reduces their ability to maintain a constant level of employment productively. They therefore move workers from activities where demand is declining (Lee, 1996). Flexible employment allows greater adaptability to meet changing circumstances.

One of the effects of change in the digital economy era is the diffusion of flexible forms of employment and non-standard employment contracts (Degryse, 2016). With increasing authentication and robotisation in manufacturing, jobs will fragment to support global and digital production. Also, emerging jobs created by digital transformation may influence the popularisation of non-standard forms of employment such as part-time, temporary, on-call, etc. instead of standard full-time employment models. Jobs in the future may become more fragmented, meaning that a worker will have to work in more than one job to compensate for the income from his or her regular job. The flexibility of work will therefore concern the forms of employment, the nature of the tasks performed and when and where they are performed.

The development of the digital economy enables the emergence of new occupations and forms of employment. One trend that has been observed concerns flexible or non-standard forms of employment, which are also referred to in the literature as non-traditional employment relationships, flexible working practices, alternative forms of work or atypical forms of employment (Giesecke, 2009; Green & Livanos, 2015). The development of flexible forms of employment was also favoured by political and social factors, which contributed to changes in labour law or unemployment benefits, and led to an increase in professional activity (Hipp & Anderson, 2015). It is worth adding that flexible forms of employment are also addressed by the European Union's policy on flexicurity, which seeks to increase the flexibility of employment on the labour market while maintaining social security (European Commission, 2007). Stability on the labour market is understood as job security, but this does not guarantee one a permanent job. In order to provide such security, it is important to equip the population with the skills to find new employment.

The growing development of flexible forms of employment create new opportunities and are sometimes convenient; however, they can also result in high employee turnover and the fragmentation of work (larger jobs are divided into micro-tasks), changing work conditions and rendering social security insufficient (Kelliher & Anderson, 2010; Putnam, Myers, & Gailliard, 2014). The increasing role of flexible forms of work is challenging the traditional organisation of work. This has important implications for the division of labour within firms. The growing demand, as well as the supply of temporary workers, is influencing the shift from labour-based to skills-based work. Thus, knowledge of new forms of flexible employment is still fragmented.

The change in the employment structure observed in highly developed countries, including EU countries, and the development of non-standard forms of employment have increased the labour market's flexibility. Research has shown that non-standard forms of employment concern especially women who combine paid work with running a home and taking care of children; young people who, despite having higher education, struggle to find stable employment, older people who prefer flexible employment, foreigners, migrants, people with reduced working capacity, people with low education and the unemployed (Hipp & Anderson, 2015; Hosking & Western, 2008). These employees decide to take up non-standard forms of employment because they have difficulties in finding permanent employment. At the same time, there is no evidence that less educated people are more likely to find employment in non-standard forms of employment. Research shows that unrealised employment potential may be attributable to the inability to secure childcare, employment protection or wage discrimination.

The need for greater flexibility in the labour market during the digital transformation stems from various factors, including population ageing and other demographic factors (Kalleberg, 2000). Moreover, non-standard forms of employment are gaining in importance as more and more people begin to appreciate work-life balance and try to clearly separate work from free time. The great advantage of non-standard forms of employment is flexible working time, which allows employees to determine their availability. This type of employment arrangement also means the possibility of flexible operation: employees can perform their duties remotely, regardless of the task or project to be carried out or the position held (Kalleberg, 2000). Non-standard forms of employment may be beneficial for the employee, if this form of employment enables the employee to develop and raise their qualifications, as well as to quickly adapt to changes in the labour market. Moreover, non-standard forms of employment allow for the integration of a greater number of people in the labour market (Hipp & Anderson, 2015). Many researchers emphasise that non-standard forms of employment are perceived as uncertain, which affects employees, e.g. there is greater uncertainty in terms of occupational safety (Laß & Wooden, 2020), employees are at risk of social inequalities (Kalleberg, 2000).

Several threats have accompanied the development of non-standard forms of employment in the era of digital transformation. One is the variety of concepts describing non-standard forms of employment, which makes it difficult to study and reach a comprehensive understanding of this phenomenon. In addition, the International Labour Organization emphasises that the definition of non-standard forms of employment will constantly evolve along with the implementation of new solutions on the labour market and the need for enterprises to adapt to these changes. Multiple definitions and discrepancies in data for different countries also make comparative analysis difficult (Schmid & Wagner, 2017).

In addition to non-standard forms of employment, there are also standard forms of employment. They are characterised by full-time employment, which has no contractual time limits and the work is carried out directly at the employer's premises (Ashford, George, & Blatt, 2007; Kalleberg, 2000). Standard forms of employment take into account both employer and employee interests. Studies show that employees in non-standard forms of employment tend to perform tasks that are peripheral to the company, while standard employees are more connected to the company (Schmid & Wagner, 2017). With standard forms of employment, the company takes full responsibility for the employee. In contrast, non-standard forms of employment involve less control over the employee (Cappelli & Keller, 2013). It should be emphasised that standard employment is still predominant in the employment structure (Hipp & Anderson, 2015). If the employment differs by more than one feature from standard employment, it can be considered a non-standard form of employment.

On this basis, it can be argued that flexible working is, on the one hand, a problem for workers, as they are often forced to work harder despite seemingly greater freedom of self-determination. From the organisation's perspective, on the other hand, supplementary work is performed without involving additional resources, thus increasing the organisation's productivity. Increased productivity has led companies to embrace employee flexibility (Bal & Izak, 2021). While numerous studies have been done on flexible forms of employment, more are needed to better understand the effects and consequences of the dynamic development of workplace flexibility, a timely subject of national and European debates on the influence of the digital economy on the labour market.

Conclusions

The aim of this chapter was to examine the impact of the digital economy on labour market dualism, and to assess how technological progress can lead to more and better jobs. The digital economy is an economy based on knowledge and technology. These characteristics are crucial for successful adaptation and, therefore, for reducing income inequality and unemployment in the long term.

Based on the analysis of the dual labour market, it can be concluded that certain characteristics of workplaces create premises for the existence of permanent inequalities in working and employment conditions. These inequalities are not eliminated or reduced by any natural tendencies. At the same time, the "good" and "bad" aspects of labour provision tend to perpetuate themselves. Highly paid labour is less likely to lose its job, the positions occupied are characterised by good health conditions, the possibility of flexible working hours and there are incentives to acquire new qualifications and professional skills (Pfeifer, 2005). In the 'worse' part of the market, low wages are accompanied by unfavourable working conditions. A person who has a job devoid of demands and learning opportunities will not have the motivation or opportunity to start or continue learning. The disadvantaged situation of some groups of workers can be seen as a result of their low spatial, occupational and skills mobility. Labour market policies should be geared towards enabling disadvantaged people on the labour market to become educated and increase their employability.

The digital economy has brought positive and negative changes to the labour market. Despite concerns about the effect automation will have, there are studies that show that jobs are being created by the digital economy. According to McKinsey, a third of the new jobs created in the United States over the past 25 years fit into new categories of work that either did not exist, or only to a small extent, in areas such as IT development, hardware manufacturing, application development and IT systems management (McKinsey Global Institute, 2017). The net impact of new technologies on employment can be very positive. A 2011 study by McKinsey's Paris office found that over the preceding 15 years, the internet had eliminated 500,000 jobs in France but created 1.2 million others, a net increase of 700,000, or 2.4 jobs for every one eliminated. The growing role of big data in the economy and business will create a significant demand for statisticians and data analysts. It has been predicted that there could be a shortage of data scientists within a decade. One of the main drivers of technological change in the foreseeable future is digitalisation, with technologies such as computers, smartphones and the internet at its heart. Smart automation will not result in a total loss of jobs, but it may lead to significant changes in the structure of employment, e.g. in terms of industries, occupations, skills and tasks. This includes changes in prerequisites (e.g. skill levels) for re-entry into the labour market, which are likely to be higher (Walwei, 2016).

This chapter points out that workers in the digital economy need to be highly skilled, flexible and adaptable. In particular, there is a need for greater flexibility in the digital economy. The labour market is forecast to globalise further, which will force more jobs to become more flexible (Turcan et al., 2014). Employment policies will be geared towards project-based tasks rather than lifelong employment for all, with the risks for employees increasing. The relationship between employer and employee will be increasingly collaborative and involve less subordination and hierarchy. There is also already a greater share of e-work in many forms of employment.

To conclude, the digital economy is considered a major source of long-term economic growth and job creation. Recent data indicate that the European economy is dynamic and increasingly innovative, i.e. knowledge-based and technology- and skills-intensive. It can be assumed that the labour market dualism will be influenced by the liberalisation and globalisation of information and communication, with ever more activities being performed by e-citizens.

References

Asen, R., & Blechschmidt, B. (2016). Making digital real and rewarding. *Cognizanti, 9*(1), 2–13.

Ashford, S.J., George, E., & Blatt, R. (2007). 2 old assumptions, New Work: The opportunities and challenges of research on nonstandard employment. *The Academy of Management Annals, 1*(1), 65–117. doi:10.1080/078559807

Atkinson, J. (1984). Manpower strategies for flexible organisations. *Personnel Management, 16*(8), 28–31.

Bahl, M. (2016). *The work ahead: The future of businesses and jobs in Asia Pacific's digital economy.* Chennai: Cognizant.

Bal, P.M., & Izak, M. (2021). Paradigms of flexibility: A systematic review of research on workplace flexibility. *European Management Review, 18*(1), 37–50.

Blanchflower, D.G., Bryson, A., & Green, C. (2021). Trade unions and the well-being of workers. *British Journal of Industrial Relations.* doi: 10.1111/bjir.12627

Boeri, T. (2011). Institutional reforms in European labour markets. In O. Ashenfelter, & D. Card (Ed.), *Handbook of labor economics* (Vol. 4b, pp. 1173–1236). Amsterdam: North Holland.

Bukht, R., & Heeks, R. (2017). *Defining, conceptualising and measuring the digital economy.* Manchester: University of Manchester.

Cappelli, P., & Keller, J. R. (2013). Classifying work in the new economy. *Academy of Management Review, 38*(4), 575–596.

Chase, C. (2019). How the digital economy is impacting the supply chain. *Journal of Business Forecasting, 38*(2), 16–20.

Cruz Gómez, I., Molina Romo, Ó., Verd Pericàs, J.M., Palauskaite, E., Dumčius, R., Venckutė, M., Vacas-Soriano, C. (2019). *Labour market segmentation: Piloting new empirical and policy analyses.* Available at: https://ddd.uab.cat/record/215471 (accessed 7 September 2021).

Czaja, I., & Urbaniec, M. (2019). Digital exclusion in the labour market in European countries: Causes and consequences. *European Journal of Sustainable Development, 8*(5), 324–324.

Davidescu, A. A., Apostu, S. A., Paul, A., & Casuneanu, I. (2020). Work flexibility, job satisfaction, and job performance among Romanian employees—Implications for sustainable human resource management. *Sustainability, 12*(15), 6086.

Degryse, C. (2016). Digitalisation of the economy and its impact on labour markets. *ETUI research paper-working paper.* Brussels: ETUI.

Deloitte. (2021). *Raport: Global Human Capital Trends 2021. The social enterprise in a world disrupted.* Available at: https://www2.deloitte.com/ie/en/pages/human-capital/articles/irish-human-capital-trends-report-2021.html (accessed 7 October 2021).

Doeringer, P.B., & Piore, M.J. (1971). *Internal labor markets and manpower analysis: With a new introduction.* New York: Routledge.

Doeringer, P.B., & Piore, M.J. (1975). Unemployment and the dual labor market. *The Public Interest, 38*, 67–79.

Dyer-Witheford, N. (2010). Digital labour, species-becoming and the global worker. *Ephemera: Theory & Politics in Organization, 10*(3/4), 484–503.

Eichhorst, W., & Kendzia, M.J. (2016). Workforce segmentation in Germany: From the founding era to the present time. *Journal for Labour Market Research, 49*(4), 297–315.

Eltamimi, A. (2020). The impact of new technologies in the current labour market of selected Arab states. In J. Carby-Hall, & L. Mella Méndez (Eds.), *Labour law and the gig economy* (pp. 90–124). London: Routledge.

Epicoco, M. (2020). Technological revolutions and economic development: Endogenous and exogenous fluctuations. *Journal of the Knowledge Economy.* doi:10.1007/s13132-020-00671-z

Esteban-Pretel, J., & Kitao, S. (2021). Labor market policies in a dual economy. *Labour Economics, 68*, 101956. doi:10.1016/j.labeco.2020.101956

Eurofound. (2021). *Working conditions and sustainable work: An analysis using the job quality framework*. Luxembourg: Publications Office of the European Union.

European Commission. (2007). *Towards common principles of flexicurity. More and better jobs through flexibility and security* (Vol. COM(2007) 359 final).

Federal Ministry for Economic Affairs and Energy (2014). *Monitoring-report: Digital economy 2014: ICT as innovation driver*. Berlin: Federal Ministry for Economic Affairs and Energy.

Fuchs, C. (2014). *Digital labour and Karl Marx*. New York: Routledge.

Fuchs, C., & Sevignani, S. (2013). What is digital labour? What is digital work? What's their difference? And why do these questions matter for understanding social media? *TripleC: Communication, Capitalism & Critique. Open Access Journal for a Global Sustainable Information Society, 11*(2), 237–293.

Gandini, A. (2020). Digital labour: An empty signifier? *Media, Culture & Society, 43*(2), 369–380. doi:10.1177/0163443720948018

Garz, M. (2013). Labour market segmentation: Standard and non-standard employment in Germany. *German Economic Review, 14*(3), 349–371. doi:10.1111/geer.12008

Giesecke, J. (2009). Socio-economic risks of atypical employment relationships: Evidence from the German labour market. *European Sociological Review, 25*(6), 629–646. doi:10.1093/esr/jcp012

Green, A.E., & Livanos, I. (2015). Involuntary non-standard employment and the economic crisis: Regional insights from the UK. *Regional Studies, 49*(7), 1223–1235. doi:10.1080/00343404.2013.825712

Heery, E., & Salmon, J. (Eds.). (2000). *The insecure workforce*. London: Routledge.

Hipp, L., & Anderson, C.J. (2015). Laziness or liberation? Labor market policies and workers' attitudes toward employment flexibility. *International Journal of Social Welfare, 24*(4), 335–347.

Hosking, A., & Western, M. (2008). The effects of non-standard employment on work—family conflict. *Journal of Sociology, 44*(1), 5–27.

House of Commons. (2016). *The digital economy*. Second Report of Session 2016–17. London: House of Commons.

Hunter, L., McGregor, A., Maclnnes, J., & Sproull, A. (1993). The 'flexible firm': Strategy and segmentation. *British Journal of Industrial Relations, 31*(3), 383–407. doi:10.1111/j.1467-8543.1993.tb00404.x

Imdorf, C., Helbling, L.A., & Inui, A. (2017). Transition systems and non-standard employment in early career: Comparing Japan and Switzerland. *Journal of Education and Work, 30*(5), 486–500.

Kalleberg, A.L. (2000). Nonstandard employment relations: Part-time, temporary and contract work. *Annual Review of Sociology, 26*(1), 341–365. Available at: https://www.annualreviews.org/doi/abs/10.1146/annurev.soc.26.1.341 (accessed 7 September 2021).

Kelliher, C., & Anderson, D. (2010). Doing more with less? Flexible working practices and the intensification of work. *Human Relations, 63*(1), 83–106.

Klimczuk, A., & Klimczuk-Kochańska, M. (2016). Dual labor market. In M.W.A. Wong, R. Hoogland, N.A. Naples (Ed.), *The Wiley Blackwell encyclopedia of gender and sexuality studies* (pp. 1–3). Available at: https://onlinelibrary.wiley.com/doi/book/10.1002/9781118663219 (accessed 7 October 2021).

Kling, R., & Lamb, R. (1999). IT and organizational change in digital economies: a socio-technical approach. *Acm Sigcas Computers and Society, 29*(3), 17–25.

Kogan, I. (2007). *Working through barriers: Host country institutions and immigrant labour market performance in Europe*. London: Springer.

Lane, N. (1999). Advancing the digital economy into the 21st century. *Information Systems Frontiers, 1*(3), 317–320.

Laß, I., & Wooden, M. (2020). Trends in the prevalence of non-standard employment in Australia. *Journal of Industrial Relations, 62*(1), 3–32.

Lee, D. R. (1996). Why is flexible employment increasing? *Journal of Labor Research, 17*(4), 543–553. doi:10.1007/BF02685798

Lommerud, K.E., Sandvik, B., & Straume, O.R. (2004). Good jobs, bad jobs and redistribution. *Scandinavian Journal of Economics, 106*(4), 703–720.

Małkowska, A., Urbaniec, M., & Kosała, M. (2021). The impact of digital transformation on European countries: Insights from a comparative analysis. *Equilibrium. Quarterly Journal of Economics and Economic Policy, 16*(2), 325–355.

Manzerolle, V. (2010). Mobilizing the audience commodity: Digital labour in a wireless world. *Ephemera: Theory & Politics in Organization, 10*(4), 455.

Matt, C., Hess, T., & Benlian, A. (2015). Digital transformation strategies. *Business & Information Systems Engineering, 57*(5), 339–343.

McKinsey Global Institute. (2017). *Technology, jobs and the future of work*. Available at: https://www.mckinsey.com/featured-insights/employment-and-growth/technology-jobs-and-the-future-of-work (accessed 7 September 2021).

Morel, N. (2015). Servants for the knowledge-based economy? The political economy of domestic services in Europe. *Social Politics: International Studies in Gender, State & Society, 22*(2), 170–192.

Morgan, G. (1997). *Imaginization: New mindsets for seeing, organizing, and managing*. San Francisco, CA: Berrett-Koehler Publishers.

Morgan, G. (2011). Reflections on images of organization and its implications for organization and environment. *Organization & Environment, 24*(4), 459–478.

Mueller, S.C., Bakhirev, A., Böhm, M., Schröer, M., Krcmar, H., & Welpe, I.M. (2017). Measuring and mapping the emergence of the digital economy: A comparison of the market capitalization in selected countries. *Digital Policy, Regulation and Governance, 19*(5), 367–382. doi:10.1108/DPRG-01-2017-0001

OECD. (2014). *Measuring the digital economy: A new perspective*. Paris: OECD Publishing.

OECD. (2020). *A roadmap toward a common framework for measuring the digital economy. Report for the G20 Digital Economy Task Force*. Paris: OECD.

Palier, B. (2019). Work, social protection and the middle classes: What future in the digital age? *International Social Security Review, 72*(3), 113–133.

Pfeifer, C. (2005). Flexibility, dual labour markets, and temporary employment. Empirical evidence from German establishment data. *Management Revue, 16*(3), 404–422.

Piore, M.J. (1969). On-the-job training in the dual labor market: public and private responsibilities in on-the-job training of disadvantaged workers. In A.R. Weber, F.H. Cassell, & W.L. Ginsburg (Eds.), *Public-private manpower policies* (pp. 101–132). Madison, WI: Industrial Relations Research Association.

Postigo, H. (2016). The socio-technical architecture of digital labor: Converting play into YouTube money. *New Media & Society, 18*(2), 332–349.

Putnam, L.L., Myers, K.K., & Gailliard, B.M. (2014). Examining the tensions in workplace flexibility and exploring options for new directions. *Human Relations, 67*(4), 413–440.

Raghuram, S., London, M., & Larsen, H. H. (2001). Flexible employment practices in Europe: country versus culture. *International Journal of Human Resource Management, 12*(5), 738–753.

Rubbers, B. (2020). Mining boom, labour market segmentation and social inequality in the Congolese Copperbelt. *Development and Change, 51*(6), 1555–1578.

Schmid, G., & Wagner, J. (2017). Managing social risks of non-standard employment in Europe. *ILO – working paper, Conditions of Work and Employment Series*, No. 91.

Selwyn, N. (2004). Reconsidering political and popular understandings of the digital divide. *New Media Society, 6*(3), 341–362. doi:10.1177/1461444804042519

Song, M., Zheng, C., & Wang, J. (2021). The role of digital economy in China's sustainable development in a post-pandemic environment. *Journal of Enterprise Information Management, 35*(1), 58–77.

Storey, J., Quintas, P., Taylor, P., & Fowle, W. (2002). Flexible employment contracts and their implications for product and process innovation. *International Journal of Human Resource Management, 13*(1), 1–18.

Tapscott, D. (1996). *The digital economy: Promise and peril in the age of networked intelligence.* New York: McGraw-Hill.

Teague, P., & Grahl, J. (1998). Institutions and labour market performance in Western Europe. *Political Studies, 46*(1), 1–18.

Turcan, V., Gribincea, A., & Birca, I. (2014). Digital economy-a premise for economic development in the 20th century. *Economy and Sociology: Theoretical and Scientifical Journal, 2*, 109–115.

Valenduc, G., & Vendramin, P. (2016). *Work in the digital economy: Sorting the old from the new.* Available at: https://www.etui.org/Publications2/Working-Papers/Work-in-the-digital-economy-sorting-the-old-from-the-new (accessed 7 September 2021).

Van Doorn, N. (2017). Platform labor: On the gendered and racialized exploitation of low-income service work in the 'on-demand'economy. *Information, Communication & Society, 20*(6), 898–914.

Wachter, M.L., Gordon, R., Piore, M.J., & Hall, R.E. (1974). Primary and secondary labor markets: A critique of the dual approach. *Brookings Papers on Economic Activity, 1974*(3), 637–693.

Walwei, U. (2016). *Digitalization and structural labour market problems: The case of Germany.* Geneva: International Labour Office.

Woodcock, J., & Graham, M. (2019). *The gig economy. A critical introduction.* Cambridge: Polity.

Yamaguchi, S. (2018). Changes in returns to task-specific skills and gender wage gap. *Journal of Human Resources, 53*(1), 32–70. doi:10.3368/jhr.53.1.1214-6813R2

2 Opportunities and consequences of digital transformation for the labour market

A systematic literature review

Michał Głuszak

Introduction

Ongoing digital transformation has profound implications for society and the economy. In recent decades, numerous scholars have tackled the diffusion of digital technologies and investigated how they are embedded in products, services and company operations (Yoo et al., 2012). These digitisation processes have become so radical that they have been called a digital revolution. Other terms used in this context include digitisation, digital transformation and the Fourth Industrial Revolution, though they are not entirely synonymous. In spite of the growing number of projects dealing with seemingly similar and related issues, the literature on digital transformation remains fragmented (Osterrieder, Budde, & Friedli, 2020).

The complexity of this multifaceted phenomenon has caused some problems with defining and setting the boundaries of the scientific debate, which revolves around the increasing automation of business undertakings, practices, procedures and models in response to the increasing influence and opportunities of information and computing technologies (Betz, Olagunju, & Paulson, 2016). Gong and Ribiere (2021) reviewed 134 definitions used in research and argue that most of them are flawed (by lacking conceptual clarity, to take one example). Based on the literature review and critical analysis, they define digital transformation as

> a fundamental change process enabled by digital technologies that aims to bring radical improvement and innovation to an entity (an organisation, a business network, an industry, or society) to create value for its stakeholders by strategically leveraging its key resources and capabilities.
> (Gong & Ribiere, 2021, p. 10)

Defining a digital transformation is not an easy challenge, and neither is assessing its impact on various markets. The introduction of digital technologies into business operations creates various opportunities and poses several

DOI: 10.4324/9781003254638-4

challenges on labour market. Both positive and negative impacts have been discussed in the economic literature.

The chapter presents the results of a systematic literature review to capture the most relevant problems identified in prior empirical studies. Based on previous economic and business research, it synthesises the current evidence on the impact of digital transformation on major actors of the labour market in various industries. This review shows how digital transformation disrupts traditional business models, and how innovative business opportunities impact the labour market. The following section of the chapter presents the research methods and the literature selection process. Based on the systematic review, I reflect on the opportunities digital transformation presents for the labour market in Section "Opportunities of digital transformation for the labour market" and consequences identified in the literature in Section "Consequences of digital transformation for the labour market". The final section of the chapter summarises the main conclusions and suggests directions for further research.

Methods

Systematic literature review methodology

This systematic literature review was done to examine how digital transformation disrupts traditional business models, and how innovative business opportunities impact the labour market. The need for a methodical synthesis of findings from multiple independent studies was recognised by Pearson (1904), who is often credited with the first attempt at meta-analysis. Since then, different approaches have been used to synthesise the body of empirical evidence in various research fields. Grant and Booth (2009) identify 14 different types of review including: critical reviews, scoping reviews, systematic literature reviews, state-of-the-art reviews, umbrella reviews or meta-analysis.

Scoping reviews apply a qualitative approach and are used to examine the extent, range and nature of research activity of a body of literature, and can be of particular use when the topic has not yet been extensively reviewed or is of a complex or heterogeneous nature, and in a topic area (Pham et al., 2014). Modern meta-analysis stems from the pioneering work of Glass (Glass, 1976) and Rosenthal (1978), who used sophisticated econometric techniques to compare and investigate potential differences between empirical findings (Leamer & Leonard, 1983). Rader, Mann, Stansfield, Cooper and Sampson (2014) explored the concerns and research documentation issues related to systematic literature reviews.

The modern understanding of meta-analysis owes much to the work of Glass (1976), who first used the term, and Rosenthal (1978). In the early 1980s, it was noted that the spread of econometric tools, access to empirical data and publication practices (emphasis on the use of quantitative methods) had resulted a wealth of studies describing economic phenomena from different perspectives. The difficulty of agreeing on the results of empirical studies, which are often contradictory, hinders the development of economics as a science. Moreover, some theorists point to the inability to create empirical generalisations and to test theoretical concepts on the basis of scattered and often incomparable empirical research results as a source of crisis in economics science (Stanley, 1989). Another threat is Stanley's arbitrariness in selecting evidence to support a given thesis and the rejection as contradictory of some empirical findings that are unjustifiably considered unreliable or biased (Stanley, 2001). A further issue is the relatively low representation of empirical research from outside the Anglo-Saxon cultural circle in mainstream economics journals. All these considerations often lead to subjective and unwarranted conclusions from critical reviews of the literature. It is also not always possible to identify the causes of discrepancies that make it difficult to generalise the results of independent studies conducted in different economic, social and cultural contexts.

Despite the numerous advantages of systematic reviews as a tool for synthesising the results of empirical studies, they are relatively rarely used in economics, especially compared to the medical or psychological sciences. Nevertheless, an exponential increase in systematic reviews investigating various economic phenomena has been observed (Stanley & Doucouliagos, 2012). Systematic literature reviews investigating business and management issues have grown in popularity (Walecka & Zakrzewska-Bielawska, 2016).

The exponential growth of studies investigating digital transformation, as well as the substantial body of empirical evidence, have allowed for several systematic reviews that synthesised major findings. Some of the papers have addressed various facets of digital economy or Industry 4.0. Based on their extensive literature review, Verhoef et al. (2021) distinguish between digitisation, digitalisation and digital transformation. They suggest a research agenda that will promote empirical research on phases of digital transformation (what is the optimal level of digital transformation companies should pursue? How does digital transformation affect economic performance?); digital resources (how can a company create digital resources? What is the connection between resources and digital transformation?); digital growth strategies (what strategies are energy efficient?) (Karki & Porras, 2021). A recent systematic review explored the link between the concept of the smart factory and industry 4.0 smart manufacturing, the internet of things and digital transformation (Osterrieder et al., 2020).

Data collection and data analysis

The systematic literature review presented in this chapter explores how digital transformation disrupts traditional business models, and how innovative business opportunities impact the labour market. Preferred Reporting Items for Systematic Reviews and Meta-Analyses (PRISMA) protocols are applied for systematic review and MAXQDA software is used to quantify the relations found in prior papers indexed in two major scientific databases: Scopus and Web of Science (WoS).

The review follows several steps in two distinct research stages: (1) data collection and management and (2) data analysis. In the stage of data collection and management, four areas are identified:

- the objective of the research and research questions;
- research areas;
- key search criteria;
- inclusion and exclusion criteria for in-depth analysis.

Procedures for elimination of redundant papers were also developed at this stage.

The study contributes to the debate on the interrelations between digital transformation and the labour market. Three main research questions were considered:

- What are the opportunities of digital transformation for various actors on the labour market (mostly employers and employees)?
- What are the consequences of the digital transformation for the labour market?
- What are the research gaps in the field and what topics are the most important for a future research agenda?

Based on the literature screening process, the systematic literature review in this chapter focuses on selected research areas: economics, business studies, management and social studies. Relevant papers on education and training (especially concerning skills, competences and knowledge required by workers) were also included. The next step was to add specific search criteria that would narrow the scope of the review to a manageable and relevant number of items. In the search process, the phrases "labour market" and "digital" were used to cover all occurrences of the digital economy, digitalisation and digital transformation in combination with the labour market in titles, keywords or article abstracts. Only original scientific papers written in English – conference papers, articles, chapters in books and books – were included, while editorials and reviews were excluded. The issue of whether to include work in languages other than English has been widely discussed in papers on methodology. A major point of criticism is that the failure to do so leads to substantial sample selection and potential bias. However, as most research in this field is published in English, the risk of omitting relevant work is limited.

In the final step, high-quality literature was searched in two major scientific databases: Clarivate Web of Science and Elsevier Scopus. The results only included relevant and original research. Table 2.1 explains the data gathering and management procedure.

Table 2.1 Search criteria in the Scopus and WoS databases

Search criteria	*Description*	*No*
Searching in WoS database		
Searching for articles on digital transformation in the context of the labour market	TS = ("labour market" or "labor market") and digital*)	801
Limiting search to articles, books, book chapters and conference papers (excluding review papers)		776
• excluding non-English literature		663
• excluding research areas		527
Searching the Scopus database		
Searching for articles on digital transformation in the context of the labour market	TITLE-ABS-KEY (digital*) AND ("labour market" OR "labor market")	988
Limiting search to articles, books, book chapters and conference papers		943
• excluding non-English literature		834
• excluding research areas (only social science, business)		574
Merging, screening and preparing final dataset		
Merging the Scopus and WoS literature		1102
Screening the database for irrelevant data and preparing the final dataset		71

Source: the author's own research.

The results of the search process revealed a considerable number of papers within our interest both in the WoS database (527 items after applying inclusion and exclusion criteria) and Scopus (574). The aforementioned papers include articles, conference proceedings, book chapters and books. Statistical studies show that there has been a significant increase in the sample of source materials in recent years (Figure 2.1).

The topic of digital transformation on the labour market is relatively new, only recently drawing scholarly interest. From 2011 to 2020 the number of papers published and indexed in Scopus or WoS grew exponentially. However, in the last two years there has been a significant decrease in the dynamics of published work in this field. Notably, the papers addressing digital economy or digital transformation in the context of the labour market come from Russia (which placed the most papers in both the WoS and Scopus), Romania, the UK, the US, Spain, Germany and Italy (Table 2.2).

In a further step, the initial sample was refined by examining the exact content of the source material. Articles, conference papers and book chapters that did not directly investigate the digital transformation on labour market were dropped, but for some reason the search phrases were present in abstracts, titles or key words. Papers that solely covered the technical side of

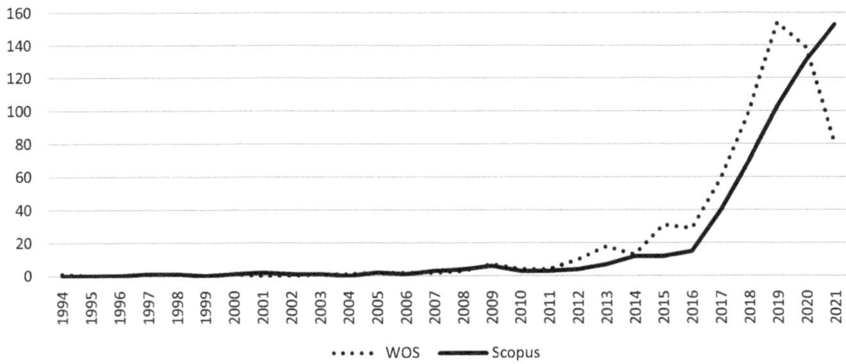

Figure 2.1 Sample of the number of source materials
Source: the author's own research.

Table 2.2 Basic statistics from the literature on the digital transformation of the labour market

Type	*WoS*	*Scopus*
Type of publication		
Article	290	397
Conference paper	267	104
Book Chapter	6	57
Book		16
Leading countries in publications in the study area		
Sweden	17	14
Romania	18	17
Canada	25	18
Australia	25	24
Italy	27	34
Spain	33	41
Germany	42	52
United Kingdom	43	59
United States	52	61
Russia	97	89

Source: the author's research.

the digital transformation (mostly related to computer science) were also excluded, as they did not discuss the opportunities and challenges of the ongoing digital revolution on the labour market. The dataset ultimately included 71 papers, which were examined in detail in the final phase of the systematic literature review.

Opportunities of digital transformation for the labour market

The literature shows that the ongoing digital transformation presents opportunities that fall into three distinct categories: economic, social and environmental. A recent review indicates that most (around 60%) of the benefits discussed fall into the broad economic category (Ghobakhloo, Fathi, Iranmanesh, Maroufkhani, & Morales, 2021). These can be summarised as follows:

- employment and security on the labour market – the biggest opportunity linked to digital transformation is that it potentially stimulates employment. New developments including the gig economy and remote work may lead to more participation in the labour market. This study investigates this relationship empirically, using aggregate data from European countries. The results suggest that higher adoption of digital technologies (measure by DESI index) leads to lower long-term unemployment and a higher overall employment rate. This research indicates that successful digital transformation can reduce the labour market's insecurity (Basol & Yalcin, 2021, Małkowska, Urbaniec, & Kosała, 2021);
- digital transformation and competitiveness – the greater competitiveness digital transformation promises will bear major economic opportunities. Although business competitiveness has not been fully conceptualised (Wach, 2014), the literature does provide multiple channels that can boost business competitiveness. One of them is digital monitoring and supervision, which helps companies assess performance, optimise processes and increase efficiency on an unprecedented scale and in real time;
- digital transformation and labour productivity – labour productivity is another major issue raised by multiple papers. The employee's role in the company may evolve towards one of greater responsibility thanks in large part to digital transformation. The ultimate outcome of the transformation may be the inclusion of employees in the decision-making processes of companies (Fantini, Pinzone, & Taisch, 2020);
- digital transformation and equality on the labour market – several papers have demonstrated that mastering digital skills may help newcomers and immigrants integrate into the labour market (Joshi, Koulolias, Moran, & Loeffler, 2018; Melnikova, Grunwald, Ahrens, & Zascerinska, 2018). A Hungarian study shows that digital platforms provide additional work opportunities to older people (Berde & Tokes, 2019). Gender researchers argue that digitalisation may provide new opportunities for female labour force for two reasons: the lower risk of being replaced by machines compared to men, and the comparative advantage when combining social and digital skills compared to men (Krieger-Boden & Sorgner, 2018). Additionally, access to work platforms and expansion of remote work has increased labour market accessibility for women with small children, as well as immigrant women (Webster & Zhang, 2020).

Consequences of digital transformation for the labour market

Multiple overall benefits have been reported in empirical papers dealing with the consequences of digital transformation on the labour market. However, in many cases the generally positive effect of the digital economy for the labour market often comes at the cost of at least part of labour force. The main consequences are:

- digital transformation and employment imbalances – another problem reported in the literature is that uneven levels of digital technology adoption across sectors will lead to substantial changes in the labour markets. Estimates show that automation will affect nearly half of the labour force. First, the various job categories will be either fully automated or replaced by digital technologies. Second, digital transformation will lead to a significant change of job characteristics and competences required (Ljubica & Quintini, 2018). The body of empirical evidence suggests that there is a link between ongoing digital revolution and the unemployment rate in selected industries, where human are being replaced by machines (Stephany, 2021). Several papers have addressed this issue using general statistics (Basol & Yalcin, 2021; Finkelstein Shapiro, & Mandelman, 2021; Rudskaya & Konnikov, 2020) or investigating case studies from selected industries (Dengler & Matthes, 2018). The problem of regional imbalances on labour markets has been addressed (Zhuravleva, Grigoryan, & Riet, 2019);
- the digital divide on the labour market. One of the issues identified in the literature has been described as digital exclusion, a term coined after social exclusion. The latter refers to the lack of access to goods and services that are necessary in everyday life – and may manifest itself in labour markets, housing conditions, consumption patterns, participation in culture (Haddon, 2000). Similarly, digital exclusion refers to the lack of access to digital services that are necessary to function in society and actively participate in the labour market. This polarising phenomenon has been addressed to compare differences between countries (developed vs developing), as well as in the context of technological inequalities (in urban vs rural areas). Empirical investigation suggests that access to digital technology is not the only reason for digital exclusion to occur. Digital exclusion and its consequences for the labour market – inferior job opportunities, the inability to apply for certain positions, worse career prospects – are also caused by the lack of digital skills and the willingness to use technology (Czaja & Urbaniec, 2019). The literature has addressed the impact of digital isolation and the loss of digital skills on labour market outcomes (Novo-Corti & Barreiro-Gen, 2017). Several papers tried to identify vulnerable groups that are adversely affected by digital transformation (Vasilescu, Serban, Dimian, Aceleanu, & Picatoste, 2020).

Labour market inequalities caused by the digital transformation have contributed to yet another interesting phenomenon investigated in the literature – the digital divide. According to the OECD's, the term "digital divide" refers to the gap between individuals, households, businesses and geographic areas at different socio-economic levels with regard to both their opportunities to access information and communication technologies (ICTs) and to their use of the internet for a wide variety of activities (OECD, 2001, p. 5). The digital divide and, more generally, the digital transformation polarises labour market participants. On the upside of the digital divide are those who benefit from digital trends and are able to achieve superior earnings and work-life balance thanks to the usefulness of the skills they offer. All those whose skills are easily replaced and may be automated at low cost end up losing out, ultimately struggling to find career opportunities, which will lead to personal and social problems;

- digital skills and the labour market. Some papers have reported on catalysts for successful digital transformation. Among the opportunities created by the digital transformation is the creation of new categories of employment as the result of the shift in needs and demand in the new digital economy. At the same time, there are several caveats that come with the new job categories created by industry 4.0. For example, several papers discuss job quality issues and social policy challenges. Research suggest that a highly skilled workforce is one of the key factors explaining faster digital transformation on the labour market (Suciu, Pelinescu, Cristea, & Noja, 2019). Several papers have investigated the correlation between digital skills and employability (Bejakovic & Mrnjavac, 2020; Souza, Ferreira Dias, & Amorim, 2020), while others have looked at what skills, competences and knowledge are required on the rapidly changing labour market (Labanauskaite, Zuperkiene, Kumpf, Simanskiene, & Koller, 2021). Finally, research has been done with a view to bridging the gap between economics and education, investigating the role of education on labour markets undergoing digital transformation (Titan, Burciu, Manea, & Ardelean, 2014);
- digital transformation and Covid-19. Digital transformation, the Covid-19 pandemic and labour market resilience are also widely studied (Brugiavini, Buia, & Simonetti, 2021). During the Covid-19 pandemic the revolution towards remote work has transformed labour markets worldwide, and promoted global outsourcing of labour on an unprecedented scale (Gousev & Yurevich, 2021). Many authors have argued that remote work and digital work platforms have strengthened the labour market's resilience during the pandemic's shock. This effect will outlast the pandemic and foster the market's recovery (Zamfir & Aldea, 2020);
- digital transformation and regulatory issues. Last but not least, there are policy implications. The process of digital transformation is inevitable, so effort must be made to mitigate possible risk and minimise the negative

externalities that will arise as the result of adoption of digital technologies in a growing number of sectors. One of the most pressing challenges identified in the literature is how labour standards and regulation can be used to reduce tensions between companies and workers while allowing for smooth digital transition. The issue of training, digital skills development and worker re-employment is also addressed widely. Finally, the literature contains commentary on social protection (Andrews, Criscuolo, & Gal, 2016). New institutional economics theory has explained that new flexible forms of employment created by digital transformation are not aligned with the old and less flexible regulatory environment (Kychko, Samiilenko, Khudolei, Bondar, & Kravchyk, 2021).

Conclusions

The systematic literature review allowed me to summarise the debate on the impact of digital transformation on the labour market, particularly in the context of Europe. The first goal of the paper was to identify the opportunities related to digital transformation for various actors on the labour market. The review shows that researchers have focused on opportunities related to higher employment rates and lower labour market risk, potential benefits related to increased labour productivity and competitiveness, as well as empowerment and greater equality (related to gender, age or ethnicity).

The second objective was to identify and assess the changes on the labour market related to digital transformation. The literature examines different facets of the transformation: the evolution of skills needed on the labour market, imbalances in employment (across regions and sectors), the problem of the digital divide and digital exclusion, and regulatory issues mitigating the negative consequences caused by the gig economy. Extensive empirical research has also been done on the Covid-19 pandemic. Finally, a synthesis of key themes for future research was also done. There is a further need for research to understand regional differences in digital labour markets in European countries, which can play an important role in the further integration of the EU. An important and still understudied issue is the role the gig economy may play for immigrants in European countries.

References

Andrews, D., Criscuolo, C., & Gal, P.N. (2016). *The best versus the rest. The global productivity slowdown, divergence across firms and the role of public policy* (OECD Productivity Working Papers No. 2016/5).

Basol, O., & Yalcin, E.C. (2021). How does the digital economy and society index (DESI) affect labor market indicators in EU countries? *Human Systems Management, 40*(4), 503–512.

Bejakovic, P., & Mrnjavac, Z. (2020). The importance of digital literacy on the labour market. *Employee Relations, 42*(4), 921–932.

Berde, E., & Tokes, L. (2019). The platform economy as a working opportunity for older people The case of the Hungarian carpooling company Oszkar. *Journal of Enterprising Communities-People and Places in The Global Economy, 14*(1), 76–90.

Betz, C., Olagunju, A.O., & Paulson, P. (2016). The impacts of digital transformation, agile, and devOps on future IT curricula. In *Proceedings of the 17th Annual Conference on Information Technology Education* (p. 106). New York, NY, USA: Association for Computing Machinery.

Brugiavini, A., Buia, R.E., & Simonetti, I. (2021). Occupation and working outcomes during the Coronavirus Pandemic. *European Journal of Ageing*. 1–20. https://doi.org/10.1007/s10433-021-00651-5

Czaja, I., & Urbaniec, M. (2019). Digital exclusion in the labour market in European countries: Causes and consequences. *European Journal of Sustainable Development, 8*(5), 324–336.

Dengler, K., & Matthes, B. (2018). The impacts of digital transformation on the labour market: Substitution potentials of occupations in Germany. *Technological Forecasting and Social Change, 137*, 304–316.

Fantini, P., Pinzone, M., & Taisch, M. (2020). Placing the operator at the centre of Industry 4.0 design: Modelling and assessing human activities within cyber-physical systems. *Computers & Industrial Engineering, 139*, 105058. doi:10.1016/j.cie.2018.01.025

Finkelstein Shapiro, A., & Mandelman, F. S. (2021). Digital adoption, automation, and labor markets in developing countries. *Journal of Development Economics, 151*(February 2020), 102656. doi:10.1016/j.jdeveco.2021.102656

Ghobakhloo, M., Fathi, M., Iranmanesh, M., Maroufkhani, P., & Morales, M.E. (2021). Industry 4.0 ten years on: A bibliometric and systematic review of concepts, sustainability value drivers, and success determinants. *Journal of Cleaner Production, 302*, 127052. doi:10.1016/j.jclepro.2021.127052

Glass, G.V. (1976). Primary, secondary, and meta-analysis of research. *Educational Researcher, 5*(10), 3–8.

Gong, C., & Ribiere, V. (2021). Developing a unified definition of digital transformation. *Technovation, 102*, 102217. doi:10.1016/j.technovation.2020.102217

Gousev, A.B., & Yurevich, M.A. (2021). Globalization of employment amid COVID-19 pandemic. *MGIMO Review of International Relations, 14*(1), 148–173.

Grant, M.J., & Booth, A. (2009). A typology of reviews: An analysis of 14 review types and associated methodologies. *Health Information and Libraries Journal, 26*(2), 91–108.

Haddon, L. (2000). Social exclusion and information and communication technologies: Lessons from studies of single parents and the young elderly. *New Media & Society, 2*(4), 387–406.

Joshi, S., Koulolias, V., Moran, F.G., & Loeffler, E. (2018). *Case study-how public services in Sweden help newcomers to integrate in the labour market and society through the digital platform mobilearn*. In T. Brandsen, T. Steen, & B. Verschuere (Eds.), *Co-production and Cocreation: Engaging citizens in public services*. New York: Routledge. doi:10.1007/978–981-13–1156–7

Karki, B.R., & Porras, J. (2021). Digitalization for sustainable maintenance services: A systematic literature review. *Digital Business, 1*(2), 100011. doi: 10.1016/j.digbus.2021.100011

Krieger-Boden, C., & Sorgner, A. (2018). Labor market opportunities for women in the digital age. *Economics: The Open-Access, Open-Assessment E-Journal, 12*(28), 1–8. doi:10.5018/economics-ejournal.ja.2018–28

Kychko, I., Samiilenko, H., Khudolei, V., Bondar, N., & Kravchyk, Y. (2021). Risks of digital transformations of labour relations and the labour market. *Laplage Em Revista, 7*, 650–660.

Labanauskaite, D., Zuperkiene, E., Kumpf, A., Simanskiene, L., & Koller, S.M. (2021). Development of digital and entrepreneurial competences for the future labour market needs. *Entrepreneurship and Sustainability Issues, 8*(3), 565–581.

Leamer, E., & Leonard, H. (1983). Reporting the fragility of regression estimates. *The Review of Economics and Statistics, 65*(2), 306–317.

Ljubica, N., & Quintini, G. (2018). *Automation, skills use and training. OECD Social, Employment, and Migration Working Papers*. Paris: OECD. doi:10.1787/2e2f4eea-en.

Małkowska, A., Urbaniec, M., & Kosała, M. (2021). The impact of digital transformation on European countries: Insights from a comparative analysis. *Equilibrium. Quarterly Journal of Economics and Economic Policy, 16*(2), 325–355.

Melnikova, J., Grunwald, N., Ahrens, A., & Zascerinska, J. (2018). Digital entrepreneurship as a means of integration of immigrants and asylum seekers into labour market in Baltic countries. In N. Grunwald & M. Zakrzewska (Eds.), *Proceedings of the 5th International Scientific Conference on Modern Economics* (pp. 119–128). Wismar: Robert-Schmidt-Institut.

Novo-Corti, I., & Barreiro-Gen, M. (2017). Additional barriers to access to labour market for prisoners due to digital isolation. In F.C. Freire, X.R. Araujo, V.A. M. Fernandez, & X.L. Garcia (Eds.), *Media and metamedia management* (Vol. 503, pp. 391–396). doi:10.1007/978-3-319–46068-0_51

OECD. (2001). *Understanding the digital divide.* OECD Digital Economy Papers No. 49, Paris. https://doi.org/10.1787/236405667766

Osterrieder, P., Budde, L., & Friedli, T. (2020). The smart factory as a key construct of industry 4.0: A systematic literature review. *International Journal of Production Economics, 221*(July), 1–16. doi:10.1016/j.ijpe.2019.08.011

Pearson, K. (1904). Report on certain enteric fever inoculation statistics. *British Medical Journal, 2*, 1243–1246.

Pham, M.T., Rajić, A., Greig, J.D., Sargeant, J.M., Papadopoulos, A., & Mcewen, S. A. (2014). A scoping review of scoping reviews: Advancing the approach and enhancing the consistency. *Research Synthesis Methods, 5*(4), 371–385.

Rader, T., Mann, M., Stansfield, C., Cooper, C., & Sampson, M. (2014). Methods for documenting systematic review searches: A discussion of common issues. *Research Synthesis Methods, 5*(2), 98–115.

Rosenthal, R. (1978). Combining results of independent studies. *Psychological Bulletin, 85*(1), 185–193.

Rudskaya, I.A., & Konnikov, E.A. (2020). Digital transformation of the labor market. *Revista Inclusiones,* 7(3), 188–199.

Souza, A., Ferreira Dias, M., & Amorim, M. (2020). Recent empirical results of the impact of digitalisation on the labour market. In K.S. Soliman (Ed.), *Education excellence and innovation management: A 2025 vision to sustain economic development during global challenges*. Proceedings of the 35th International Business Information Management Association Conference (IBIMA), 1–2 April 2020 Seville, Spain.

Stanley, T. (1989). Meta-regression analysis: A quantitative method of literature surveys. *Journal of Economic Surveys, 3*(2), 161–170.

Stanley, T. (2001). Wheat from Chaff: Meta-analysis as quantitative literature review. *Journal of Economic Perspectives, 15*(3), 131–150.

Stanley, T., & Doucouliagos, H. (2012). *Meta-regression analysis in economics and business. Meta-Regression Analysis in Economics and Business.* London: Routledge.

Stephany, F. (2021). One size does not fit all: Constructing complementary digital reskilling strategies using online labour market data. *Big Data & Society, 8*(1). doi:10.1177/20539517211003120.

Suciu, M.C., Pelinescu, E., Cristea, M., & Noja, G.G. (2019). Digital transformation and the EU labour markets. In P. Griffiths, & M.N. Kabir (Eds.), *Proceedings of the European conference on the impact of artificial intelligence and robotics (ECIAIR 2019).* Oxford: Academic Conferences and Publishing International.

Titan, E., Burciu, A., Manea, D., & Ardelean, A. (2014). From traditional to digital: The labour market demands and education expectations in an EU context. *Procedia Economics and Finance, 10*, 269–274, doi:10.1016/S2212-5671(14)00302-5.

Vasilescu, M.D., Serban, A.C., Dimian, G.C., Aceleanu, M.I., & Picatoste, X. (2020). Digital divide, skills and perceptions on digitalisation in the European Union-Towards a smart labour market. *Plos One, 15*(4). doi:10.1371/journal.pone.0232032

Verhoef, P.C., Broekhuizen, T., Bart, Y., Bhattacharya, A., Qi Dong, J., Fabian, N., & Haenlein, M. (2021). Digital transformation: A multidisciplinary reflection and research agenda. *Journal of Business Research, 122*(July 2018), 889–901.

Wach, K. (2014). The theoretical modelling of the firm-level international competitiveness in business studies. In K. Wach, & D. Kiendl-Wendner (Eds.), *International competitiveness in Visegrad countries: Macro and micro perspectives* (pp. 101–124). Graz: Fachhochschule Joanneum.

Walecka, A., & Zakrzewska-Bielawska, A. (2016). Metodyka metaanalizy – egzemplifikacja wykorzystania w naukach o zarządzaniu. *Zeszyty Naukowe Uniwersytetu Ekonomicznego w Krakowie, 6*(954), 63–80.

Webster, N.A., & Zhang, Q. (2020). Careers delivered from the kitchen? Immigrant women small-scale entrepreneurs working in the growing Nordic platform economy. *Nora-Nordic Journal of Feminist and Gender Research, 28*(2), 113–125.

Yoo, Y., Boland, R.J., Lyytinen, K., Majchrzak, A., Lyytinen, K., & Majchrzak, A. (2012). Organizing for innovation in the digitized world. *Organization Science, 23*(5), 1398–1408.

Zamfir, A.M., & Aldea, A.B. (2020). Digital skills and labour market resilience. *Postmodern Openings, 11*(1), 188–195.

Zhuravleva, N.A., Grigoryan, M.G., & Riet, K.G. (2019). The influence of digital technologies on regional labour market structure (The case of St Petersburg). In E. Tikhonovich & V. Batmanova (Eds.), *Proceedings of the Volgograd State University International scientific Conference: Competitive, sustainable and safe development of the regional economy (CSSDRE 2019)* (pp. 442–446). Dordrecht: Atlantis Press.

3 Labour markets in the age of digital transformation

Evidence from EU countries

Joanna Kudełko

Introduction

The digital transformation has an impact on all areas of the economy and human life. Rapid technological advancement has given rise to the concept of Industry 4.0, which is another turning point in the development of civilisation, comparable to the invention of the steam engine, the mass use of electricity or the use of computer-aided production lines. The concept of Industry 4.0 is founded on the integration of computer systems and people's cooperation with digitally controlled machines, based on the extensive use of the internet and modern information technologies (Schwab, 2016).

Digital transformation affects business processes and social relations (Kergroach, 2017). Advanced technologies supporting production processes modify the functioning of contemporary enterprises (Gracel & Makowiec, 2017). Changes mainly result from an extensive use of information and digital technologies in production and services (Yin, Stecke, & Li, 2018). The digital transformation is identified with such phenomena as automation, robotisation, Big Data, artificial intelligence, the Internet of Things and 3D technology (Davenport & Harris, 2007; Gupta, 2007; Henke et al., 2016; Singh, Mishra, & Sagar, 2013).

The digital transformation modifies classical business principles as it offers new business models allowing for value to be captured at each stage of the value chain and for competitive advantage to be gained (Bharadwaj, Sawy, Pavlou, & Venkatraman, 2013; Mithas & Lucas, 2010). The use of new technologies enables economies to create value with lower investment expenditure, while older technologies and organisational approaches become less importance (Manyika et al., 2013).

Digitalisation moves into an increasing number of social and economic spheres, and technological advancement has a major impact on the labour market. Changes can be observed in production methods, interactions between employees and intelligent machines, and the fact that people's work is more closely monitored and supervised. At the same time, employer-employee relations change as the use of new phenomena increase: flexible forms of employment and non-standard job contracts as well as new work

DOI: 10.4324/9781003254638-5

methods and new trends in workstation and the organisation of working hours (Degryse, 2016).

Digital transformation creates new labour market conditions to which both employers and employees must adapt. While technological advancement offers opportunities, it also poses threats. New opportunities result from the emergence of new professions characterised by a high degree of innovativeness and creativity. At the same time, demand decreases for routine and work that can be done with algorithms instead of human labour (Charles, Hurst, & Notowidigdo, 2013; Jaimovich & Siu, 2012). Employment is mainly threatened by automated production and service delivery processes, although not all professions are vulnerable to the same extent (Arnold, Arntz, Gregory, Steffes, & Zierahn, 2018). Automation poses a risk to those professions in which the performance of tasks is based on routine and repetition. It does not pose such threats to professions based on creativity, negotiation and interpersonal skills (Frey & Osborne, 2013). Manual work will be gradually replaced by robots controlled by humans. The complementary character of human skills and competences and the functionalities of machines will enable employees to focus on non-routine activities and the use of human creativity (Bisello & Fernandez-Macias, 2018; Jelonek & Urbaniec, 2019). Labour market changes are reflected in various phenomena (Degryse, 2016):

- job creation – resulting from new sectors, products and services;
- job change – resulting from digitalisation, new forms of management and interactions between humans and intelligent machines;
- job destruction – resulting from work positions being automated and performed by robots;
- job shift – along with a wide use of digital platforms, crowd sourcing and the sharing economy.

Technological advancement is accompanied by increased expectations of employees in terms of the competencies they possess. Employees must gain new qualifications, including digital skills, to meet the requirements of contemporary labour markets. The quality of human capital remains a major driver in the development of digital economies (Małkowska, Urbaniec, & Kosała, 2021; Pereira, Temouri, & Patel, 2020). Employees are expected to have competencies relevant to specific sectors. Moreover, it is necessary to acquire new additional skills required by digitalisation, automation and the use of artificial intelligence (Bughin et al., 2018). In the years to come, demand is likely to increase for high-level cognitive competencies such as the ability to analyse text, quantitative and statistical skills, project management skills and the ability to process and interpret information. Apart from technological competencies, an equally important role will be played by soft skills: critical thinking and problem solving (Griffiths, Inman, Rojas, & Williams, 2018), social and emotional skills, i.e., teamwork skills, the ability to adapt to change as well as attitudes and emotions expressed by effective communication and interactions with other people (Adams, 2013; Sisson & Adams, 2013).

Better-educated and qualified workers will be at an advantageous on the labour market and they can expect higher compensation. This will lead to pay gaps between qualified and unqualified workers, which may result in social stratification (Autor, 2003). Activities aimed at increasing people's employability include education (Didier 2021, Nivea, Andreea-Gabriela, & Romeo, 2017). Indeed, the development of competencies should be a lifelong process. Employers should share the costs of developing their employees' professional qualifications as high-quality human capital increases a company's capital as well as its competitiveness. Development within the framework of Industry 4.0 should promote lifelong learning and the acquisition of new skills by people who hold their current positions (Piątkowski, 2020). In the context of changes in labour markets, this chapter assesses the diversification of EU countries in terms of labour market resources. This will allow for an evaluation of their readiness to adapt to contemporary labour market challenges.

The diversification of EU countries in terms of labour market resources

Research methodology

It bears repeating that societies that can meet digital economy challenges tend to have employees and enterprises in possession of high quality labour resources. Human capital relates to employees' knowledge and competencies, with digital skills and their practical application playing a key role. This concerns natural persons as well as the business sector. In order to describe the specificity of labour markets in particular EU countries, I will look at variables which characterise labour resources. The ratios used describe the adaptation of resources, i.e., human capital and enterprises, to labour markets' contemporary challenges. The choice of indicators was determined by their factual value and the availability of comparable data. A detailed list of the variables is presented in Table 3.1. The data accepted for the analysis describes the education levels of human resources (variable 3), readiness to improve qualifications (variable 4) and participation of highly skilled employees in the employment structure (variables 1 and 2). It also indicates society's digital skills (variable 6) and their practical application (variables 5 and 7), as well as the degree of the use of digital technologies in the business sector (variables 8, 9 and 10). The accepted data also includes labour market ratios (variables 11 and 12) and the general level of the countries' development (variable 13), all of which are used in comparative analyses. The variables describing labour market resources and development levels in EU countries in 2020 are presented in Appendix 3.1.

Table 3.1 Variables used for the analysis of labour resources and development levels in EU countries

Number of variable	*Name of variable*	*Description of variable*
1	Employment in high- and medium-high technology manufacturing sectors and knowledge-intensive service sectors	The data shows the employment in high- and medium-high technology manufacturing sectors and in knowledge-intensive service sectors as a share of total employment. The source of the data is the European Labour force survey (LFS) (Percentage of total employment)
2	Human resources in science and technology	The data shows the active population in the age group 25–64 that is classified as HRST (having successfully completed an education at the third level or being employed in science and technology) (Percentage of total active population aged 25–64)
3	Tertiary educational attainment	The indicator measures the share of the population aged 25–34 who have successfully completed tertiary studies (e.g., university, higher technical institution). This educational attainment refers to ISCED (International Standard Classification of Education) 2011 level 5–8 for data from 2014 onwards and to ISCED 1997 level 5–6 for data up to 2013. The indicator is based on the EU Labour Force Survey (EU-LFS) (Percentage)
4	Adult participation in learning	The indicator measures the share of people aged 25 to 64 who stated that they received formal or non-formal education and training in the four weeks preceding the survey. Data comes from the EU Labour Force Survey (EU-LFS) (Percentage)
5	Individuals regularly using the internet	Regular use: at least once a week on average within the last three months before the survey. Use includes all locations and methods of access and any purpose (private or work/business related) (Percentage of individuals)
6	Individuals who have basic or above basic overall digital skills	Basic or above basic overall digital skills represent the two highest levels of the overall digital skills indicator, a composite indicator based on selected activities performed by individuals aged 16–74 on the internet in four areas (information, communication, problem solving, content creation). The indicator is based on the EU survey on ICT usage in households and by individuals (Percentage of individuals)

7	Individuals having ordered/bought goods or services for private use over the internet in the last three months	This indicator covers all individuals aged 16 to 74. Financial investments are excluded (Percentage of individuals)
8	Enterprises having received orders online (at least 1%)	Enterprises with at least 10 persons employed in NACE sectors C-N, having received orders online within the last calendar year before the survey (Percentage of enterprises)
9	Share of enterprises turnover on e-commerce	Enterprises' receipts from sales through electronic networks within the last calendar year before the surveys, percentage of total turnover. Enterprises with at least 10 persons employed in NACE sectors C-N (Percentage of turnover)
10	Enterprises using software solutions like CRM to analyse information about clients for marketing purposes	Enterprises using software solutions like CRM to analyse information about clients for marketing purposes, in January of the survey year (Percentage of enterprises)
11	Employment rate in the age group 20–64	The employment rate is calculated by dividing the number of persons aged 20 to 64 in employment by the total population of the same age group. The indicator is based on the EU Labour Force Survey (Percentage of total population)
12	Total unemployment rate	Unemployment rates represent unemployed persons as a percentage of the labour force. The labour force is the total number of people employed and unemployed (Percentage of population in the labour force)
13	GDP per capita in PPS	The volume index of GDP per capita in Purchasing Power Standards (PPS) is expressed in relation to the European Union average set to equal 100. If a country's index is higher than 100, its level of GDP per head is higher than the EU average and vice versa. Basic figures are expressed in PPS, a common currency that eliminates the differences in price levels between countries and allowing meaningful volume comparisons of GDP between countries (in PPS_EU27_2020=100)

Source: own elaboration based on Eurostat (2021).

The first stage of the study is an analysis of the internal diversification in the group of EU countries with respect variables 1–10. The analysis uses a single diversification measure – the diversification coefficient calculated as the relation between standard deviation and arithmetic mean. It is used to assess various characteristics and the degree of their diversification.

The statistical ratios allowed for the creation of a synthetic measure of labour market resources in particular countries. The values of the synthetic measure were the basis for ranking the countries. The synthetic measure of labour market resources was determined using Hellwig's taxonomic spatial measure of development (Hellwig, 1968; Kudełko, & Rynio, 2020). This method makes it possible to order groups of objects (countries) described by a predefined set of diagnostic properties. Hellwig's method is a model method, meaning that it adopts an ideal model of an object, i.e., one characterised by the highest (for the stimulating factors) or the lowest values (for the hampering factors). The synthetic measure is construed from measurements of distance between the object being studied and the model representation of an ideal object, expressed in standard Euclidean metrics. The resulting measure usually takes values in the range of (0;1), with higher values signifying closer proximity to the model. However, in this method of calculating the value of the synthetic measure, the likelihood of obtaining negative values is low. The distance of the country to the ideal model representation was calculated from the following formula each time:

$$d_{i0} = \left(\sum_{j=1}^{m} \left(z_{ij} - z_{oj} \right)^2 \right)^{\frac{1}{2}},$$

where:

z_{oj} – coordinates of the model object, determined from the standardised input variables,

z_{ij} – coordinates of the standardised input variables,

m – the number of variables.

The value of synthetic measure for each country was calculated from the following formula:

$$d_i = 1 - \frac{d_{i0}}{d_0},$$

where

$$d_0 = \overline{d_0} + 2s_{(d_0)},$$

$$\overline{d_0} = \frac{1}{n} \sum_{i=1}^{n} d_{i0},$$

$$s_{(d_0)} = \left(\frac{1}{n} \sum_{i=1}^{n} \left(d_{i0} - \overline{d_0} \right)^2 \right)^{\frac{1}{2}}.$$

The values of the synthetic measure were used to rank EU countries from the highest to the lowest value, resulting in an overall ranking. The last stage of the study analysed correlations between the values of the synthetic measure of labour market resources and employment rates, unemployment rates and GDP. The study explored whether the quality of labour market resources translates into the functioning and general economic condition of the countries. The analysis of correlations was based on the Pearson linear correlation coefficient, which allows for the strength and direction of two measurable features to be determined. Statistical data used in the study was obtained from the Statistical Office of the European Union – Eurostat. Statistical analyses were performed using standard formulas of the MS Excel and IBM's SPSS Statistics suite.

Research findings

The situation in the EU's labour markets was analysed on the basis of the selected ratios (variables 1–10), used to determine the adaptability to contemporary labour market requirements (Table 3.1, Appendix 1). These features point to differences between the countries. The measure adopted in the study is the changeability coefficient.

The largest gap between EU countries was recorded for the number of adults learning in the population aged 25–64. The changeability coefficient for this ratio reaches a high value of 71.9% (Appendix 1). The highest percentage of adult learning population is recorded in Sweden, Finland and Denmark: 28.6%, 27.3% and 20.0%, respectively. The lowest percentage is recorded in Romania (1%), Bulgaria (1.6%) and Slovakia (2.8%). Another differentiating feature in EU countries is employment in high- and medium-high technology manufacturing sectors and knowledge-intensive service sectors, for which the changeability coefficient amounts to 59.5%. In this category, the leading countries include Czechia, Slovakia and Slovenia (11.5%, 11.2% and 10.4%, respectively). The lowest percentage of employees in high- and medium-high technology manufacturing sectors and knowledge-intensive service sectors is recorded in Luxembourg (0.7%), Cyprus (0.9%) and Greece (1.7%).

Another differentiating feature characterised by a high value of changeability is the share of enterprises' turnover on e-commerce (46.6%). The highest share of e-commerce is recorded in Ireland (44%), Belgium (31%) and Czechia (30%), while the lowest were in Greece (4%), Cyprus (6%) and Bulgaria (6%). Unlike the above ratios, the least differentiating variable is the percentage of individuals who regularly use the internet – the value of the changeability coefficient is 8.5%, with some differences in particular countries. In Denmark, Luxembourg, Finland and Sweden more than 95% of individuals use the internet, while the respective figure for Bulgaria is only 69%, and in Romania, Portugal and Italy – 76%. A low value of changeability is recorded for human resources employed in science and technology (changeability coefficient – 18.9%). The largest share of employees in science and technology in the total active population aged 25–64 is recorded in Luxembourg (65.0%), Finland (61.6%) and Sweden (61.4%), while the lowest is in Romania (28.4%), Italy (38.0%) and Bulgaria (38.0%).

The next stage of the study calculated the value of the synthetic measure on the basis of the ten input variables. Calculations are based on Hellwig's pattern of economic development, which allows an overall/combined assessment of resources available in European labour markets to be presented. On the basis of the calculations, the EU countries were ranked by the value of the synthetic measure from the best to the weakest countries in terms of development. Top positions are held by Denmark, Sweden, Ireland, Finland and Belgium (Table 3.2).

Table 3.2 EU countries ranked by labour market resources in 2020

Ranking position	*Country*	*Value of the synthetic measure of labour market resources*
1	Denmark	0.670
2	Sweden	0.639
3	Ireland	0.596
4	Finland	0.549
5	Belgium	0.528
6	Netherlands	0.512
7	Austria	0.454
8	Spain	0.445
9	Germany	0.437
10	France	0.434
11	Estonia	0.408
12	Czechia	0.401
13	Malta	0.384
14	Luxembourg	0.383
15	Lithuania	0.369
16	Slovenia	0.364
17	Slovakia	0.327
18	Poland	0.274
19	Portugal	0.271
20	Cyprus	0.221
21	Hungary	0.218
22	Croatia	0.215
23	Latvia	0.194
24	Italy	0.141
25	Greece	0.138
26	Romania	0.026
27	Bulgaria	0.023

Source: own elaboration based on Eurostat (2021).

Denmark holds the EU's overall highest rank for the value of labour resources, with a synthetic measure of 0.67, and, further, it ranks first for three variables: individuals regularly using the internet, individuals having ordered/bought goods or services for private use over the internet in the last three months, and enterprises having received orders online. Denmark also holds top positions in the remaining variables.

Sweden took second place overall (with a score of 0.64), first place in adult participation in learning, and high positions in five other categories: human resources employed in science and technology, individuals regularly using the internet, individuals who have basic or above basic overall digital skills, individuals having ordered/bought goods or services for private use over the internet and enterprises having received orders online.

With a score of 0.60, Ireland rounds out the top 3, the country having taken first in the share of enterprises' turnover on e-commerce. It also holds high positions for enterprises having received orders online, tertiary educational attainment, human resources in science and technology and enterprises using software solutions like CRM to analyse information about clients for marketing purposes.

Bulgaria, Romania, Greece, Italy and Latvia returned the lowest rankings. With a negative value of −0.03, Bulgaria's synthetic measure is the lowest among all EU Member States. It returned the lowest scores in 4 out of 10 of the variables: individuals regularly using the internet, individuals who have basic or above basic overall digital skills, individuals having ordered/bought goods or services for private use over the internet and enterprises having received orders online. Bulgaria also ranked the lowest in all of the other categories with the exception of employment in high- and medium-high technology manufacturing sectors and knowledge-intensive service sectors, for which it finished in 13th place among all EU countries.

With a synthetic measure of 0.03, Romania finished just ahead of Bulgaria at the bottom of the rankings. It had the worst scores for three categories: human resources in science and technology, tertiary educational attainment and adult participation in learning. Greece was second from the bottom with an overall score of 0.14, and the worst score in the EU for share of enterprises' turnover on e-commerce, employment in high- and medium-high technology manufacturing sectors and knowledge-intensive service sectors.

The analysis shows that countries admitted to the EU in 2004 and later achieve worse results than the "old" Member States, though Greece and Italy, holding bottom ranking positions, are exceptions.

Another interesting question is how the quality of labour resources translates to employment and unemployment rates and general development levels in EU countries. To answer this question, we analyse correlations between the synthetic measure of labour market resources and the following variables:

- the employment rate among individuals 20–64 years of age (% of total population) – (variable 11 in Table 3.1);

- the overall unemployment rate (% of population in the labour force) – (variable 12 in Table 3.1);
- GDP per capita in PPS (In PPS_EU27_2020=100) – (variable 13 in Table 3.1);
- the results point to a strong correlation between the synthetic measure and
- GDP per capita (the Pearson linear correlation coefficient – 0.56);
- the employment rate (the Pearson linear correlation coefficient – 0.46);
- no visible correlation is found between the synthetic measure and
- the total unemployment rate (the Pearson linear correlation coefficient – (−0.11).

Conclusions and future directions

The ongoing rapid digital transformation is having and will continue to have a major impact on social and economic relations, including labour market interactions. This poses a number of challenges: meeting new requirements and improving the quality of labour market resources, including employees' and companies' knowledge and qualifications, particularly in the area of digital skills.

This chapter analyses the situation in EU labour markets on the basis of ratios describing human resources' educational attainment, readiness to increase qualifications, the participation of highly skilled labour in the employment structure, as well as digital skills and the extent to which digital technologies are used in the business sector.

EU countries vary in terms of their labour market resources. The largest gaps between countries relate to indicators including the percentage of the adult learning population, employees in high- and medium-high technology manufacturing sectors and knowledge-intensive service sectors, and the share of enterprises' turnover on e-commerce. Slight differences occur in areas including individuals regularly using the internet, and human resources employed in science and technology. Denmark, Sweden and Ireland led the rankings for all of the aspects analysed, and stand apart for their ability with and use of digital skills. Bulgaria, Romania and Greece returned the lowest scores. The results of the study clearly point to a correlation between the quality of labour market resources and employment rates as well as development levels measured by GDP per capita.

The conclusions of this work open the way for further in-depth studies of more specific issues related to the employment structure of EU countries. Changes in labour market resources and conditions over longer periods of time are pressing topics for future analyses. Comparative analyses of the development of European and other labour markets would be valuable.

Appendix 3.1

Variables describing labour market resources and development level in EU countries in 2020

Country	*Employment in high- and medium-high technology manufacturing sectors and knowledge-intensive service sectors (% of total employment)*	*Human resources in science and technology (% of total active population aged 25–64)*	*Tertiary educational attainment (% of the population aged 25–34)*	*Adult participation in learning (% of people aged 25 to 64)*	*Individuals regularly using the internet (% of individuals)*	*Individuals who have basic or above basic overall digital skills (% of individuals)*[a]
Austria	6.1	52.2	41.4	11.7	86	66
Belgium	4.4	56.6	48.5	7.4	90	61
Bulgaria	4.3	38.0	33.0	1.6	69	29
Croatia	3.6	40.0	36.6	3.2	78	53
Cyprus	0.9	53.0	57.8	4.7	91	45
Czechia	11.5	40.6	33.0	5.5	86	62
Denmark	4.9	59.3	47.1	20.0	97	70
Estonia	4.3	54.7	43.1	17.1	88	62
Finland	5.0	61.6	43.8	27.3	95	76
France	4.1	55.2	49.4	13.0	94	57
Germany	10.1	50.7	35.1	7.7	93	70
Greece	1.7	40.7	43.7	4.1	77	51
Hungary	9.6	39.9	30.7	5.1	84	49
Ireland	4.2	60.8	58.4	11.0	89	53
Italy	6.4	38.0	28.9	7.2	76	42
Latvia	2.2	47.7	44.2	6.6	87	43
Lithuania	2.6	52.4	56.2	7.2	82	56
Luxembourg	0.7	65.0	60.6	16.3	96	65
Malta	3.3	47.6	40.2	11.0	86	56
Netherlands	2.8	60.8	52.3	18.8	93	79
Poland	5.4	46.6	42.4	3.7	81	44
Portugal	3.3	40.9	41.9	10.0	76	52
Romania	6.3	28.4	24.9	1.0	76	31
Slovakia	11.2	39.7	39.0	2.8	88	54
Slovenia	10.4	50.6	45.4	8.4	85	55
Spain	4.0	47.8	47.4	11.0	91	57
Sweden	4.2	61.4	49.2	28.6	95	72
Maximum value	11.5	65	60.6	28.6	97	79
Minimum value	0.7	28.4	24.9	1	69	29
Arithmetic mean	5.1	49.3	43.5	10.1	86.3	55.9
Changeability coefficient (%)	59.5	18.9	21.1	71.9	8.5	22.1

Source: own calculations based on Eurostat (2021).
a data for 2019.

Individuals having ordered/ bought goods or services for private use over the internet in the last three months (% of individuals)[a]	*Enterprises having received orders online (at least 1%) (% of enterprises)*	*Share of enterprise turnover on e-commerce (% of turnover)*	*Enterprises using software solutions like CRM to analyse information about clients for marketing purposes (% of enterprises)*[a]	*Employment rate in the age group 20–64 (% of total population)*	*Total unemployment rate (% of population in the labour force)*	*GDP per capita in PPS (In PPS_ EU27_2020=100)*
54	22	17	22	75.5	5.4	124
55	26	31	25	70.0	5.6	117
14	8	6	11	73.4	5.1	55
35	31	14	10	66.9	7.5	64
31	15	6	19	74.9	7.6	87
43	30	30	15	79.7	2.6	94
74	38	29	23	77.8	5.6	136
56	17	14	16	78.8	6.8	86
55	19	20	26	76.5	7.8	115
58	14	23	15	72.1	8.0	103
71	18	18	20	80.0	3.8	121
32	13	4	16	61.1	16.3	64
35	14	23	7	75.0	4.3	74
59	33	44	25	73.4	5.7	211
28	12	13	15	62.6	9.2	94
34	12	10	12	77.0	8.1	72
38	28	14	24	76.7	8.5	87
63	10	15	18	72.1	6.8	266
50	25	15	25	77.4	4.3	97
70	19	17	26	80.0	3.8	133
41	14	17	21	73.6	3.2	76
28	20	20	17	74.7	6.9	77
15	18	12	14	70.8	5.0	72
47	17	21	15	72.5	6.7	71
45	18	18	10	75.6	5.0	89
47	25	19	24	65.7	15.5	86
70	31	24	21	80.8	8.3	123
74	38	44	26	80.8	16.3	266
14	8	4	7	61.1	2.6	55
46.2	20.3	18.3	18.2	73.9	6.8	103.5
35.6	38.4	46.6	30.5	6.9	46.4	43.9

References

Adams, C.J. (2013). Soft skills seen as key element for higher ed. *Education Digest, 78*(6), 18–22.

Arnold, D., Arntz, M., Gregory, T., Steffes, S., & Zierahn U. (2018). *No need for automation angst but automation policies.* Available at: https://policynetwork.org/opinions/essays/no-need-automation-angst-automation-policies (accessed 15 August 2021).

Autor, D.H. (2003). Outsourcing at will: The contribution of unjust dismissal doctrine to the growth of employment outsourcing. *Journal of Labor Economics, 21*(1), 1–42.

Bharadwaj, A.S., Sawy, O.E., Pavlou, P.A., & Venkatraman, N. (2013). Digital business strategy: Toward a next generation of insights. *Management Information Systems Quarterly, 37*(1), 471–482.

Bisello, M., & Fernandez-Macias, E. (2018). *Are blue-collar jobs turning white?* LSE Business Review. Available at: https://blogs.lse.ac.uk/businessreview/2018/10/18/are-blue-collar-jobs-turning-white (accessed 18 August 2021).

Bughin, J., Hazan, E., Lund, S., Dahlström, P., Wiesinger, A., & Subramaniam, A. (2018). *Skill shift: Automation and the future of the workforce.* Brussels: McKinsey Global Institute.

Charles, K.K., Hurst, E., & Notowidigdo, M.J. (2013). Manufacturing decline, housing booms, and non-employment. *National Bureau of Economic Research Working Paper, 18949.* Available at: https://www.nber.org/system/files/working_papers/w18949/revisions/w18949.rev1.pdf (accessed 10 August 2021).

Davenport, T., & Harris, J. (2007). *Competing on analytics.* Boston, MA: Harvard Business.

Degryse, C. (2016). *Digitalisation of the economy and its impact on labour markets.* Working Paper 2016.02. Brussels: ETUI.

Didier, N. (2021). Are we ready? Labour market transit to the digital economy. *Journal of Adult and Continuing Education.* doi:10.1177/1477971420983347

Eurostat (2021). Available at: https://ec.europa.eu/eurostat (accessed 30 August 2021).

Frey, C.B., & Osborne, M.A. (2013). *The future of employment: How susceptible are jobs to computerisation.* Available at: http://bit.ly/2D5bQBy (accessed 15 September 2021).

Gracel, J., & Makowiec, M. (2017). Core competencies of managers in the fourth industrial revolution (Industry 4.0). *Acta Universitatis Nicolai Copernici, 44*(4), 105–129.

Griffiths, D.A., Inman, M., Rojas, H., & Williams, K. (2018). Transitioning student identity and sense of place: Future possibilities for assessment and development of student employability skills. *Studies in Higher Education, 43*(5), 891–913.

Gupta, A.K. (2007). *Industrial automation and robotics.* New Delhi: University Science Press, Laxmi Publications.

Hellwig, Z. (1968). The application of the taxonomic method for the typological division of countries regarding the development level as well as the resources and structure of qualified personnel. *Przegląd Statystyczny, 15*(4), 307–327.

Henke, N., Bughin, J., Chui, M., Manyika, J., Saleh, T., Wiseman, B., & Sethupathy, G. (2016). *The age of analytics: Competing in a data-driven world.* Available at: https://www.mckinsey.com/business-functions/mckinsey-analytics/our-insights/the-age-of-analytics-competing-in-a-data-driven-world# (accessed 12 September 2021).

Jaimovich, N., & Siu, H.E. (2012). The trend is the cycle: Job polarization and jobless recoveries. *National Bureau of Economic Research Working Paper, 18334*, 1–36.

Jelonek, M., & Urbaniec, M. (2019). Development of sustainability competencies for the labour market: An exploratory qualitative study. *Sustainability, 11*(20), 5716.

Kergroach, S. (2017). Industry 4.0: New challenges and opportunities for the labour market. *Foresight and STI Governance, 11*(4), 6–8. doi:10.17323/2500–2597.2017.4.6.8.

Kudełko, J., & Rynio, D. (2020). Level of regional development and the dynamics of unemployment during the COVID-19 crisis, based on observations of German and polish regions. In K.S. Soliman (Ed.), *Sustainable economic development and advancing education excellence in the era of global pandemic*: Proceedings of the 36th International Business Information Management Association Conference (IBIMA), 4–5 November 2020, Granada, Spain. International Business Information Management Association, 1890–1904.

Małkowska, A., Urbaniec, M., & Kosała, M. (2021). The impact of digital transformation on European countries: Insights from a comparative analysis. *Equilibrium. Quarterly Journal of Economics and Economic Policy, 16*(2), 325–355.

Manyika, J., Chui, M., Bughin, J., Dobbs, R., Bisson, P., & Marrs, A. (2013). *Disruptive technologies: Advances that will transform life, business, and the global economy*. Washington, DC: McKinsey Global Institute.

Mithas, S., & Lucas, H. (2010). What is your digital business strategy? *IT Professional, 12*(6), 4–6. doi:10.1109/MITP.2010.154.

Nivea, M., Andreea-Gabriela, D., & Romeo, D. (2017). Continuous education and training of adults–Purpose of an active life on the labour market. *Junior Scientific Researcher, 3*(2), 9–18.

Pereira, V., Temouri, Y., & Patel, C. (2020). Exploring the role and importance of human capital in resilient high performing organisations: Evidence from business clusters. *Applied Psychology, 69*(3), 769–804.

Piątkowski, M. (2020). Expectations and challenges in the labour market in the context of industrial revolution 4.0. The agglomeration method-based analysis for Poland and other EU member states. *Sustainability, 12*, 5437. doi:10.3390/su12135437.

Schwab, K. (2016). The fourth industrial revolution. *World Economic Forum*, Geneva. Available at: http://luminariaz.files.wordpress.com/2017/11/the-fourth-industrial-revolution-2016-21.pdf (accessed 10 August 2021).

Singh, G., Mishra, A., & Sagar, D. (2013). An overview of artificial intelligence. *SBIT Journal of Sciences and Technology, 2*(1), 1–4.

Sisson, L.G., & Adams, A.R. (2013). Essential hospitality management competencies: The importance of soft skills. *Journal of Hospitality & Tourism Education, 25*, 131–145.

Yin, Y., Stecke, K.E., & Li, D. (2018). The evolution of production systems from Industry 2.0 through Industry 4.0. *International Journal of Production Research, 56*(1), 848–861. doi:10.1080/00207543.2017.1403664.

Part II

The labour market and employment relations in the digital economy

Theoretical background

4 Labour market segmentation theory and the digital economy

Maria Urbaniec

Introduction

Labour market segmentation is a pressing topic in Europe's policy debate. The issue has gained importance since the asymmetric impact of the 2008/2009 crisis on young people began to occur. That impact has led to labour market reforms, especially in countries affected by the crisis. While in the aftermath of the Great Recession the European Union (EU) Member States adopted various strategies to tackle segmentation, these initiatives did not lead to a significant reduction in labour market segmentation (Baimbridge, Litsios, Jackson, & Lee, 2017; Rubery & Piasna, 2016). EU Member States have acted to reduce labour market segmentation in four dimensions: employment protection legislation, unemployment benefits, active labour market policies and working time flexibility (Eichhorst, Marx, & Wehner, 2017).

Labour market segmentation refers to a clear division between secure and insecure jobs and raises issues in important areas, including macroeconomic efficiency, worker welfare and effects on social cohesion. The attractiveness of segmentation theory lies in its focus on the role of organisations in shaping labour market inequalities. Labour market segmentation is treated as an effect of the introduction and increasing use of other-than-typical forms of employment and work organisation. Particularly in the digital economy, the development of flexible forms of employment and work organisation increases labour market segmentation (Schmid, 2016). In Europe, segmentation mainly takes the form of a division between permanent and temporary work. This results in an expanding market area in which occupational stability, protection of workers' interests and promotion opportunities are significantly reduced. Furthermore, the employee's situation will depend more and more on the changing economic situation. In recent years, segmentation has contributed to deregulation in the labour market, reducing employment protections (Rubery & Piasna, 2016). In addition to deregulation, another way to overcome segmentation is the flexicurity approach, which allows employment insecurity to be compensated through social protection and investment in human capital (Cazes & Nešporová, 2007; Schmid, 2016; Svetek, 2020). This raises the question: what factors can contribute to overcoming

DOI: 10.4324/9781003254638-7

labour market segmentation? One of the factors that support the creation of an inclusive digital economy providing good quality jobs is workplace innovation. Workplace innovation enhances an organisation's innovation capacity through a dual focus on promoting both high-quality jobs and good organisational performance.

This chapter examines how the digital economy affects labour market segmentation and what factors determine the development of flexible employer-employee relations? It assesses the extent to which the dualisation and flexibility of labour markets can be reduced and enhanced through the concept of workplace innovation. This chapter is structured as follows. The first section introduces segmentation theory and patterns of temporary employment, highlighting the significant segmentation between secure and unsecure jobs. Then factors affecting labour market and flexible employer-employee relations in the digital economy will be identified. Next section looks at the limitations of labour market segmentation theory in explaining the consequences of the digital economy. The final section contains the concluding remarks.

The relevance of labour market segmentation theory

Modern labour market segmentation theory emerged in the early 1960s (Hayter & Barnes, 1992; Leontaridi, 1998). It changed the view of many economists who considered the labour market as a market of individuals with different characteristics, such as education and motivation. This perspective was intended to help explain the demand side of the market, as well as the nature and strategies of employers, as employer strategies implemented at the organisational level for selecting, investing, rewarding and retaining employees create segmented or divided labour markets (Rubery, 2007; Rubery & Piasna, 2016). Labour market segmentation theory draws on various theoretical traditions that have proved valuable in articulating the causes, features and consequences of inequality in work and employment (Grimshaw Fagan, Hebson, & Tavora, 2017). The segmentation approach to labour market problems derives from institutionalism, and the precursor of segmentation theory is considered to be Clark Kerr (1977). According to Kerr, two processes take place in the labour market: employees change jobs and the level and structure of wages evolve. These two processes are not interrelated. Thus, Kerr (1950, 1977) distinguished between the wage market, describing the phenomenon of wage formation, and the labour market, in the sense of describing the mechanism behind the allocation of labour resources.

An important contribution to the development of the labour market segmentation theory was also made by German researchers Lutz and Sengenberger (1974). Drawing on research conducted on the labour market in the Augsburg area, they built their own variant of the labour market segmentation concept (Lutz, 1987). They divided the labour market into three parts, within which different types of behaviour of market participants were observed:

- a segment comprising supply and demand of young workers in the labour force – while the supply is made up of graduates from different types of schools at all levels of education, the demand is created by employers interested in hiring a new, qualified workforce;
- a demand and supply segment of people with standard, universal professional qualifications not related to the needs of a specific enterprise. People who often perform traditional professions (carpenter, bricklayer) can be found in this part of the labour market. They are characterised by high mobility. This is due to the high adaptability of this group to seasonal and cyclical fluctuations in the demand for their labour, as well as their own interest in developing and moving up the professional hierarchy;
- the segment of supply and demand for all qualifications, i.e. the unskilled labour market. This segment constitutes a significant part of the working population and is characterised by high mobility and the ability to adapt general professional predispositions and preferences to the current situation on the labour market.

These three segments are isolated from each other and the possibilities of movement between them are very limited. In addition to the segments mentioned above, Lutz and Sengenberger (1974) observed clear tendencies towards the formation of atypical, specific (company-based) and partial labour markets. Their formation grew out of the increasing differentiation of production structures as a result of the progressive division of labour, the consolidation of enterprises, the organisation of practical vocational training and the shortage of certain types of labour. The distinction of these segments of the labour market became the basis for the three-part division of the labour market (Lutz & Sengenberger, 1974; Sengenberger, 1978). Qualifications were adopted as the criterion for division, among which three types were distinguished: universal, professional and specific for one job. Professional qualifications are the only criterion determining the size of the segments and the boundaries between them. The three-part division of the labour market distinguishes: (1) the unskilled labour market, (2) the skilled labour market (the occupational labour market) and (3) a labour market with qualifications adapted to the needs of individual enterprises (the enterprise labour market).

The term labour market segmentation has been used in various ways in recent decades (Eichhorst & Kendzia, 2016; Gray & Chapman, 2018). The security of the job often depends on the form of employment used, with some forms offering greater security than others. It refers to a clear division in labour markets between secure and insecure jobs, which are related to forms of employment. The issue of forms of employment has for years been of interest to labour law specialists and labour market researchers. Starting with the economic crisis of the late 1970s and early 1980s, traditional solutions of collective and individual employment relations, which had been used during the industrial era, were eroding (Wilkinson, Wood, & Deeg, 2014). Flexible, task-specific contracts, which do not contain a typical social package or contain one only partially, have now started to appear on labour markets. Such contracts are used with highly skilled, dynamic and well-paid freelancers who value flexibility and independence, and to unskilled or low-skilled mass production or simple service workers (often called 'junk jobs') (Kalleberg, 2003). These are two very different situations, with various objectives for the use of flexible contracts and a completely diverse distribution of benefits for the employer and employee. There are new dimensions of the segmentation of labour markets not only as "better" and "worse" industries from the workers' point of view, but also of a general division between occupations that favour a more permanent relationship with the worker and those where employment flexibility is more important, where workers rotate frequently.

With the emergence of these phenomena, and especially the liberalisation and flexibilisation of legal regulations concerning employment conditions in the "weaker" segment of the labour market, a discussion has started in the European Union on the limits of the changes that can be introduced (Cardoso & Branco, 2018; Ibsen & Tapia, 2017; Orel, Dvouletý, & Ratten, 2021). While policymakers agree with the need to make employment more flexible in response to the need to ensure enterprise competitiveness and the recurrent problem of high unemployment, they have also identified the need to adapt the social security system and public employment services to the workforce that is at risk of frequent job losses and requires assistance to re-enter employment. This has given rise to the idea of flexicurity – a policy by which workers that have been made redundant have employment flexibility with social security together with an active public service policy for retraining and helping them find new jobs (Eichhorst et al., 2017; Muffels & Wilthagen, 2013; Schmid, 2016).

To conclude, segmentation and its causes have been studied from a number of perspectives. It was originally seen as a consequence of employer strategies reinforcing socio-structural divisions (Doeringer & Piore, 1971). Since the 1990s, however, the dominant perspective has been to explain segmentation as a result of labour market institutions (Schmid, 2016). In contrast to the mainstream, the modern segmentation theory argues for a more positive role of employment regulation in reducing the problems, at both macro- and micro-economic levels.

Factors affecting labour market and employer-employee relations in the digital economy

The theory of labour market segmentation deals with the recognition of divisions into component markets and the search for arguments confirming the different functioning of separate segments. Segmentation of individual labour markets may be caused by: (1) specific requirements of various jobs (such as qualifications), which excludes certain categories of employees from applying for a specific position; (2) factors created artificially – for example, excluding individuals not belonging to given trade unions or associations from the possibility of obtaining employment; (3) cultural and moral factors; (4) other obstacles that the potential employee cannot overcome (Eichhorst & Kendzia, 2016; Loveridge & Mok, 2012; Wilkinson, 1981).

Given current developments in the digital economy, other factors may also play an important role. New digital technologies have created an increasingly rapidly changing environment, which has been heralded as the fourth industrial revolution (Schwab, 2016). Predictions about jobs and job quality as a result of this transformation are mixed. For example, between 40% and 90% of jobs are predicted to become obsolete (Frey & Osborne, 2013). Positive alternatives for the future are also possible if we can assess the impact of new technologies on jobs, business models and welfare in the EU. It can be argued that technology is not deterministic, but socially negotiated by key social actors at different levels, including the firm, industry, regional, national and EU levels (Child & Mansfield, 1972; Douglas, 2012). Different stakeholders, including companies and employees, can collectively contribute to promoting the creation of an inclusive digital economy that provides quality jobs and decent working conditions if a "strategic choice" is made (Child, 1972).

One of the strategic factors influencing the employee-employer relationship in the digital economy is workplace innovation. Workplace innovation enhances an organisation's innovation capacity through a dual focus on promoting both high-quality jobs and good organisational performance (McMurray, Muenjohn, & Scott, 2021; Oeij, Rus, & Pot, 2017). Workplace innovation is partially rooted in interpersonal relationships and approaches to sociotechnical systems in the 1950s. At the time, technological innovation was seen as the opposite of social innovation. Today, a resurgence of thinking about sociotechnical systems suggests that technological innovation alone is no longer sufficient for innovation to "happen", as successful innovation requires wider acceptance and embedding. This, in turn, suggests that technological innovations are more likely to "stick" if they are accompanied by social and organisational renewal. While this in itself is not a new observation, the integration of socio-organisational elements with technological innovation and business models seems particularly relevant in the current digital economy.

Given that the digital, knowledge-based and service-oriented economy (including in manufacturing) depends on highly skilled workers who are willing and motivated to use their skills for the good of the firm, a focus on employee engagement (Boxall & Macky, 2014) is paramount, as is technological innovation and business models. Therefore, workplace innovation provides a link between the (market) need of an organisation to change (e.g. through technological or business model innovation) in order to remain competitive while pursuing outcomes that benefit both employees and the organisation itself. Workplace innovation is perceived as a means, not an end. Workplace innovation interventions are therefore concrete socio-organisational innovations or measures that improve both quality and productivity at work. At the same time, they represent a process in which workers are actively involved in the co-creation and implementation of these measures.

Workplace innovation involves an integral set of participatory mechanisms for intervening on structural (organisational design, for example) and cultural (leadership, coordination and organisational behavioural) aspects of an organisation and its employees in order to simultaneously improve operating conditions (productivity, innovation, quality) and quality of work life (well-being at work, competence development, employee engagement). In this definition, "participatory intervention mechanisms" are synonymous with employee involvement in decision-making processes and are a prerequisite for workplace innovation (Oeij, Dhondt, Žiauberytė-Jakštienė, Corral, & Totterdill, 2016; Oeij & Dhondt, 2017).

In addition to being shaped by new technologies, the economy and society are being transformed by new business models. Business model innovations represent both a threat to established companies and industries and an opportunity to create new services, thus providing the potential for new business opportunities and jobs (Christensen, Bartman, & Bever, 2016). In the digital economy, for example, the most visible manifestations of these new types of business models are the collaborative economy, the platform economy, the gig economy and Industry 4.0 (Filser, Kraus, Breier, Nenova, & Puumalainen, 2021; Kaine & Josserand, 2019; Trabucchi, Buganza, Muzellec, & Ronteau, 2021). The success of these business models is driven by digitalisation, automation and robotisation. Furthermore, in some sectors, such as the bioeconomy, Key Enabling Technologies (KETs) are becoming increasingly important in creating new services and jobs. KETs include new materials and nanotechnology, photonics and micro- and nanoelectronics, life sciences technologies, artificial intelligence and digital security and connectivity (European Commission, 2018; Laibach, Börner, & Bröring, 2019; Sołtysik, Urbaniec, & Wojnarowska, 2019).

Parallel to technological change and the emergence of new business models, rapid demographic changes, including population ageing and migration, are also affecting the labour market (Pawera & Jancikova, 2018; Walwei, 2016). Demographic change affects not only the supply of labour and skills, but also the demand for new services and social care, for example in health, education and training. To conclude, a range of interrelated factors, from technological advances through workplace innovations and new business models to demographic changes, affect the future of jobs, the well-being of employees and the overall quality of work.

Implications and limitations of labour market segmentation theory in the digital economy

Labour market segmentation generates challenges in important areas, including macroeconomic efficiency, employee well-being and the impact on social cohesion. The issues arising from segmentation are complex and include macroeconomic efficiency on the one hand, and employee well-being on the other. In terms of macroeconomic effects, there are indications that the growth of temporary employment has impeded productivity growth (it discourages investment in the workforce) and has not contributed to employment growth (because secure employment is replaced by temporary work) (Boeri, 2011). In the literature, there is also evidence that job insecurity, and in particular fixed-term contracts, negatively affects workers' health and well-being (Benach et al., 2014). This leads to stress as a result of such social problems, not only damaging health but also disrupting various aspects of people's lives, e.g. cognitive abilities, family formation (Mani, Mullainathan, Shafir, & Zhao, 2013). The same is true for unemployment and poverty, which are inevitable if there is a lack of mobility to get out of precarious jobs.

Precarisation is defined as mechanisms that produce, reproduce or spread disadvantaged segments of the labour market through: (1) low wages; (2) limited access to social security; (3) low job security; (4) other conditions that make work less stable than under standard (permanent) contracts (Bereswill & Neuber, 2016). Moreover, Grimshaw et al. (2017) indicates key forms of inequality at work and employment: low wages, gender pay inequality and segmentation patterns between standard and non-standard forms of employment. The effect of job insecurity is frustration and anger, which can lead to vulnerability to radical and populist slogans, such as those related to hostility towards immigrants, who constitute an important subcategory of the precariat (Standing, 2014). The stress of labour market segmentation stems from the fact that many European welfare states are poorly equipped to deal with non-standard workers in the digital economy. Eligibility criteria for social benefits, based on assumptions underlying the post-war employment model, often disadvantage workers with short and intermittent working lives (Berton & Richiardi, 2012). As Palier and Thelen (2010) highlight, in countries with strong segmentation, policy makers have an incentive to design social exclusion policies.

Especially in the wake of the 2008/2009 crisis and rising youth unemployment, EU Member States have started to take segmentation seriously. EU Member States are taking action to reduce labour market segmentation in four dimensions: employment protection legislation, unemployment benefits, active labour market policies and working time flexibility (Eichhorst et al., 2017). There are therefore many policy initiatives aimed at overcoming labour market divisions, though they have yet to prove very successful: temporary employment continues to grow and youth unemployment remains worryingly high. Measures taken to date have been insufficient to significantly improve the labour market situation. An analysis done by Eichhorst et al. (2017) arrived at the following conclusions:

- segmentation – measured as the share of temporary work – is a constant feature of many, though not all, European labour markets. So far, no Member State has managed to reverse this trend to a significant extent;

- segmentation is more acute in Member States with high youth unemployment – this concerns both the share of temporary work and the prospects for mobility to permanent jobs;
- while many temporary workers successfully transition to permanent employment, segmentation exists – it appears that a significant share of temporary workers are "trapped", even in the long term.

Furthermore, the labour market is segmented when there are significant barriers to mobility. In particular, employment protection legislation has been identified as a barrier to mobility into the core labour market (Bentolila, Dolado, & Jimeno, 2012). This is because employers anticipate turnover costs, which encourages reliance on a core labour force supplemented by temporary workers. The large number of temporary workers in the labour market is not a problem if mobility towards secure employment is high. In fact, many temporary workers successfully make this transition. However, segmentation occurs when workers are stuck in unstable and insecure jobs accompanied by repeated periods of unemployment.

Apart from the economic background of the existence of "worse" and "better" jobs in the economy, the consequences of the emerging divisions for workers are also important. These result from the dual concept within labour market segmentation theory, among other sources. Analysing the changes in work organisation as a cause of the spread of flexibility, Sennett (1998) notes numerous negative changes in the situation of workers. While these changes are supposed to deliver a break from the work routines of the Fordist period, in reality they mainly lead to an increase in uncertainty, forcing workers to negotiate permanent risks. The constant fluctuations resulted from the restructuring of companies, changes in their owners and mergers leading to the downsizing or liquidation of organisational units all introduce discontinuity into professional life. This is often associated with the need to relocate and, from the point of view of the employees' outlook, means the loss of a narrative that gave meaning to a career and determined the direction of their development. Employee insecurity is also affected by organisational change: large corporations no longer have a hierarchical organisation (Hickman & Silva, 2018). The pyramidal structure has been replaced by a loose network whose individual elements can be exchanged and removed. The model of managerial power has changed: managers no longer give clear orders, but manage communication within the team, which limits their responsibility in case of failure.

In the digital economy, new ways of managing and a changed organisational structure hinder employees' ability to make sound career choices. Horizontal moves, or promotion within the structure turns out to be a sham, consisting of a transfer to a parallel position, are a leading example here, as are "retrospective losses" (due to a knowledge deficit, the new job turns out to be based later on worse conditions than the previous one) and unpredictable salaries. Sennett (1998) also sees digitalisation as the cause of frequent underemployment as automation and computerisation become more ubiquitous. This can be particularly true for occupations requiring manual labour, e.g. bakers. However, both blue-collar workers and higher-skilled workers with tasks that require more creativity may lose out to digitalisation due to a superficial approach to their work.

Nowadays, the computer makes it possible not to think about the essence of technological processes or design activities once carried out with a pencil and paper (think engineers using CAD software). Devices that make work more convenient are causing the traditional work ethos, the desire to develop and a sense of pride in one's work, to disappear. Instead, there is a desire to frequently change positions and the nature of work, even if this does not lead to a better professional position. The flexibility promoted in the digital economy does not give employees more freedom, and often even limits their subjectivity and control over their own working lives (Litvinenko, 2020). In the corporate culture, older employees turn out to be superfluous, with those as young as 40 stereotypically perceived as professionally burnt-out, less attractive and uncreative and their experience in conditions of rapid technological and organisational changes seen more as a liability than an asset (Kroon, Van Selm, ter Hoeven, & Vliegenthart, 2018). However, the relatively better situation young people enjoy results in part from the fact that they resist superiors less frequently than their older colleagues and are more susceptible to modern methods of control in the workplace.

Conclusions

The aim of the chapter was to analyse how the digital economy affects labour market segmentation and what factors determine the development of flexible employer-employee relationships? The term labour market segmentation has been used in various ways in recent decades. It refers to a clear division in labour markets between secure and insecure jobs, which are related to forms of employment. One form of segmentation is the division between workers on fixed-term and temporary contracts. In practice, there are various precarious forms of flexible employment, including part-time employment, temporary work and quasi-independent self-employment. Part-time employment is mainly voluntary in most European countries (OECD, 2021). Although temporary work and dependent self-employment can be very precarious, they represent a much smaller share of the European labour force than standard employment. This division has been institutionalised by the creation and expansion of flexible forms of employment, especially temporary work.

Alongside the economic background of the existence of "worse" and "better" jobs in the economy, the consequences of the emerging divisions from the workers' perspective are also important. These arise from the dual concept within labour market segmentation theory, among other sources. What is important here is first and foremost the issue of the consolidation of positions within the two segments: workers in the 'worse' part of the labour market have relatively little opportunity for promotion to the "better" part. Participation in the "better" or "worse" segment of the labour market may also depend on the nature of the employment – whether it is permanent or temporary (Rubery & Piasna, 2016). Being among temporary employees at the beginning of one's career largely determines the further path of that career. People with average professional qualifications, employed in positions with high turnover, have a strong chance of remaining in the "marginal" sector. This may be due to the low quality of their formal education, and subsequent work in inferior and unstable positions perpetuates job insecurity.

Furthermore, this chapter has attempted to assess the extent to which the dualisation and flexibility of labour markets can be constrained and enhanced through, among other things, the concept of workplace innovation. Workplace innovation enhances an organisation's innovation capacity through a dual focus on promoting both high-quality jobs and good organisational performance. Particularly in the digital economy, disruptive technologies and social transformation require workplace innovation. The main areas of the digital economy include the digitalisation of production through automation/robotics (also referred to as "Industrie 4.0") (Howaldt, Kopp, & Schultze, 2017) and the digitalisation of work through the platform economy (also referred to as "uberisation") (Warhurst, Mathieu, & Wright, 2017). Both have the capacity to eliminate jobs: the former by replacing jobs with technology; the latter by using technology to replace jobs with micro-jobs. Both can also make existing skills, tax and welfare systems highly vulnerable to disruption. Current academic and policy discourse is dominated by predictions of mass unemployment and social upheaval (Brynjolfsson & McAfee, 2014; Frey & Osborne, 2013; Fuchs & Sevignani, 2013). However, new business models and accompanying technological advances can either lead to "dystopia" (Fuchs, 2019), which much of the current discourse predicts, or alternatively to increased job quality, wealth creation and socio-economic inclusiveness. Although the current understanding of these changes and their socio-economic impacts suffers from a lack of systematic evidence, technological advances can mitigate the potentially negative social impacts of technology-driven innovation (Oeij & Dhondt, 2017).

To conclude, segmented labour markets, operating at multiple scales and spaces, are leading to increasingly flexible worker-employer relationships. These trends continue with the emergence of digital work, which can be performed globally by workers separated by large physical distances and by workers who do not share the characteristics endowed by a shared culture. This is also largely related to the technical structure of platforms, digital work transactions over the internet and geographically dispersed global workers.

References

Baimbridge, M., Litsios, I., Jackson, K., & Lee, U.R. (2017). Segmentation across Europe. In M. Baimbridge, I. Litsios, K. Jackson, & U.R. Lee (Eds.), *The segmentation of Europe* (pp. 1–33). London: Palgrave Macmillan.

Benach, J., Vives, A., Amable, M., Vanroelen, C., Tarafa, G., & Muntaner, C. (2014). Precarious employment: Understanding an emerging social determinant of health. *Annual Review of Public Health, 35*, 229–253.

Bentolila, S., Dolado, J.J., & Jimeno, J.F. (2012). Reforming an insider-outsider labor market: The Spanish experience. *IZA Journal of European Labor Studies, 1*(1), 1–29.

Bereswill, M., & Neuber, A. (2016). Marginalised masculinity, precarisation and the gender order. In M.T. Herrera Vivar, & H. Lutz (Eds.), *Framing intersectionality* (pp. 83–102). London: Routledge.

Berton, F., & Richiardi, M. (2012). *The political economy of work security and flexibility: Italy in comparative perspective*. Bristol: Policy Press.

Boeri, T. (2011). Institutional reforms in European labour markets. In O. Ashenfelter & D. Card (Eds.), *Handbook of labor economics* (pp. 1173–1236). Amsterdam: North Holland.

Boxall, P., & Macky, K. (2014). High-involvement work processes, work intensification and employee well-being. *Work, Employment and Society, 28*(6), 963–984.

Brynjolfsson, E., & McAfee, A. (2014). *The second machine age: Work, progress, and prosperity in a time of brilliant technologies*. New York: WW Norton & Company.

Cardoso, D., & Branco, R. (2018). Liberalised dualisation. Labour market reforms and the crisis in Portugal: A new departure. *European Journal of Social Security, 20*(1), 31–48.

Cazes, S., & Nešporová, A. (2007). *Flexicurity: A relevant approach in Central and Eastern Europe*. Geneva: International Labour Organization.

Child, J. (1972). Organizational structure, environment and performance: The role of strategic choice. *Sociology, 6*(1), 1–22.

Child, J., & Mansfield, R. (1972). Technology, size, and organization structure. *Sociology, 6*(3), 369–393.

Christensen, C.M., Bartman, T., & Bever, D. v. (2016). The hard truth about business model innovation. *MIT Sloan Management Review, 58*, 31–40.

Doeringer, P.B., & Piore, M.J. (1971). *Internal labor markets and manpower analysis: With a new introduction*. New York: Routledge.

Douglas, D.G. (2012). *The social construction of technological systems: New directions in the sociology and history of technology*. Cambridge, MA: MIT Press.

Eichhorst, W., & Kendzia, M.J. (2016). Workforce segmentation in Germany: From the founding era to the present time. *Journal for Labour Market Research, 49*(4), 297–315.

Eichhorst, W., Marx, P., & Wehner, C. (2017). Labor market reforms in Europe: Towards more flexicure labor markets? *Journal for Labour Market Research, 51*(1), 1–17.

European Commission. (2018). *A sustainable bioeconomy for Europe: Strengthening the connection between economy, society and the environment. Updated Bioeconomy Strategy* (EC RTD/F. 2018). Available at: https://ec.europa.eu/research/bioeconomy/pdf/ec_bioeconomy_strategy_2018.pdf#view=fit&pagemode=none (accessed 7 August 2021).

Filser, M., Kraus, S., Breier, M., Nenova, I., & Puumalainen, K. (2021). Business model innovation: Identifying foundations and trajectories. *Business Strategy and the Environment, 30*(2), 891–907.

Frey, C.B., & Osborne, M. (2013). *The future of employment*. Oxford: Oxford Martin Programme on Technology and Employment, University of Oxford.

Fuchs, A. (2019). *Precarious times: Temporality and history in modern German culture.* Ithaca, NY: Cornell University Press.

Fuchs, C., & Sevignani, S. (2013). What is digital labour? What is digital work? What's their difference? And why do these questions matter for understanding social media? *TripleC: Communication, Capitalism & Critique. Journal for a Global Sustainable Information Society, 11*(2), 237–293.

Gray, J., & Chapman, R. (2018). The significance of segmentation for institutionalist theory and public policy. In D.L Champlin, & J.T. Knoedler (Eds.), *The institutionalist tradition in labour economics* (pp. 117–130). London: Routledge.

Grimshaw, D., Fagan, C., Hebson, G., & Tavora, I. (2017). A new labour market segmentation approach for analysing inequalities: Introduction and overview. In D. Grimshaw, C. Fagan, G. Hebson, & I. Tavora (Eds.), *Making work more equal* (pp. 1–32). Manchester: Manchester University Press.

Hayter, R., & Barnes, T. J. (1992). Labour market segmentation, flexibility, and recession: A British Columbian case study. *Environment and Planning C: Government and Policy, 10*(3), 333–353.

Hickman, C.R., & Silva, M.A. (2018). *Creating excellence: Managing corporate culture, strategy, and change in the new age.* London: Routledge.

Howaldt, J., Kopp, R., & Schultze, J. (2017). Why Industrie 4.0 needs workplace innovation—A critical essay about the German debate on advanced manufacturing. In P. Oeij, D. Rus, & F. Pot (Eds.), *Workplace innovation. Aligning perspectives on health, safety and well-Being* (pp. 45–60). Cham: Springer.

Ibsen, C.L., & Tapia, M. (2017). Trade union revitalisation: Where are we now? Where to next? *Journal of Industrial Relations, 59*(2), 170–191.

Kaine, S., & Josserand, E. (2019). The organisation and experience of work in the gig economy. *Journal of Industrial Relations, 61*(4), 479–501.

Kalleberg, A.L. (2003). Flexible firms and labor market segmentation: Effects of workplace restructuring on jobs and workers. *Work and occupations, 30*(2), 154–175.

Kerr, C. (1950). Labor markets: Their character and consequences. *American Economic Review, 40*(May), 278–291.

Kerr, C. (1977). *Labor markets and wage determination: The Balkanization of labor markets and other essays.* Berkeley: University of California Press.

Kroon, A.C., Van Selm, M., ter Hoeven, C.L., & Vliegenthart, R. (2018). Reliable and unproductive? Stereotypes of older employees in corporate and news media. *Ageing and Society, 38*(1), 166–191.

Laibach, N., Börner, J., & Bröring, S. (2019). Exploring the future of the bioeconomy: An expert-based scoping study examining key enabling technology fields with potential to foster the transition toward a bio-based economy. *Technology in Society, 58*, 101118. doi:10.1016/j.techsoc.2019.03.001

Leontaridi, M. (1998). Segmented labour markets: Theory and evidence. *Journal of Economic Surveys, 12*(1), 103–109.

Litvinenko, V. (2020). Digital economy as a factor in the technological development of the mineral sector. *Natural Resources Research, 29*(3), 1521–1541.

Loveridge, R., & Mok, A.L. (2012). *Theories of labour market segmentation: A critique.* Boston, MA: Springer.

Lutz, B. (1987). *Arbeitsmarktstruktur und betriebliche Arbeitskräftestrategie: eine theoretisch-historische Skizze zur Entstehung betriebszentrierter Arbeitsmarktsegmentation.* Frankfurt am Main: Campus Verlag.

Lutz, B., & Sengenberger, W. (1974). *Arbeitsmarktstrukturen und öffentliche Arbeitsmarktpolitik: eine kritische Analyse von Zielen und Instrumenten* (Vol. 26). Göttingen: Verlag Otto Schwartz & Co.

Mani, A., Mullainathan, S., Shafir, E., & Zhao, J. (2013). Poverty impedes cognitive function. *Science, 341*(6149), 976–980.

McMurray, A.J., Muenjohn, N., & Scott, D. (2021). Measuring workplace innovation: Scale development. *Journal of Small Business Management*, 1–20. doi:10.1080/00472778.2020.1844490

Muffels, R., & Wilthagen, T. (2013). Flexicurity: A new paradigm for the analysis of labor markets and policies challenging the trade-off between flexibility and security. *Sociology Compass, 7*(2), 111–122.

OECD. (2021). *OECD employment outlook 2021*. Paris: OECD.

Oeij, P., Dhondt, S., Žiauberytė-Jakštienė, R., Corral, A., & Totterdill, P. (2016). Implementing workplace innovation across Europe: Why, how and what? *Economic and Social Changes: Facts, Trends, Forecast, 5*(47), 195–218.

Oeij, P., Rus, D., & Pot, F. (2017). *Workplace innovation: Theory, research and practice*. Cham: Springer.

Oeij, P.R., & Dhondt, S. (2017). Theoretical approaches supporting workplace innovation. In P. Oeij, D, Rus, & F. Pot (Eds.), *Workplace innovation: Theory, research and practice* (pp. 63–78). Cham: Springer.

Orel, M., Dvouletý, O., & Ratten, V. (Eds.). (2021). *The flexible workplace: Coworking and other modern workplace transformations*. Cham: Springer.

Palier, B., & Thelen, K. (2010). Institutionalizing dualism: Complementarities and change in France and Germany. *Politics & Society, 38*(1), 119–148.

Pawera, R., & Jancikova, E. (2018). An issue of age in the labour market in Slovakia. *Economic Annals-XXI, 168*(11–12), 93–99.

Rubery, J. (2007). Developing segmentation theory: A thirty year perspective. *Economies et sociétés, 28*(6), 941–964.

Rubery, J., & Piasna, A. (2016). Labour market segmentation and the EU reform agenda: Developing alternatives to the mainstream. *ETUI Research Paper, 2016.10*.

Schmid, G. (2016). *Flexible and secure labour market transitions: Towards institutional capacity building in the digital economy*. Available at: https://www.econstor.eu/handle/10419/162527 (accessed 7 September 2021).

Schwab, K. (2016). *The forth industrial revolution*. Cologny/Geneva: World Economic Forum.

Sengenberger, W. (1978). *Der gespaltene Arbeitsmarkt*. Frankfurt am Main: Campus.

Sennett, R. (1998). *The corrosion of character: The personal consequences of work in the new capitalism*. New York: WW Norton & Company.

Sołtysik, M., Urbaniec, M., & Wojnarowska, M. (2019). Innovation for sustainable entrepreneurship: Empirical evidence from the bioeconomy sector in Poland. *Administrative Sciences, 9*(3), 50.

Standing, G. (2014). The Precariat-The new dangerous class. *Amalgam, 6*(6–7), 115–119.

Svetek, M. (2020). The promise of flexicurity: Can employment and income security mitigate the negative effects of job insecurity? *Economic and Industrial Democracy*. doi:10.1177/0143831X20975474

Trabucchi, D., Buganza, T., Muzellec, L., & Ronteau, S. (2021). Platform-driven innovation: Unveiling research and business opportunities. *Creativity and Innovation Management, 30*(1), 6–11.

Walwei, U. (2016). *Digitalization and structural labour market problems: The case of Germany.* Geneva: International Labour Office.

Warhurst, C., Mathieu, C., & Wright, S. (2017). Workplace innovation and the quality of working life in an age of Uberisation. In P. Oeij, D, Rus, & F. Pot (Eds.), *Workplace innovation: Theory, research and practice* (pp. 245–259). Cham: Springer.

Wilkinson, A., Wood, G., & Deeg, R. (2014). *The Oxford handbook of employment relations: Comparative employment systems.* Oxford: Oxford University Press.

Wilkinson, F. (1981). *The dynamics of labour market segmentation.* London: Academic Press.

5 New institutional economics and the digital economy

Michał Głuszak

Introduction

The nascence of new communication channels and development of the internet at the end of the 20th century intensified transnational economic activity to the extent that the new era is often referred to as digital capitalism or digital economy (Schiller, 2000, p. xiv). In the first two decades of the 21st century, several new ideas emerged, some of which initiated profound changes in technology, economics, society and international relations. From a historical perspective, the adoption of technology has driven industrial revolutions. In this light, it seems plausible that the 21st century will prove turbulent one in human history. Alongside the ongoing shift in the balance of geopolitical power from the West to the East, threats and ongoing challenges spurred by climate change, we are now witness to the beginning of the Fourth Industrial Revolution (Revolution 4.0).

The emergence of this new digital era is marked by a profound expansion of communication channels (the internet), digitalisation, artificial intelligence, robotics and other technological advancements, which together are driving a revolution in how human society operates. However, it is extremely hard to predict the extent and direction of those changes. As Eggertsson (2013) has written, the most pressing challenges digitalisation processes are bring to bear include intellectual property rights issues, business models, political structure and changes in lifestyle. Digital transformation has changed labour relations. There are various labour market consequences of digital economy reported and assessed in the economics literature: labour market inequality, job insecurity, precarity, income irregularity, balance between property rights and work rights, new job creation, the length of both the work day and one's career and work-life balance.

The ongoing digital transformation has a distinctive and multifaceted impact on the labour market, both in terms of the nature of work, types of tasks performed and employment relations (Marginson, 2016; Sozinova, 2021). One phenomenon that has arisen in recent years is the 'gig economy'. The term is used to describe temporary and flexible work arrangements taken by freelancers (independent contractors) rather than employees, and perform

DOI: 10.4324/9781003254638-8

project-based tasks for a variety companies rather than a single employer (Pichault & McKeown, 2019; Tran & Sokas, 2017). This is a stark contrast to the traditional model of work relations, in which people are full-time employees with regulated rights (often protected by unions). In the traditional (old) model, employees changed their positions (or employer) relatively rarely, and focused on a longer period in planning a career over the lifecycle. That model seems a thing of the past, at least in several sectors. As with most social and economic trends involving institutional changes, the gig economy comes with both opportunities and threats (Hinings, Gegenhuber, & Greenwood, 2018; Lehdonvirta, 2018; Pulignano, Thompson, & Doerflinger, 2020).

One benefit of the gig economy for both employees and employers is its flexibility. Thanks to the digital revolution, people are no longer forced to commute to the office, instead working remotely from home, saving both time and costs (Rainnie & Dean, 2020). The Covid-19 pandemic has increased the flexibility even further. Due to the threats and needs for social distancing Covid-19 imposed, remote work has become the standard in numerous sectors where services are provided easily. Additionally, some services are not limited geographically, and can be effectively delivered around the world.

Remote work has also benefitted employers. Expenditures on renting and operating office facilities have fallen, allowing companies to be more cost effective (both in terms of fixed and average costs). Companies are no longer forced to recruit employees where their office premises are located, or to require them to move. Thanks to the expansion of the internet, remote work can be performed by employees (but also individual contractors) from around the world at negligible cost, and companies can recruit from a wider pool of talent. This creates a completely new set of challenges for human resource management (Donnelly & Johns, 2021; Méndez, 2020).

At the same time, the digital economy presents the labour market with a range of challenges (Coyle, 2017; Drahokoupil & Jepsen, 2017; Greve, 2019; Jepsen & Drahokoupil, 2017) Firstly, contrary to common beliefs, remote work and the gig economy can weaken the work-life balance, not only failing to provide more leisure time, but also blurring the boundaries between work and private life. Second, improved information technologies have significantly reduced the cost of supervising work and monitoring performance, thus making extensive control over employees easy and inexpensive. Third, with various modes and contracts binding relations between companies and workers, employment status needs clarification. This could be addressed with sensible regulations to protect employees (Méndez, 2020). The Covid-19 pandemic has demonstrated that external disruptions may have severe consequences for the majority of people working in the gig economy. Institutional change is needed to provide a fairer balance between flexibility and security. A blended approach, where employees of the company cooperate with a pool of independent contractors, would be advisable (Mahato, Kumar, & Jena, 2021). The literature demonstrates that an institutional perspective can

neoclassical economics assumes that in general individuals have access to perfect information and unlimited computational capabilities to process it and make rational decisions. In contrast, new institutional economics does not impose those constraints, and it acknowledges that agents (*homo sapiens* rather than *homo economicus*) typically operate with incomplete information and do not make optimal decisions. Those types of behaviour are typically attributed to bounded rationality, a term that came to prominence following the contributions of Simon (1955) and his successors.

The digital economy has significantly reduced the costs of information. These costs are a major component of transaction costs, a category long overlooked by mainstream economics. To understand the impact transaction cost may have for the labour market, one needs to adopt a different perspective. Neoclassical economics and new institutional economics treat transaction costs differently. The former neglects them as if they were irrelevant and generally assumes that the market is frictionless and operate smoothly at the micro level. New institutional economics takes a completely different stance regarding transaction costs. It acknowledges the existence of nontrivial transaction costs that shape the decisions of economic agents. The incurrence of transactions costs in the face of uncertainty, searching for new information and operating in a turbulent economic environment encourages the creation of institutions. One way to reduce risk and costs related to uncertainty and transactions costs is to introduce regulations, laws and contracts (formal institutions). Another is to introduce and enforce social norms and habits (informal institutions).

The functional nature of the firm is to be a system which processes and coordinates economic transactions (Coase, 1937). This logic can be extended to non-profit organisations devised to satisfy other goals society considers important. Organisations operate within an institutional framework, and institutions set up the rules of the game at the macro-, meso- and micro-levels. As an analytical framework, the new institutional economics explains complex and interrelated changes on the labour market caused by digital revolutions. In particular, the theory helps explain: (1) the evolution and emergence of new arrangements on the labour market, especially those governing employer-employees relations; (2) the impact of both formal and informal institutions on the adoption of digital technologies on the labour market, as well as the consequences of inefficient legal rules and social norms for economic development and social welfare; (3) the effect of labour market changes on the emergence of a new institutional framework that will help to achieve economic growth and soothe social tensions brought about by the digital economy.

Factors determining employment relations from a new institutional theory in the digital economy

Formal institutions and employer-employee relations

Digital economy has had a profound influence on business operations worldwide – from company organisation to the creation of new networks and modes of operation (Moriset & Malecki, 2009). Empirical evidence from various countries suggests that the effect of digital transformation on labour markets is moderated by the alignment between legal institutions (rules of the game) and organisational governance. The formal institutions that affect the labour market include constitutions, laws, markets, contracts and arrangements and property rights. Most of these institutions are instrumental to the adoption of digital economy on the labour market and its consequences – both positive and negative. Addressing formal institutions – that is, creating and enforcing laws – helps to explain the consequences of digital transformation on labour market as well as the differences between countries and sectors that are subject to specific regulations.

In their systematic review, Kreshpaj et al. (2020) explain what is meant by the term precarious employment. On the basis of a systematic analysis of the relevant literature, they identify three dimensions: (1) employment insecurity (contractual relation insecurity, contractual temporariness, contractual underemployment, multiple jobs/sectors), (2) income inadequacy and (3) lack of rights and protection (due to the lack of unions, social security, regulatory support and workplace rights) (Kreshpaj et al., 2020). At least two of the three points fall within the purview of the new institutional economics.

Patel (2020) argues that the Fourth Industrial Revolution is characterised by the automation of work. The emergence of digital technologies and artificial intelligence portends upheaval in numerous sectors that have traditionally depended upon routine and well-defined work. A growing body of evidence suggests that digitalisation and automation are likely leading to the replacement of humans by machines, at least to some extent. In some instances, automatisation reduces labour time and leads to different contractual arrangements, while in more extreme cases, particularly in sectors dependent on routine jobs, employees are made redundant. The arrangements within business organisations are not in line with existing formal institutions. The ongoing reduction of routine jobs typically performed by less affluent and educated people with lower economic, social and cultural capital was not preceded, nor has it been followed, by institutional change. The introduction of new modes of industrial organisations related to digital technologies is not in perfect alignment with existing laws and social norms and it may have a detrimental effect on economic growth and social stability (Teague & Grahl, 1998). The further infringement of already underprivileged groups within society, whose jobs are automated by machines and positions made redundant, leads to growing inequalities and social policy problems. Comparative analysis shows that this problem is not evenly distributed across countries, with some more affected by digital transformation. Patel (2020) argues that policy measures may limit the negative externalities caused by digital transformation. Doing so would require institutional evolution so that formal institutions (legal regulations, e.g. constitutions, legal contracts) are adopted to the new reality, one in which a significant share of society is not active on the labour market, as their jobs will have been automated (Gahan & Harcourt,

1998). Evidence from Middle-Eastern countries shows that changes in labour law and training programmes on a large scale may limit the negative effects of digital transformation (Eltamimi, 2020).

Based on the regulatory measures and court practice, Chernyaeva (2020) demonstrates that formal institutions play a vital role in the adoption of digital technologies in the labour market. The most important issues are related to labour relationships and the contractual arrangements between employer and employee. These include regulations governing remote work, electronic documentation, health policy and safety requirements. Tomassetti (2020) addresses tensions between workers and companies caused by the digital revolution. Digitalised work may shift the balance from worker rights (employees) towards property rights (companies) at least from a legal perspective. Well-documented evidence shows that companies attempt to decrease the level of protection of workers providing their services remotely. The growing empirical evidence suggest that relations between labour markets and institutions is strong (Wilthagen & Rogowski, 2002), especially when new trends (such us the digital economy) emerge, and are absorbed by individuals and organisations. Both historical and current economic development suggests that the topic deserves more attention (Fudge, 2017).

Informal institutions and employer-employee relations

Informal institutions that have an impact on the adoption of digital technologies on the labour market include: norms, traditions, customs, religion, taboos, codes of conduct and social theories. The set of informal institutions is hierarchical in nature, but different layers of informal institutions overlap across countries, regions and industries. Some norms and customs are exclusive to certain industries (long-established traditional artisans, for example) and have limited impact on the labour market as a whole. The other informal institutions are typical to societies, because value systems and religion can be shared by a large number or even the vast majority of a population.

The digital transformations of a labour market and integration of information technologies into every sphere of human activity change relatively stable social norms, beliefs and lifestyles. These changes raise general concerns, including the following: (1) excessive control of employers over employees' private lives and working time, (2) potential work-life (im)balance caused by the lines between work and leisure time blurring, (3) the automation of work and potential technological unemployment, (4) the emergence of global labour market where work is provided through digital platforms, (5) the gig economy, precarity and uncertainty (Śledziewska & Włoch, 2021).

Several problems and social tensions related to the new modes of work arrangement that typify the gig economy are caused by the misalignment of digital transformation with informal institutions shared by society: social theories (religion, philosophy, social science and other beliefs and expectations) and social norms (rules of behaviour). Those informal rules of the game are relatively stable over time (compared to the ever-changing rules of law) and "are a part of the heritage that we call culture" (North, 1990, p. 37). They affect human behaviour on the labour market, but are modified by the strategic and collective decisions of individuals or organisations (Greif & Kingston, 2011).

In the context of digital economy and its consequences for the labour market, in the long-run organisations and individuals make a collective effort to adapt the rules of the game to new circumstances, increase social welfare and spur economic growth. Nonetheless, the profound and effective changes of an informal institutional framework are usually stepwise. Informal institutions are relatively more rigid than rules of law and evolve gradually (Eggertsson, 2013, p. 1). The empirical examples show that informal institutions are very influential in emerging economies (Olsen & Morgan, 2010), and changes in cultural and social norms tend to lag behind regulatory evolution. Unfortunately, comprehensive social theory on the formation of informal institutions and their evolution has yet to be proposed (North, 1993).

A recent study based on the longitudinal data and applications suggests that the evolution of informal institutions is path-dependent (Nunn, 2009). A growing body of empirical evidence provides solid support for the old hypothesis that history matters. In the economic context, empirical evidence has shown that historical events have their long-run consequences and economic development exhibits a marked path dependence. Still, despite the substantial progress made in the field, the new institutional economics has not provided a sound theoretical explanation of path dependence-related causality mechanisms (Nunn, 2009).

Comparative studies show that informal institutions play an instrumental role in economic development. Tabellini (2010) argues that certain norms and values (i.e. trust, individualism, respect) are positively linked with economic growth, while other values (obedience, for example) may postpone development. In the same line of argument, Tamanaha (2015) suggests that cultures promoting discipline, hard work and education outperform those that do not. Moreover, informal roles play a vital role in the enforcement of rules of law and other formal institutions present on a labour market. An interesting paper uses Hofstede's cultural indices to explain labour-market flexibility in various countries. The results suggest that informal institutions embedded in national cultures may have a strong influence on rigidities on the labour market (i.e. employment terms, wages, unemployment policy). For example, feminine gender traits in social and cultural norms were positively related with labour-market inflexibility (Black, 1999).

Digital economy, institutional change and the labour market

According to new institutional economics, institutions play an important role in economic development. The institutional framework influences transaction costs, labour market arrangements and resource allocation in digital economy and therefore has an indirect impact (positive or negative) on economic growth (Nabli & Nugent, 1989). As discussed previously, the comparative quality of institutions may explain why digital economy works in some sectors and countries but not in the others. Nonetheless, digital transformation also leads to changes in the institutional framework of the employer-employee relations.

The new institutional economics provides some interesting insights into potential future institutional changes related to digital transformation in the context of the labour market. Institutions, while relatively stable, are also transformed over time. To reflect this, several efforts have been made to model institutional changes. From a theoretical perspective, the institutional change on the labour market may be caused by both endogenous and exogenous factors (the digital revolution belonging to the latter group). Changes in the institutional framework can be induced (voluntary, collective agreement on new rules of the game) or imposed (if introduced by acts of law). Institutional change is also a path-dependent and complex process, which explains why institutions differ across economies or industry sectors, and why it is hard to replicate/recreate beneficial institutions based on their relative performance in seemingly similar cases. According to the economics literature, institutional change on the labour market can be caused by three categories of factors: functional, political and social (Mcguire et al., 2002). The first incentive for institutional change is related to the inefficiency and failures of the labour market, which affect the performance of the industry. The second group of incentives is related to political agendas and the balance of power groups representing the interest of employees or employers. Indirect or direct influence of changing beliefs and expectations in society may cause social pressure. (Mcguire et al., 2002, p. 10)

Theoretical models and empirical evidence suggest that ongoing digital transformation on the labour market may not result in positive institutional change. In a negative scenario, adverse externalities of digital economy on the labour market – precarity, job inequality, lack of labour security, problems with work-life-balance – will not be eradicated by adjusting the institutional framework. Researchers have identified several reasons why institutional change does not lead to improved economic performance. Based on historical evidence, Ostrom (2005) demonstrated that influence groups (elites, corporations, policy makers) may promote social or economically inefficient institutional changes or halt efficient changes if their particular profit is not aligned with general welfare. Acemoglu (2006) explains the persistence of inefficient economic institutions, arguing that groups with political influence tend to promote policies that indirectly or directly transfer resources from society in a bid to increase their own income. If enforced, policies lead to inefficient institutional changes that decrease welfare. According to Lin (Lin, 1987), other reasons that ineffective institutional changes are imposed include the bounded rationality of the government, ideology, bureaucracy, group interest conflicts and limited knowledge of social science. The evolution of economic institutions in part resembles natural selection and evolution (Loasby, 2005), and arguably does not always mean that emerging institutions are best fit for survival (Hodgson, 2005)

Limitations of the new institutional economic theory for the labour market and the directions of future research

Current knowledge suggests that the new institutional economy may provide a powerful theoretical and analytical framework for understanding scarce evidence from the labour market in the dawn of the digital economy. It may be used to analyse the consequences of digital transformation, and address the threats and opportunities that characterise the gig economy: increasing job insecurity, increasing precarity and worsening income irregularity and tensions between property and labour rights. Nonetheless, there are some limitations of the theory as an explanatory tool.

The first major challenge is the problem of informal institutions. The new institutional economics emphasises the importance of informal rules (such as social and cultural norms, beliefs and social theories) for economic development and business operations. Nevertheless as Eggertsson (2013) points out, economy generally treats them as exogenous. In particular, mainstream economists have tended to overlook the problem (Stigler & Becker, 1977) and to treat social norms and theories (as well as preferences and needs) as given and relatively stable. Meanwhile the evidence from all industrial revolutions suggests that social norms change and adapt to new industrial organisation and technological advancements. A broader, more general theory to explain the formation and evolution of informal institutions is needed. Another problem with informal institutions concerns measurement issues. Despite their apparent importance, the instruments used to compare industries, societies and cultures based on important institutions are rather vague and imprecise (Tamanaha, 2015).

The new institutional economics does not explain well why some formal institutions do not work; nor why certain rules of the game are obeyed and others are not (Hindrics & Guala, 2015). Greif and Kingston (2011) advocate for the development of new theory that treats enforcement of the rules as an endogenous process rather than an exogenous one. They argue that treating institutions as a rules framework, where incentives to obey the rules are given, must be substituted with a general theory that coherently explains the enforcement of the rules (Greif & Kingston, 2011). The generalisation of institutions theory would help explain a number of puzzling results from empirical evidence provided by comparative studies: first, why in some countries a similar legal institutional framework generates different outcomes on the labour market (regarding protection of employees, work-life balance) and, second, how to fully incorporate formal rules into organisational practices and arrangements in the gig economy.

Conclusions

This chapter has discussed the validity of the new institutional economics as an analytical framework to be used when investigating changes on labour market caused by digital revolution. The theoretical analysis suggest that the new institutional economics is a useful tool in explaining ongoing integration of digital technologies on the labour market. The transaction cost analytical framework explains why digital technologies transform traditional work relations between employers and employees. The adequate institutional framework – both formal and informal – facilitates the smooth transition of the labour market in response to the digital economy, and mitigates risks related to the gig economy, precarious employment and other related phenomena. The most notable threats as well as growth potential are observed in developing countries that have quickly adopted digital economy, but lack appropriate institutional arrangements to effectively utilise them (Eggertsson, 2013).

As also discussed in the chapter, further analysis revealed that both formal institutions (legal rules created by laws and contracts) and informal institutions (norms, customs, beliefs) play a vital role in labour market transitions. In the former case, the role of a legal framework is to provide fair rules of the game – that is, allowing for flexible arrangements but not eliminating social security. Informal institutions are crucial for the successful adoption of new technologies on the labour market and explain why a similar legal environment generates different outcomes in seemingly similar cases.

The compatibility of technological advancements, induced by digital economy with formal institutions as well as general alignment with beliefs and social norms, facilitates their adoption on the labour market and partially negates potential social and economic turbulence. The scattered and relatively recent empirical evidence from across the world suggests that challenges related to digital transformation arise within sectors with established and traditional work arrangements, especially within a rigid and inelastic institutional setting. Institutional change may be difficult even when current industrial organisation is suboptimal and substantial efficiency gains may be achieved by proper implementation of digital technologies in arrangements and contracts between workers and companies. As the past has shown, and is well explained by new industrial economic theory, several factors may cause inefficient economic institutions, including the conflicting interests of power groups or the bounded rationality of government.

References

Acemoglu, D. (2006). A simple model of inefficient institutions. *The Scandinavian Journal of Economics, 108*(4), 515–546.

Black, B. (1999). National culture and labour-market flexibility. *The International Journal of Human Resource Management, 10*(4), 592–605.

Chen, S.C.Y., & Webster, C. (2012). *Institutional economics. New. International Encyclopedia of Housing and Home* (Vol. 4). Elsevier Ltd. doi:10.1016/B978-0-08-047163-1.00640-8

Chernyaeva, D. (2020). The 4th Industrial Revolution and its impact on the individual employment relationship: general considerations and the regulatory context in Russia. In J. Carby-Hall & L.M. Méndez (Eds.), *Labour Law and the Gig Economy* (pp. 66–78). Abingdon, Oxon; New York, NY: Routledge.

Coase, R.H. (1937). The nature of the firm. *Economica, 4*(16), 386–405. doi:10.1111/j.1468-0335.1937.tb00002.x

Coase, R. (1998). The new institutional economics. *American Economic Review, 88*(2), 72–74.

Coyle, D. (2017). Precarious and productive work in the digital economy. *National Institute Economic Review, 240*(1), R5–R14.

Donnelly, R., & Johns, J. (2021). Recontextualising remote working and its HRM in the digital economy: An integrated framework for theory and practice. *The International Journal of Human Resource Management, 32*(1), 84–105.

Drahokoupil, J., & Jepsen, M. (2017). The digital economy and its implications for labour. 1. The platform economy. *Transfer: European Review of Labour and Research, 23*(2), 103–107.

Eggertsson, T. (2013). Quick guide to new institutional economics. *Journal of Comparative Economics, 41*(1), 1–5.

Eltamimi, A. (2020). The impact of new technologies in the current labour market of selected Arab states. In J. Carby-Hall & M.L. Mendez (Eds.), *Labour law and the gig economy* (pp. 90–124). London: Routledge.

Fudge, J. (2017). The future of the standard employment relationship: Labour law, new institutional economics and old power resource theory. *Journal of Industrial Relations, 59*(3), 374–392.

Gahan, P., & Harcourt, T. (1998). Labour markets, firms and institutions: Labour economics and industrial relations. *Journal of Industrial Relations, 40*(4), 508–532.

Greif, A., & Kingston, C. (2011). Institutions: Rules or equilibria? In N. Schofield & G. Caballero (Eds.), *Political economy of institutions, democracy and voting* (pp. 13–43). Berlin Heidelberg: Springer-Verlag.

Greve, B. (2019). The digital economy and the future of European welfare states. *International Social Security Review, 72*(3), 79–94.

Hindrics, F., & Guala, F. (2015). Institutions, rules, and equilibria: A unified theory. *Journal of Institutional Economics, 11*(3), 459–480.

Hinings, B., Gegenhuber, T., & Greenwood, R. (2018). Digital innovation and transformation: An institutional perspective. *Information and Organization, 28*(1), 52–61.

Hodgson, G.M. (2005). Evolution and institutional change: On the nature of selection in biology and economics. In U. Maki, B. Gustafsson, & C. Knudsen (Eds.), *Rationality, institutions & economic methodology* (pp. 225–245). London: Routledge.

Jepsen, M., & Drahokoupil, J. (2017). The digital economy and its implications for labour. 2. The consequences of digitalisation for the labour market. *Transfer: European Review of Labour and Research, 23*(3), 249–252.

Kreshpaj, B., Orellana, C., Burström, B., Davis, L., Hemmingsson, T., Johansson, G., & Bodin, T. (2020). What is precarious employment? A systematic review of definitions and operationalizations from quantitative and qualitative studies. *Scandinavian Journal of Work, Environment and Health, 46*(3), 235–247.

Lehdonvirta, V. (2018). Flexibility in the gig economy: Managing time on three online piecework platforms. *New Technology, Work and Employment, 33*(1), 13–29.

Lin, J.Y. (1987). *An economic theory of institutional change: Induced and imposed change.* Discussion Papers No. 545. Yale: Yale University.

Loasby, B.J. (2005). Institutional stability and change in science and the economy. In U. Maki, B. Gustafsson, & C. Knudsen (Eds.), *Rationality, institutions & economic methodology* (pp. 206–224). London: Routledge.

Mahato, M., Kumar, N., & Jena, L.K. (2021). Re-thinking gig economy in conventional workforce post-COVID-19: A blended approach for upholding fair balance. *Journal of Work-Applied Management, ahead-of-p*(ahead-of-print). doi:10.1108/jwam-05-2021-0037

Marginson, P. (2016). Governing work and employment relations in an internationalized economy: The institutional challenge. *ILR Review, 69*(5), 1033–1055.

Mcguire, D., Garavan, T., O'Donnell, D., & Dineen, D. (2002). *Labour market flexibility: An institutional theory perspective.* Paper presented at the Irish Academy of Management Conference. Waterford: Waterford Institute of Technology.

Ménard, C. (2018). Research frontiers of new institutional economics. *RAUSP Management Journal, 53*(1), 3–10.

Menard, C., & Shirley, M.M. (Eds.). (2005). *Handbook of new institutional economics.* Dordrecht: Springer.

Méndez, L.M. (2020). Areflection on the challenges posed by digitalisation of labour markets. In J. Carby-Hall & M.L. Mendez (Eds.), *Labour law and the gig economy* (pp. 1–13). London: Routledge.

Moriset, B., & Malecki, E.J. (2009). Organization versus space: The paradoxical geographies of the digital economy. *Geography Compass, 3*(1), 256–274.

Nabli, M.K., & Nugent, J.B. (1989). The new institutional economics and its applicability to development. *World Development, 17*(9), 1333–1347.

North, D.C. (1990). *Institutions, institutional change and economic performance. Political economy of institutions and decisions.* Cambridge: Cambridge University Press. doi:10.1017/CBO9780511808678

North, D.C. (1993). *The new institutional economics and development* (Economic History). University Library of Munich, Germany. Available at: https://econpapers.repec.org/RePEc:wpa:wuwpeh:9309002 (accessed 30 August 2021).

Nunn, N. (2009). The importance of history for economic development. *Annual Review of Economics, 1*(1), 65–92.

Olsen, W., & Morgan, J. (2010). Institutional change from within the informal sector in Indian rural labour relations. *International Review of Sociology, 20*(3), 533–553.

Ostrom, E. (2005). Doing institutional analysis digging deeper than markets and hierarchies. In C. Menard, & M.M. Shirley (Eds.), *Handbook of new institutional economics* (pp. 819–848). Boston, MA: Springer.

Patel, D.A. (2020). Digitalisation vis-à-vis the Indian labour market: pros and cons. In J. Carby-Hall & L.M. Méndez (Eds.), *Labour Law and the Gig Economy* (pp. 79–89). Abingdon, Oxon; New York, NY: Routledge.

Pichault, F., & McKeown, T. (2019). Autonomy at work in the gig economy: Analysing work status, work content and working conditions of independent professionals. *New Technology, Work and Employment, 34*(1), 59–72.

Pulignano, V., Thompson, P., & Doerflinger, N. (2020). Workplace change and institutional experimentation: A case study of service-sector work in Europe. *Transfer: European Review of Labour and Research, 26*(2), 175–187.

Rainnie, A., & Dean, M. (2020). Industry 4.0 and the future of quality work in the global digital economy. *Labour & Industry: A Journal of the Social and Economic Relations of Work, 30*(1), 16–33.

Revina, S.N., Paulov, P.A., & Sidorova, A.V. (2020). Regulation of tax havens in the age of globalization and digitalization BT – Digital transformation of the economy: Challenges, trends and new opportunities. In S. Ashmarina, A. Mesquita, & M. Vochozka (Eds.), *Digital Transformation of the Economy: Challenges, Trends and New Opportunities* (pp. 88–95). Cham: Springer International Publishing.

Schiller, D. (2000). *Digital capitalism: Networking the global market system*. Cambridge, MA: MIT Press.

Shanahan, M. (1999). Australian labour market institutions through time: A perspective from the new institutional economics. *Australian Economic History Review, 39*(3), 213–238.

Simon, H.A. (1955). A behavioral model of rational choice. *The Quarterly Journal of Economics, 69*(1), 99–118.

Śledziewska, K., & Włoch, R. (2021). *The economics of digital transformation. The disruption of markets, production, consumption, and work*. London: Routledge. doi:10.4324/9781003144359

Sozinova, A.A. (2021). Investigating the prospects of new institutional theory in the smart economy BT – Modern global economic system: Evolutional development vs. revolutionary leap. In E.G. Popkova, & B.S. Sergi (Eds.), *Digital economy: Complexity and variety vs. rationality* (pp. 2075–2081). Cham: Springer International Publishing.

Stigler, G.J., & Becker, G.S. (1977). De Gustibus Non Est Disputandum. *The American Economic Review, 67*(2), 76–90. Available at: http://www.jstor.org/stable/1807222 (accessed 30 August 2021).

Tabellini, G. (2010). Culture and institutions: Economic development in the regions of Europe. *Journal of the European Economic Association, 8*(4), 677–716.

Tamanaha, B.Z. (2015). The knowledge and policy limits of new institutional economics on development. *Journal of Economic Issues, 49*(1), 89–109.

Teague, P., & Grahl, J. (1998). Institutions and labour market performance in Western Europe. *Political Studies, 46*(1), 1–18.

Tomassetti, J. (2020). Rebalancing worker rights and property rights in digitalised work. In J. Carby-Hall & L.M. Méndez (Eds.), *Labour Law and the Gig Economy* (pp. 139–155). Abingdon, Oxon; New York, NY: Routledge.

Tran, M., & Sokas, R.K. (2017). The gig economy and contingent work: An occupational health assessment. *Journal of Occupational and Environmental Medicine, 59*(4), e63–e66.

Williamson, O.E. (2000). The new institutional economics: Taking stock, looking ahead. *Journal of Economic Literature, 38*(3), 595–613.

Wilthagen, A., & Rogowski, R. (2002). Legal regulation of transitional labour markets. In S. Günther & B. Gazier (Eds.), *The dynamics of full employment: Social integration through transitional labour markets* (pp. 233–273). Cheltenham: Edward Elgar Publishing.

6 Behavioural economics and the digital economy

Agnieszka Małkowska

Introduction

Humans live in a world where the boundaries between the physical, digital and biological worlds are increasingly blurred. This blurring is characteristic for the Fourth Industrial Revolution (Schwab, 2016), which has already become a reality and is gaining momentum. Technological innovations and digitalisation are profoundly transforming societies and economies worldwide. In fact, every area of human life has been affected to some extent by these processes. This progressive and multifaceted impact of technological innovations is also reflected in the labour market and in the relations between its agents. In the era of digital economy, the labour market is facing new opportunities and challenges. Technological progress has swung open the door to new business models (OECD, 2018), flexible work arrangements (Eurofound, 2015) and transnational forms of work (Konkolewski, 2017). Ongoing robotisation, automation and ever-improving artificial intelligence (AI) are supporting and sometimes displacing human work.

While technological transformation boosts labour productivity, product quality and worker safety, it also poses risks and concerns. These arise from changes in the demand for human labour, which lead to a reduction in jobs, especially those based on physical and routine tasks, but also to the decline of some professions. The need to conduct multiple job searches and retraining, engage in lifelong learning and undertake non-traditional forms of work are some of the challenges facing current and future workers (Konkolewski, 2017). In spite of the gains created by the digital economy, transitions in the labour market can lead to greater unpredictability and instability of workers' career paths, earnings irregularity and labour market inequality. The deep and multi-directional changes anticipated in the labour market point to the need for public policies to address these issues. Among the most rapidly developing fields of economics, behavioural economics can explain labour market issues, intra-organisational relations and labour policy as it focuses on human behaviour, interactions and decision-making. By providing psychological insights into human nature, it helps us better understand and overcome the challenges that the digital economy brings to the realm of work.

DOI: 10.4324/9781003254638-9

Behavioural economics was developed on a critique of standard economic assumptions lying under the concept of *homo oeconomicus*. However, it does not stand in opposition to mainstream economics, but complements it with more realistic foundations. Insofar as it involves minor changes made to standard economic models as a result of findings provided by behavioural economics, Pesendorfer (2006) considers the relationship between mainstream and behavioural economics to be a symbiotic one.

Tomer (2007) identifies six dimensions – (1) narrowness; (2) rigidity; (3) intolerance; (4) mechanicalness; (5) separateness; and (6) individualism – containing important distinctions between the two schools of thought. While mainstream economics is perceived as highly narrow, rigid, intolerant, mechanistic, separate and individualistic, behavioural economics and its major sub-strands are markedly different in these respects, exhibiting medium to low degrees of these characteristics (Tomer, 2007). The narrowness of a particular scientific discipline – that is, the methodological and/or substantive limitations of its inquiry – is one of the most important comparative dimensions, and is worth examining in greater detail. Mainstream economics is considered very narrow, due mainly to the adoption of three basic assumptions about human preferences and behaviour: rationality, self-interest and self-control. The methodological narrowness that results from formal mathematical modelling-based methods is another crucial issue. Behavioural economics takes a much broader approach, although its various subfields differ in the detail and scope. The key contribution that behavioural economics has made to economy is in providing a more realistic view of the nature of human beings, directed by bounded rationality, selfishness and limited willpower (Tomer, 2007). In contrast to the quantitative and formal mathematical approaches of the mainstream, behavioural economics relies more on evidence from experiments (Camerer & Loewenstein, 2004).

Technological transformation is profoundly changing the landscape of work and human relations, posing challenges to employees, employers, managers and policy-makers alike. Understanding and responding to these processes is not possible without a behavioural perspective, which essentially governs the world of work. This chapter adopts this perspective. Behavioural labour economics is a thriving field; yet the number of publications and amount of research being done on it remains insufficient. The aim of this chapter, therefore, is to identify the contribution that behavioural economics can provide to addressing problems emerging from the technological changes taking place thanks to the digital economy. The chapter seeks to answer the following questions: (1) which concepts and findings of behavioural economics are applicable to the digital economy of work? (2) which behavioural factors explain conduct, relationships and decisions in a changing labour market? (3) which solutions proposed by behavioural economics can be helpful in influencing agents' actions in the digital labour economy.

The relevance of the behavioural economics for the labour market and industrial relations in the digital economy

Behavioural economics framework

Looking back at the development of behavioural economics, two beginnings can be distinguished – the well-known first, associated with the groundbreaking articles by Tversky and Kahneman (1974) and Kahneman and Tversky (1979), followed by Thaler's seminal publications (1980). And the second (but first in time) associated with the publications of George Katona from the 1940s, Herbert Simon in 1950 and Harvey Leibenstein in 1966. The recent output of behavioural economics is associated with scholarly contributions from several sub-branches as well as individual practitioners (Tomer, 2007).

Behavioural economics developed around the neoclassical paradigm of *homo oeconomicus*. The main assumptions of economics – about the perfectly rational behaviour of individuals characterised by unlimited cognitive abilities and willpower, fully informed, guided by their own narrowly defined self-interest, characterised by consistency of preferences and stability of goals over time, making decisions based on the calculation of inputs and outputs and the pursuit of optimal results that maximise utility or profit – have been challenged. By looking for anomalies in people's behaviour, behavioural economics identifies the limitations of human nature, the errors arising from them and the actual patterns in behaviour and decision-making. It formulates the perceived boundaries and behavioural traits in the form of concepts, hypotheses and research paths that find application in various fields of economics and beyond. These include the following:

- *bounded rationality* is a concept originating from Herbert Simon (1955, 1979) that contests the assumption of human rationality that is integral to the *homo oeconomicus* paradigm. Simon observed that decision-makers did not have access to all the information that is relevant to the problem at hand, but neither were they able to perceive all the information they had access to. They are also limited in their information processing when dealing with complex problems. In his model, utility maximisation was replaced by a satisficing solution (Altman, 2008). The concept of bounded rationality was extended by Kaufman (1999), noting that human behaviour is not only conditioned by limited knowledge and cognitive abilities, but also by one's emotional state;
- *the heuristic and biases approach* was brought into economics by Daniel Kahneman and Amos Tversky (Tversky and Kahneman, 1974). In their publication, *judgment under uncertainty: heuristics and biases*, the authors show that people use intuition when solving complex tasks and making decisions, using simplified inference rules unconsciously. Shortcuts and

simplifications, or heuristics (representativeness, availability, anchoring and adjustment heuristics) are useful because they meaningfully facilitate judgment processes. However, they can also give rise to serious cognitive biases;

- *prospect theory* by Daniel Kahneman and Amos Tversky (Kahneman & Tversky, 1979) arose as a critique of expected-utility theory. Based on a series of experiments, Kahneman and Tversky documented how people systematically violate the basic predictions of expected-utility theory in their actual decision-making behaviour and developed an alternative model of choice under risk–prospect theory. Prospect theory comprises four main elements:

    1 reference dependence, or the act of deriving utility from gains and losses and measured relatively to some reference point, rather than from absolute levels of wealth;
    2 loss aversion, or people's greater sensitivity to losses than to gains;
    3 decreasing sensitivity, or the diminishing sensitivity people exhibit to gains and losses;
    4 probability weighting, or the tendency to weigh outcomes not according to their objective probabilities but rather by subjective, transformed probabilities or decision weights, overweighting low probabilities and underweighting high probabilities (Barberis, 2013);

- *endowment effect* is a term coined by Thaler (1980) and based on the observation that "(...) *goods that are included in the individual's endowment will be more highly valued than those not held in the endowment, ceteris paribus.*" Thus, because people value the good they possess more highly (simply by virtue of that fact) than the one they do not, they often demand much more to give up the former than they would be willing to pay to acquire it. One possible explanation for the endowment effect is the value asymmetry Kahneman and Tversky (1974) called *loss aversion* (Kahneman, Knetsch, & Thaler, 1991);
- *hyperbolic discounting* refers to the act of applying decreasing discount rates over time to trade-offs between present and future consumption. There is a general tendency that people more often choose a smaller reward that occurs earlier than a larger reward that occurs later. The value of the later reward is discounted by a factor that increases with the length of the delay (Frederick, Loewenstein, & O'Donoghue, 2002).

All these concepts and insights from behavioural economics play a momentous role in explaining human behaviour in a variety of domains and relationships, both within and outside of economics. The development of behavioural labour economics and the empirical output of this field affirms the contribution of psychological and sociological findings to a better understanding of labour issues, e.g. with respect to relations between labour market participants (principal-agent relations or interactions between employees), decision-making by individuals (job search, trade-off between work and leisure), motives driving employees (fairness, reciprocity, altruism, peers comparisons and so on). This, in turn, leads to solutions based on behavioural approaches to human resource management and public policy-making in the labour market.

Behavioural labour economics and its relevance to digital economics

In recent decades, the contribution of behavioural economics to its subfields has become influential and significant. This also applies to labour economics, which, drawing on psychological observations and findings from behavioural economics, has developed the extensive and expanding subfield of behavioural labour economics. Labour economics encompasses different schools of thought, but the behavioural approach is a particular application. Indeed, labour market issues have a strong psychological and sociological background (Winter-Ebmer, 2014), and individual behaviour and decisions, their motives and outcomes, as well as the agents' relationships are all important issues. Thus, the labour market has become a test ground for the verification of psychological hypotheses developed in behavioural economics and for initiating new research streams.

A psychological perspective on the labour market also seems useful in light of the profound changes the market is currently facing due to the digital economy. Although the impact of technological development on the labour market has received a great deal of attention in recent years, this area is still unexplored (Kurt, 2019) and the effects of the transformations are uncertain. The driver of the changes impacting society, business and the economy is technology, which has come a long way in a short time. The COVID-19 pandemic is another factor leaving its mark on the labour market and accelerating its transformation.

The digital economy is expected to profoundly reshape labour relations, change employment structures, force a re-evaluation of skills and competences, and affect approaches to education and professional behaviour. All technological advances have winners and losers. It is anticipated that the benefits available primarily to those who succeed in the new circumstances will be an increase in wages in skilled occupations, new job opportunities in emerging occupations, shorter working hours, flexibility in working arrangements, better working conditions and improved work-life balance. In the case of low-skilled occupations, employment and wages are expected to fall. Machines will claim some jobs, leading to the decline of certain professions, and some workers will have to re-skill and search for new work (Kurt, 2019). Challenges for labour market actors and policy-makers will include increasing inequalities, job insecurity, income irregularity, unemployment and threats to social security and pension systems. A number of these anticipated implications and risks can be successfully explored and addressed through behavioural economics.

How behavioural economics can help better understand the labour market and outcomes can be found mainly at the microeconomic level. In summarising the contribution of behavioural economics to labour research, Dohmen (2014) points to several key problem areas. These include: the wage–effort relationship, wage determination, human capital accumulation, search behaviour, wage and career mobility, as well as intertemporal labour supply decisions. Behavioural labour economics sheds light on the psychological and social factors lying behind behaviours, decisions and interactions within the labour market and organisations, while also developing tools to improve attitudes, choices and outcomes. The concepts of behavioural economics that have proved fruitful in this area largely concern non-standard preferences grounded in social comparisons and preferences as well as individual differences like preference heterogeneity and personality traits. Furthermore, contributions to solving labour economics problems are based on research on non-standard beliefs and also on non-standard decision-making (DellaVigna, 2009; Dohmen, 2014). Given the challenges that the digital economy poses to employees, employers and policy-makers, it is worth citing studies that analyse the implications and provide lessons that can be applied to these issues. The relevant studies are those that explain the difficulties associated with job search, including:

- the effect of impatience on job search results (DellaVigna & Paserman, 2005);
- the impact of job seekers' faith in their employment prospects (Mueller, Spinnewijn, & Topa, 2021).

These studies are important for the structural changes expected in the labour market. Other research analyses the correlation between temporal wage fluctuations and labour supply (Camerer, Babcock, Loewenstein, & Thaler, 1997; Farber, 2005; Fehr & Goette, 2007) in occupations that have some freedom to set work schedules, such as taxi drivers and bicycle couriers. The findings of these studies can be addressed and reviewed in the light of the gig economy, in which workers engage in short-term projects or operate as freelancers. A large body of research within behavioural labour economics focuses on the impact of social norms and relationships on work behaviour, performance and outcomes. These include:

- the impact of gift-exchange on labour contracts (in terms of wages and effort provisions) (Akerlof, 1982);
- the impact of fairness on wage cuts (Kahneman, Knetsch, & Thaler, 1986);
- the impact of wage fairness on effort provision and unemployment (Akerlof, & Yellen, 1988, 1990);
- the effect of labour relations on work outcomes (product quality) (Krueger & Mas, 2004);

- the effect of social pressure (peer effect) on worker productivity (Mas & Moretti, 2009);
- the effect of peer salaries on job satisfaction and the intention to resign (Card, Mas, Moretti, & Saez, 2012).

The results of this research make an important contribution to understanding and managing human resources and shaping employee-employer and employee-employee relationships in changing and increasingly complex work environments. The findings of behavioural economics show a path for public policy to follow, which is an important factor for dealing with the risks and challenges of the digital economy in the labour market. Exemplary issues of the practical application of knowledge developed within behavioural economics concern:

- libertarian paternalism and nudging (Thaler & Shefrin, 1981);
- using behavioural tendencies such as procrastination and inertia to boost workers' retirement savings (Thaler & Benartzi, 2004);
- designing the optimal unemployment insurance based on biased beliefs about employment prospects (Spinnewijn, 2015).

Recognising the anomalies underlying human behaviour and choices helps both managers and public policy-makers design choice architectures to guide employees and job seekers towards more desirable outcomes.

Behavioural factors affecting the labour market and flexible employer-employee relations

As mentioned earlier, behavioural economics points to three basic patterns that affect human judgement, behaviour and decision-making: bounded self-control, bounded self-interest and bounded rationality, which results from individuals' limited knowledge, cognitive abilities and emotional state. The decisions and actions of people in the labour market, their attitudes towards the job and the workplace and their relations with employers and co-workers are to a large extent shaped by behavioural factors. The reality of the digital economy does not diminish the importance of behavioural insights, but rather means that the increasingly difficult and dynamically changing labour market and the growing complexity of the work environment and professional relationships can be explained and solved with a behavioural approach.

Bounded rationality and cognitive limitations

The theory of bounded rationality makes realistic the neoclassical assumption of rational human choices based on weighing costs and benefits to maximise utility. In reality, humans have limited access to information and limited cognitive abilities, in addition to having their decisions influenced by emotions.

Within behavioural labour economics, bounded rationality is explained, in particular, on the grounds of a heuristics and biases approach, prospect theory and endowment effect.

A problem area in the transition of the labour market towards a digital economy is job losses and the consequent need for workers to find new employment. The job seeker's beliefs about their prospects on the labour market are an important determinant of job search behaviour. Behavioural economics points to the causes that can lead to poor outcomes and longer-term unemployment. Individuals' expectations with error or systematic bias affect job-search outcomes. Optimistic bias has been shown to influence both the process and the effects of a job search. For example, Spinnewijn (2015) found evidence of striking optimistic biases among workers, indicating that they underestimate the risks of unemployment and in particular the risks associated with long periods of unemployment. Therefore, optimistic job seekers may do too little to get a job. Interestingly, Mueller et al. (2021) found that this optimistic tendency increases with the duration of unemployment. Another reason job seekers remain unemployed for long periods is tendency to evaluate job and wage offers in relation to a reference point, often the expectation that they will receive a salary on a par with their previous job. As people are usually loss averse, they are unwilling to accept a wage below the reference point, despite the obvious benefits. Setting an inefficiently high reference point may also be associated with moral hazard in relation to a generous unemployment compensation system that demotivates people to put in the effort needed to find a job.

Heuristics and cognitive errors can also affect the other side of the employment relationship, namely the employer or manager seeking a new employee. Representativeness heuristics can be used as an example. If a manager believes that the best salespeople are those who exhibit certain characteristics e.g. they are extroverts, ex-athletes or white males, then when looking for an employee for a sales position the manager will favour candidates who fit this image (Bazerman & Moore, 2009).

The second problem area for labour market transitions within the digital economy is the supply of labour by non-traditional workers or gig workers. Gig workers are independent contractors, online platform workers or freelancers with flexible work schedules. They generally do short-term work for multiple clients. The growing number of gig workers raises questions about their working behaviours. Previous research in the area of labour supply decisions has focused on taxi drivers, providing a sort of proxy for gig workers. Camerer and Loewenstein (2004) explain the negative relationship between hourly wage and the number of working hours. His study shows that when the hourly wage increases, the number of hours taxi drivers work decreases and, conversely, when the wage is low, taxi drivers work more hours. This is interpreted as an income-targeting effect – daily reference earnings are achieved faster on good days when wages are higher and slower on bad days when wages are lower and taxi drivers have to work longer to meet their target earnings (a reference point based on expectations) (Nielsen & Sebald, 2016). Further research by Farber (2005) on the daily supply of taxi drivers in New York City suggests that at a reference level of daily income, the probability of stopping work increases once the reference point is reached. In their research, Allon, Cohen, and Sinchaisri (2018) focused directly on gig workers from a ride-hailing online platform. They observe behavioural biases with regard to cumulative earnings and hours including (1) income-targeting behaviour, suggesting that drivers' labour decisions are affected by recent earnings and income goals, as well as (2) inertia (another behavioural bias), which reflects the fact that gig workers are more likely to work even more after working longer hours.

Bounded willpower

Bounded willpower or self-control is associated with hyperbolic discounting, or people's time inconsistent preferences, which arise from the conflict between one's present and future selves (Altman, 2008). Hyperbolic discounting boils down to underestimating rewards for our future selves relative to current ones. Indeed, people increasingly choose a smaller-sooner reward over a larger-later reward as the implicit discount rate over longer time horizons is lower than the implicit discount rate over shorter time horizons (Shane, Loewenstein, & O'Donoghue, 2002). Within the behavioural labour economy, hyperbolic discounting affects retirement saving plans (Laibson, 1996), a particularly relevant issue in the context of the digital economy and new forms of work that frequently do not offer social security. A quasi-hyperbolic discounting savings model was used in two studies on retirement saving, one by Laibson et al. (1998) and the other by Diamond and Koszegi (2003), in which consumers face a trade-off between consuming more or retiring early.

A second application of non-standard discounting that is important for the challenges of the digital labour economy (as argued above) is job search behaviour. DellaVigna and Paserman (2005) investigated the effects of impatience and hyperbolic discounting on job search outcomes. The results show that job seekers who exhibit hyperbolic preferences put less effort into search activities than they would like, ultimately lengthening their period of unemployment. Research findings on hyperbolic discounting in job searches allow for policy interventions towards individuals with consistent and inconsistent time preference to be differentiated (Paserman, 2008).

Bounded self-interest

The assumption that people make choices according to self-interest alone is a gross oversimplification and is at odds with reality. Human behaviour is often based on motivations that are contrary to pure self-interest, such as altruism, reciprocity, loyalty, aversion to inequality, fairness, seeking meaning and satisfaction. In the real world, people actually show bounded self-interest, guided by social norms and social preferences in their behaviour. Social norms are an important context for economic decisions. Social norms can be defined as "*a behavioural regularity that is based on a socially shared belief of how one ought to behave, which triggers the enforcement of the prescribed behaviour by informal social sanctions*" (Fehr & Gächter, 2000, p. 166). Dohmen (2014) points out that social comparison is a prerequisite for any model of interdependent preferences (altruism, reciprocity, fairness) because the non-egoistic behaviour resulting from them is based on a comparison of the individual's own performance with that of others. Limited self-interest arising from comparisons and social preferences is a broad strand of research within behavioural labour economics. It is used to explain phenomena in the labour market and the workplace (Dohmen, 2014). From the point of view of the digital labour economy and the changing relationships between employee and employer, as well as between employees themselves, the key social factors are ethical norms, fairness, reciprocity and loyalty. They influence work motivation, commitment, performance, effort provision, turnover intentions, job satisfaction and happiness.

Research in this area often focuses on gift-exchange, peer effect and social reference point. A key to understanding the relationship between pay and effort is the equitable wage-effort hypothesis by Akerlof and Yellen (1990), which states that workers withdraw effort proportionately when their actual pay is below a fair wage. Research in the area of the relationship between wages and employee effort has produced a number of interesting findings. For example, Gneezy and List (2006) examined a gift-exchange approach to maximising employee effort by means of an experiment. Participants were engaged in two separate jobs: data entry for a university library and door-to-door fundraising. Their findings suggest that higher pay is indeed reciprocated by greater effort from workers – but only in the early hours of the task. The study shows that after a few hours the effort level in the group receiving the gift was the same as in the group that did not receive it, suggesting the higher effort level was not sustainable.

Gächter and Thöni (2010) also investigated the effect of wage differences on effort. Using a three-person gift-exchange experiment, they measure the effects of wage comparisons on the average response of an employee's effort to an observed change in a peer's wage. One conclusion from their experiment was that workers who face unfavourable wage discrimination (are paid less than their colleagues) make significantly less effort than when wages are equal. At the same time, workers who are subject to favourable wage discrimination (are paid more than their colleagues) do not increase their level of effort on average. In another study, Card et al. (2012) report that wage comparisons between co-workers affect job satisfaction and turnover intentions. They found that workers with wages below the median report lower job satisfaction and are more likely to resign, while those with wages above the median are not affected. Social comparisons have also been widely studied in relation to non-wage issues. For example, Falk and Ichno (2006) used a controlled field experiment to discover that worker productivity is systematically affected by the productivity of one's peers, with less productive workers more affected by peer effects than high-productivity workers.

These research findings on the influence of social factors on human behaviour and decisions have momentous implications for many areas, including labour markets where incomplete contracts are a factor as well as the behaviour, relationships and expected outcomes in the workplace. They also provide a basis for the design of labour policy and human resource management in the rapidly changing environment of the digital economy with a plethora of salient problems, including wage levels in the light of changing demand for labour and skills, inequalities in the labour market, worker motivation in highly complex and non-typical work environments, productivity and quality of work.

The application and limitations of behavioural economics for the labour market

Labour behavioural economics not only detects anomalies affecting human behaviour and decisions, but also offers toolboxes to help people overcome cognitive and motivational biases. Several problems of labour economics stemming from technological transformation can be tackled using knowledge of cognitive limitations and methods developed by behavioural economists. Solutions can address labour market-related behaviours in the areas of job search, education and training, saving decisions, as well as employee-employer relationships in terms of employee commitment and performance, wage policy, motivation, use of incentives and rewards, and turnover intentions, to name just a few. Peer relations also play an essential role and can significantly change the behavioural patterns and performance of employees.

Lessons from behavioural economics suggest that people do not exhibit rational expectations, use heuristics and experience cognitive biases, show dynamic inconsistency, make choices that depend on the framing of the problem, and emotional context. This leads to choices being made under conditions of bounded rationality and the preferences of the decision-maker therefore not necessarily being reflected. The solutions proposed by behavioural economics should help individuals make better choices, i.e. choices they would make if they had full information, unlimited cognitive capacity and did not suffer from lack of willpower.

As a path to follow, libertarian paternalism (Thaler & Sustein, 2003) does not remove choice or coerce but rather encourages decisions that are more in line with actual preferences. As the authors put it, "*Libertarian paternalism is a relatively weak, soft, and nonintrusive type of paternalism because choices are not blocked, fenced off, or significantly burdened*" (Thaler & Sustein, 2008, p. 5). So, people who make bad or harmful choices for themselves are not forced by libertarian paternalists to turn away, and nor are bad choices made more difficult for them to make. Their actions are rather limited to consciously moving people in directions that will make their lives better. This is called 'nudging,' which Thaler and Sustein define (2008, p. 6) "*as any aspect of the choice architecture that alters people's behavior in a predictable way without forbidding any options or significantly changing their economic incentives.*" The assumption is that intervention must be easy and inexpensive to avoid, but at the same time not mandatory.

Nudges as a solution within choice architecture are available to anyone designing plans for others, in either the private or public sectors. In relation to labour economics, nudges are used by employers, human resource managers, labour market agencies and public authorities. Although the literature more often focuses on the use of nudges in public policy, their usefulness in organisations is also confirmed by practice. Choice architecture based on nudges uses knowledge of human nature, its limitations and motivations. Tools that are frequently studied and used in labour economics and beyond include framing, default options, simplification, commitment devices and social norms (Nielsen & Sebald, 2016). An extensive literature confirms that nudging tools work well for policies targeting jobseekers (DellaVigna, Lindner, Reizer, & Schmieder, 2017; Mühlböck, Kalleitner, Steiber, & Kittel, 2020; Spinnewijn, 2015; Stutzer & Lalive, 2004) and participants in savings plans (e.g. retirement savings plans) (Choi et al., 2004; Clark, Hammond, Morrill, & Khalaf, 2017; Madrian & Shea, 2001; Thaler & Benartzi, 2004). In organisations, effective nudging can be based on knowledge of the impact of social norms, peer-comparisons and group belonging on individual behaviour.

Conclusions and future research directions

Digital economy poses a number of challenges for the labour market, businesses and public institutions. Some are already discernible, while others have yet to emerge and are difficult to predict. However, it can be expected that the technological transformation will profoundly change the way we think about work and careers while also affecting workplace relationships. These changes and their far-reaching consequences will require the active involvement of employers, employees and public institutions to deal with them. As labour economics focuses primarily on people and their relationships, behavioural economics seems particularly well-suited to solving problems in this field.

Behavioural economics identifies anomalies in traditional economic theory and examines their impact on human behaviour, relationships and decision-making. Its conclusions point to three basic patterns governing human behaviour that deviate from the mainstream economic assumptions: bounded rationality, bounded self-interest and bounded willpower. In the field of labour economics, the insights of behavioural economics explain, among many other phenomena, people's behaviour and choices, in labour relations in companies as well as in job searches and financial commitments.

They also show how planners (politicians, public sector employees, managers) can get people to make better choices.

Choice architecture and behavioural tools such as nudging are also applicable to situations arising in response to the digital economy and its implications for work and employment. However, nudges can also have negative consequences. Thaler (2015) has established basic rules for their use: (1) all nudging should be transparent and never misleading; (2) it should be easy to opt out of; (3) there should be good reason to believe that it will improve the welfare of those being nudged. The second consideration with nudging is that, as with other tools, it must be adapted to the recipients, as people are diverse in their dispositions and preferences. It is not only the diversity but also the complexity of human behaviour and the factors influencing it that must be taken into consideration. Behavioural economics, and in particular nudging as a tool, is certainly not the key to solving all problems. The criticism of nudging that takes place in the public space points to its weaknesses, including issues of problem-fitness, effectiveness and sustainability of nudging-induced changes (Mols, Haslam, Jetten, & Steffens, 2014) as well as ethical issues (Schubert, 2015).

The tools behavioural economics give us appear to be complementary rather than alternative to traditional labour policies and human management in organisations. Looking at the changes in the labour market, there is a need for further research into the application of psychological insights into human behaviour, relationships and decisions in the rapidly changing digital economy.

References

Akerlof, G.A. (1982). Labor contracts as partial gift exchange. *The Quarterly Journal of Economics, 97*(4), 543–569.

Akerlof, G.A., & Yellen, J.L. (1988). Fairness and unemployment. *American Economic Review, 78*(2), 44–49.

Akerlof, G.A., & Yellen, J.L. (1990). The fair wage-effort hypothesis and unemployment. *The Quarterly Journal of Economics, 105*(2), 255–283. doi:10.2307/2937787.

Allon, G., Cohen, M.C., & Sinchaisri, W.P. (2018). *The impact of behavioral and economic drivers on gig economy workers*. Available at SSRN: https://ssrn.com/abstract=3274628. doi:10.2139/ssrn.3274628.

Altman, M. (2008). *Behavioral economics, economic theory and public policy*. doi:10.2139/ssrn.1152105

Barberis, N.C. (2013). Thirty years of prospect theory in economics: A review and assessment. *Journal of Economic Perspectives, 27*(1), 173–196.

Bazerman, M., & Moore, D. (2009). *Judgement in managerial decision making* (7th ed.). New York: Wiley.

Camerer, C., & Loewenstein, G. (2004). Behavioral economics: past, present, future. In C.F. Camerer, G. Loewenstein, & M. Rabin (Eds.), *Advances in Behavioral Economics* (pp. 3–52). Princeton, NJ: Princeton University Press.

Card, D., Mas, A., Moretti, E., & Saez, E. (2012). Inequality at work: The effect of peer salaries on job satisfaction. *American Economic Review, 102*(6), 2981–3003.

Choi, J.J., Laibson, D., Madrian, B.C., Metrick, A., & Poterba, J.M. (2004). For better or for worse: Default effects and 401(k) savings behavior. In D.A. Wise (Ed.), *Perspectives on the economics of aging* (pp. 81–126). Chicago, IL: University of Chicago Press. doi:10.7208/9780226903286-004

Clark, R.L., Hammond, R.G., Morrill, M.S., & Khalaf, C. (2017). *Nudging retirement savings: A field experiment on supplemental plans.* National Bureau of Economic Research. Working Paper 23679. doi:10.3386/w23679

DellaVigna, S. (2009). Psychology and economics: Evidence from the field. *Journal of Economic Literature, 47*(2), 315–372.

DellaVigna, S., Lindner, A., Reizer, R., & Schmieder, J. F. (2017). Reference-dependent job search: Evidence from Hungary. *The Quarterly Journal of Economics, 132*(4), 1969–2018. doi:10.1093/qje/qjx015

DellaVigna, S., & Paserman, M.D. (2005). Job search and impatience. *Journal of Labor Economics, 23*, 527–588.

Diamond, P., & Köszegi, B. (2003). Quasi-hyperbolic discounting and retirement. *Journal of Public Economics, 87*(9–10), 1839–1872.

Dohmen, T. (2014). Behavioral labor economics: Advances and future directions. *Labour Economics, 30*, 71–85.

Eurofound. (2015). *New forms of employment.* Luxembourg: Publication Office of the European Union.

Falk, A., & Ichino, A. (2006). Clean evidence on peer effects. *Journal of Labor Economics, 24*(1), 39–57. doi.org/10.1086/497818

Farber, H.S. (2005). Is tomorrow another day? The labor supply of New York city cabdrivers. *Journal of Political Economy, 113*(1), 46–82.

Fehr, E., & Gächter, S. (2000). Fairness and retaliation: The economics of reciprocity. *The Journal of Economic Perspectives, 14*(3), 159–181.

Fehr, E., & Goette. L. (2007). Do workers work more if wages are high? Evidence from a randomized field experiment. *American Economic Review, 97*(1), 298–317.

Frederick, S., Loewenstein, G., & O'Donoghue, T. (2002). Time discounting and time preference: A critical review. *Journal of Economic Literature, 40*(2), 351–401.

Gächter, S., & Thöni, C. (2010). Social comparison and performance: Experimental evidence on the fair wage–effort hypothesis. *Journal of Economic Behavior & Organization, 76*(3), 531–543. doi:10.1016/j.jebo.2010.08.008.

Gneezy, U., & List, J.A. (2006). Putting behavioral economics to work: Testing for gift exchange in labor markets using field experiments. *Econometrica, 74*(5), 1365–1384.

Kahneman, D., Knetsch, J.L., & Thaler, R. (1986). Fairness as a constraint on profit seeking: Entitlements in the market. *The American Economic Review, 76*, 728–741.

Kahneman, D., Knetsch, J.L., & Thaler, R. H. (1991). Anomalies: The endowment effect, loss aversion, and status quo bias. *The Journal of Economic Perspectives, 5*(1), 193–206.

Kahneman, D., & Tversky, A. (1979). Prospect theory: An analysis of decisions under risk. *Econometrica, 47*, 313–327.

Kaufman, B.E. (1999). Emotional arousal as a source of bounded rationality. *Journal of Economic Behavior & Organization, 38*, 135–144.

Konkolewski, H.H. (2017). Digital economy and the future of social security. *Administration, 65*(4), 21–30.

Krueger, A.B., & Mas, A. (2004). Strikes, scabs, and tread separations: Labor strife and the production of defective bridgestone/firestone tires. *Journal of Political Economy, 112*(2), 253–289. doi:10.1086/381479

Kurt, R. (2019). Industry 4.0 in terms of industrial relations and its impacts on labour life. *Procedia Computer Science, 158*, 590–601.

Laibson, D.I. (1996). Hyperbolic discount functions, undersaving, and savings policy. *National Bureau of Economic Research Working Paper Series*, 5635.

Laibson, D.I., Repetto, A., Tobacman, J., Hall, R.E., Gale, W.G., & Akerlof, G.A. (1998). Self-control and saving for retirement. *Brookings Papers on Economic Activity, 1*, 91–196. doi:10.2307/2534671.

Leibenstein, H. (1966). Allocative efficiency vs. 'X-Efficiency. *American Economic Review, 56*, 392–415.

Madrian, B.C., & Shea, D.F. (2001). The power of suggestion: Inertia in 401(k) participation and savings behavior. *The Quarterly Journal of Economics, 116*(4), 1149–1187.

Mas, A., & Moretti, E. (2009). Peers at work. *The American Economic* Review, *99*(1), 112–145.

Mols, F., Haslam, S. A., Jetten, J., & Steffens, N. (2014). Why a nudge is not enough: A social identity critique of governance by stealth. *European Journal of Political Research, 54*(1), 81–98. doi:10.1111/1475-6765.12073.

Mueller, A.I., Spinnewijn, J., & Topa, G. (2021). Job seekers' perceptions and employment prospects: Heterogeneity, duration dependence, and bias. *American Economic Review, 111*(1), 324–363.

Mühlböck, M., Kalleitner, F., Steiber, N., & Kittel, B. (2020). Information, reflection, and successful job search: A nudging experiment. Available at SSRN: https://ssrn.com/abstract=3576740 (accessed 7 September 2021).

Nielsen, C.S., & Sebald, A. (2016). Behavioral economics and labor market policy. Available at: https://star.dk/media/1185/behavioral-economics-and-nudging.pdf (accessed 7 September 2021).

OECD (2018). Tax challenges arising from digitalisation – Interim report 2018: Inclusive framework on BEPS, OECD/G20 base erosion and profit shifting project, OECD Publishing, Paris. doi:10.1787/9789264293083-en

Paserman, M.D. (2008). Job search and hyperbolic discounting: Structural estimation and policy evaluation. *The Economic Journal, 118*(531), 1418–1452.

Pesendorfer, W. (2006). Behavioral economics comes of age: A review essay on "Advances in Behavioral Economics". *Journal of Economic Literature, 44*(3), 712–721

Schubert, C. (2015). *On the ethics of public nudging: Autonomy and agency*. Available at SSRN: https://ssrn.com/abstract=2672970 (accessed 7 September 2021).

Schwab, K. (2016). *The fourth industrial revolution*. Geneva: World Economic Forum.

Shane F., Loewenstein, G., & O'Donoghue, T. (2002). Time discounting and time preference: A critical review. *Journal of Economic Literature, 40*(2), 351–401.

Simon, H. (1955). A behavioral model of rational choice. *The Quarterly Journal of Economics, 69*(1), 99–118.

Simon, H. (1979). Information processing models of cognition. *Annual Review of Psychology, 30*, 363–396.

Spinnewijn, J. (2015). Unemployed but optimistic: Optimal insurance design with biased beliefs. *Journal of the European Economic Association, 13*(1), 130–167.

Stutzer, A., & Lalive, R. (2004). The role of social work norms in job searching and subjective well-being. *Journal of the European Economic Association, 2*(4), 696–719.

Thaler, R. (1980). Toward a positive theory of consumer choice. *Journal of Economic Behavior & Organization, 1*(1), 39–60.

Thaler, R.H. (2015). The power of nudges, for good and bad. *The New York Times*. Available at: https://www.nytimes.com/2015/11/01/upshot/the-power-of-nudges-for-good-and-bad.html (accessed 17 August 2021).

Thaler, R.H., & Benartzi, S. (2004). Save more tomorrow™: Using behavioral economics to increase employee saving. *Journal of Political Economy, 112*(S1), S164–S187.

Thaler, R.H., & Shefrin, H.M. (1981). An economic theory of self-control. *Journal of Political Economy, 89*(2), 392–406.

Thaler, R.H., & Sunstein, C.R. (2003). Libertarian paternalism. *American Economic Review, 93*(2), 175–179.

Thaler, R.H., & Sustein, C.R. (2008). *Nudge: Improving decisions about health, wealth, and happiness*. Yale: Yale University Press.

Tomer, J.F. (2007). What is behavioral economics?. *The Journal of Socio-Economics, 36*(3), 463–479.

Tversky, A., & Kahneman, D. (1974). Judgment under uncertainty: Heuristics and biases. *Science, 185*(4157), 1124–1131.

Winter-Ebmer, R. (2014). What is (not) behavioural in labour economics? *Labour Economics, 30*, 86–87.

7 Innovation theory and the digital economy

Dariusz Żmija

Introduction

The issue of innovation is considered in various areas and contexts of meaning, as well as in terms of various scientific disciplines. To date, however, no uniform and universal definition of innovation has been developed, despite the fact that interest in this phenomenon has been rising for decades. This indicates the complex nature of innovation, its multidimensionality and that how it is perceived changes over time. Getting at the essence and meaning of innovation is not a straightforward task. It is couched in the literature in a myriad of definitions and terms. Moreover, there are different types of innovation and their classifications are quite diverse. In general, innovation is commonly perceived as something new and different from existing solutions, with the understanding of this concept focusing on such associations as change, novelty and concepts. West and Far (1990) note that a change can be considered an innovation when it has a purposeful and intentional character. At root, innovation should be positive and constitute added value for the company, client or the environment. In a similar vein, Sørensen and Torfing (2013) suggest that innovation requires change, and its essence is the development and implementation of new, creative solutions that in some way break with the past.

The digital economy has been ushered in by the acceleration and intensification of digitalisation processes that have been occurring for more than two decades, reflected in the growing use of digital technologies by companies, public institutions and non-governmental organisations, employees, consumers and citizens. The digital economy can generally be understood to comprise those economic activities that are performed using new technologies. It includes the economy of goods and services whose development, production, sale or provision is entirely dependent on digital technologies (Kling & Lamb, 2000). In other words, the digital economy incorporates all economic activity that is relies on, or is significantly enhanced by, the use of digital inputs, including digital technologies, infrastructure, services and data. It also encompasses all producers and consumers, including government, that are utilising these digital inputs in their economic activities (Borowiecki et al., 2021; OECD, 2020).

DOI: 10.4324/9781003254638-10

The links between the digital economy, innovation and the labour market are complex and have been a subject of interest in economic theory for many years. However, the research focus is shifting from trying to answer the common question of whether new technologies destroy or create jobs to determining the impact of different types of innovations on the level and structure of employment, as well as on the creation of new forms of employment and the nature of employment relations (Eurofound, 2018). The aim of this chapter is to explore what innovation-related factors are influencing the labour market and employment relations in the age of digital transformation.

The relevance of innovation theory for the labour market in the digital economy

Today, innovations are perceived as the basic instrument for stimulating the development not only of enterprises but of entire economies. The issues related to innovation were initially considered from a macroeconomic perspective, measuring the impact of technical progress on economic development, while later a microeconomic research trend appeared, where technical progress was treated as a process, and research focused on the analysis of its components, including innovation (Rydvalova & Skala, 2021).

The definition of innovation can be approached sensu largo (broad approach) or sensu stricto (narrow approach) (Jasińska-Biliczak, 2020). Innovation sensu largo includes changes involving the absorption of acquired knowledge. It includes real changes concerning various objects and phenomena, occurring in different spheres of activity, which bear the mark of novelty. When innovation is approached from a narrow point of view, on the other hand, it is mainly the technical character of innovation that is considered, particularly as a change in production methods and products (possibly in the organisation of the production process), based on new or previously unused knowledge.

In Economics, Schumpeter (1934) introduced the concept of innovation. Understanding it in a broad sense, he pointed to the role research, innovation and entrepreneurship played in an economy's development. However, in his view, each dissemination of innovation was already a separate type of change, one which he called imitation. Schumpeter's concept of creative destruction held that innovation arises from the constant destruction of old structures and the constant creation of new, increasingly efficient ones (Spencer & Kirchhoff, 2006). This understanding of innovation and the distinction Schumpeter's triad draws between innovation, invention and imitation of innovation has been widely adopted (Grafström & Lindman, 2017; Viotti 2002). Beyond Schumpeter, the growing interest in innovation has led to the development of various definitions captured in both a broad and narrow sense. The definitions initially emphasised the technological aspects of innovation, so as to finally cover very broad categories, which include social and economic life, technology and the natural world.

The transformation of the global economy has contributed to a change in the perception of innovation. For example, Drucker (1985) related the issue of innovation both to the economy, mainly business, and to certain social processes. In his opinion, innovation is an economic or social concept rather than a technical one, and innovation in business is a tool of change resulting from the needs or systematic observation of the external environment in the context of starting new business activities or providing new services. Fagerberg (2005) considered innovation an important determinant of socio-economic living conditions. Porter (1990) pointed out that the main elements of innovation are new products and services, or new applications of existing products or services, or technological improvements, better methods, ways of doing things, manifested in changes to products, processes, new approaches to marketing or distribution.

When discussing the nature of innovation, the definition included in the latest Oslo Manual (2018), developed jointly by the European Statistical Office (Eurostat) and the Organisation for Economic Co-operation and Development (OECD), is often used. The Manual defines innovation as a new or improved product or process (or combination thereof) that differs significantly from previous products or processes and that has been made available to potential users (a product) or brought into use by an entity (a process) (Oslo Manual, 2018).

In the literature, innovation us understood as an output or as a process that leads to a given outcome. In the first case, innovation is the outcome of applying the progress of knowledge and invention taking the form of a good, service or an idea, perceived by the recipient as new. In the second case, innovation is not only the outcome of a specific task, but also includes activities that preceded its creation. These two contexts of innovation are also used in the Oslo Manual, where the term "innovation activities" implies a process, while the term "innovation" is reserved for outcomes. Innovation activities are defined here as all developmental, financial and commercial activities undertaken by a company to introduce innovations (Oslo Manual, 2018).

How companies approach and create innovation change as new concepts and models of the innovation process emerge. In recent years, significant trends in this area have included the transition from a linear to a systemic model of innovation, as well as going beyond the technological aspects of innovation. The change in the paradigm of economic development, as well as the growing importance of knowledge, have led to the emphasis on the role of non-technological innovations in creating innovative processes in enterprises.

Current development trends in the digital economy relate to the implementation of various types of innovations, and are forcing all elements of the economic structure, including the labour market, to adapt them. The labour market covers the relationships between the demand for and supply of labour (Abbott & Ashenfelter, 1976; Dykes, 2005). The supply side of the labour market is represented by labour resources, while the demand side is determined by the number of jobs generated by the economy. Innovations are the main cause of changes in the labour market, as they directly influence directly the size and structure of labour demand. Moreover, changes in the structure of labour demand force adjustments on the labour supply side.

Determinants of the impact of innovation on the labour market and labour relations in the digital economy

Product and process innovation

Innovation can lead to changes in productivity, which, in turn, can result in changes in employment (Mohnen & Hall, 2013). However, the link between innovation, productivity and employment is not straightforward, as different forms of innovation may have different effects on changes in the labour market (Harrison, Jaumandreu, Mairesse, & Peters, 2014). For example, the implementation of process innovations may allow a firm to produce the same amount of goods but with less capital and/or labour input, which, in turn, may lead to an increase in productivity and a decrease in employment. However, some studies indicate that the introduction of process innovation under certain conditions may have a positive impact on employment growth in the economy (Lachenmaier & Rottmann, 2011).

The implementation of product innovation by a company and the launch of a new product on the market may create new demand for the good when consumers or other companies find it useful. The impact of product innovation on the labour market can therefore be demand-driven (Hadaya & Cassivi, 2009; Jensen & Goldberg, 2014). However, to what extent a product innovation will create new jobs depends on the price elasticity of demand and the existence of substitutes or complementary products.

The price effect is another impact of innovation on the labour market. For example, if process innovations contribute to lower production costs and, as a result of their introduction, the company reduces product prices, this may contribute to the company's market expansion and employment growth (Lachenmaier & Rottmann, 2011). It should also be noted that new products with higher utility and/or lower price will displace existing products offered by the firm or its competitors. Product innovation may therefore have a negative effect for the entity that implements it, as the demand for new goods may be at the expense of products the company already sells (the "cannibalisation" effect), but also for the competitors of a company as a result of reduced demand for their goods (the "business stealing" effect) (Pellegrino, Piva, & Vivarelli, 2017). Taken together, these phenomena may reduce the initial effect of creating new jobs in the economy through product innovation (European Parliament, 2018).

The impact of innovation on the labour market can be analysed from the point of view of the type of effect it has. We see both the reduction effect, in which living labour is replaced with capital, leading to a reduction in jobs; and the employment compensation effect, where innovations tend to neutralise the decline in employment in the economy (Dachs, Hud, Koehler, & Peters, 2017; Li, Su, Tao, & Hao, 2019). This can happen when technical progress contributes to the emergence of new products or services, new markets and thus new jobs (Węgrzyn, 2013).

How technological innovation affects jobs is a matter of some debate in the literature (Frey & Osborne, 2013). There are several transmission mechanisms that link technological innovation and job quality (Muñoz-de-Bustillo, Grande, & Fernández-Macías, 2016). Technological innovation affects the structure of industries and occupations in the economy. Product innovations, for example, can contribute to new industries replacing old ones. In contrast, process innovations may cause certain types of jobs and occupations to disappear and contribute to the emergence of others. Technological innovations directly affect the quality of jobs. They bring about changes in production processes that affect health and safety, the nature of the tasks performed and the set of skills required. Process innovations can have a significant impact on productivity, which can translate, for example, into higher wages and shorter working hours.

Regarding the impact of technological innovations on the structure of industries and occupations, as well as their direct impact on the quality of jobs, the theoretical debate focuses on the effects technological change has on occupations. Some researchers point to the skills-biased technological change thesis, which argues that technological change contributes to an increase in the number of high-skilled jobs and a decrease in the number of lower-skilled jobs (Balsmeier & Woerter, 2019). Other researchers argue for a routine-biased technological change thesis, which maintains that technological change contributes to an increase in the number of both high- and low-skilled jobs, but to a decrease in the number of medium-skilled jobs (Dolphin, Gottfried, Raikes, Silim, & Thompson, 2014; Goos, Manning, & Salomons, 2014). According to the first group of researchers, technological change helps increase the quality of jobs, resulting in the appearance of more and better jobs. The second group of researchers argues that it leads to a polarisation of job quality. More jobs with higher job quality and more jobs with lower job quality appear in the economy.

The relationship between the implementation of innovations and job creation depends on the sector in which a firm operates, as industries differ in the nature and advancement in technology they use and the economic benefits they derive from innovation (Cohen, 2010). An important impact of innovation on the labour market is also the reallocation of employment and capital between sectors. This is because not all firms implementing innovations are successful—where some grow rapidly, others stagnate or close down (Dosi & Nelson, 2010). This results in a flow of labour and capital from declining to rapidly growing industries.

Digital innovation and the organisation of work

Innovations affect labour relations in different ways. This applies to tasks performed at work, work organisation, wages, employment levels, the nature of employment relations and trade union organisations. Innovations implemented by enterprises affect the tasks performed by employees and are more likely to increase the skill level of workers engaged in work tasks than to reduce it. They may lead to increased responsibility, for example due to the increased value of the modern equipment used. With the introduction of innovations, workers need higher skills, especially intellectual ones, which is partly offset by some reduction in manual skill requirements. This is the result of work becoming less physical and more mental. Consider the work performed in manufacturing and service companies. Once more physical, it now increasingly involves working with machines or robots using artificial intelligence and operating IT systems. On a related note, AI-based automation is competency discriminatory, as it strengthens the position of people with competencies that allow them to work in an environment saturated with new technologies, excluding those without such competencies (Todolí-Signes, 2019).

The practices supporting innovation in the workplace also include innovations in work organisation, Human Resource Management (HRM) practices and direct employee participation (Rus, Oeij, Pot, & Totterdill, 2019). For example, in the case of a work organisation, employees are encouraged to constantly look for solutions to improve products, services or work processes. Internal discussions are a source of inspiration for teams as well as individual employees, which can contribute to the creation of new ideas and solutions. Failures are accepted by company management as they are seen as part of the innovation process and thus learning opportunities. Cooperation with other entities, such as suppliers, partners or research institutions is important at the stage of formulating and defining the problem to be solved. With regard to HRM practices, specific practices for innovative enterprises can be distinguished. These include interdepartmental cooperation and an atmosphere of open communication, which encourages cooperation between individual departments in the company, the willingness to learn and appropriate adaptation to the position. Training is perceived by the employer as an investment in employees. Managers organise internal training sessions and encourage informal learning between employees. Employees are encouraged to participate in research and scientific conferences, international fairs and training courses offered by suppliers, which are an important source of knowledge. Another issue is direct employee participation, which is practiced in different ways and at different stages of innovation. For example, employees are often involved in making management decisions regarding the selection of innovative projects and in the preparation of joint reports assessing the suitability, market potential, technological requirements, investment needs and profitability of a new product or service. Ideas that have been approved are usually implemented by the originators themselves in cooperation with others. Employees can also influence decisions about changes in the production process. Regular meetings are held where management and employees share information about new products and services as well as project experiences (Eurofound & Cedefop, 2021).

Innovations can affect the organisation of work directly, requiring the reallocation of labour, or indirectly, creating opportunities to adjust control strategies. Work organisation concerns the how employees are distributed according to the technical requirements of the production system and the employer's control strategy. Such changes affect the cohesiveness of workgroups, for example by increasing interaction between members of a particular group of workers. Innovations also affect aspects of remuneration such as level, differentiation and relativity and sometimes the rules governing remuneration systems. (Martin, 1995).

New technologies have given rise to platformisation, which has changed the labour market (Hinings, Gegenhuber, & Greenwood, 2018). Online platforms that link labour supply and demand operate on the same principles as other types of platforms. They enable transactions (exchange of labour for payment via online payment environments), impose rules governing the relations between the parties to the market and apply a recommendation or assessment system, which helps build and maintain trust between the parties (Choudary, 2018). The growing popularity of platforms has helped encourage the spread of new forms of employment and is thus one of the reasons for their increasing flexibility, especially within the secondary labour market (Karanović, Berends, & Engel, 2021). Thanks to platforms, in addition to the classic form of a full-time job or various variants of the contract-mandate, new forms of employment relations are emerging, such as the possibility of several employees sharing a single job or employers sharing an employee.

The new forms of employment also include "voucher work," which involves the purchase of a package of work from an intermediary organisation bringing together employers and employees. However, self-employment and working for multiple clients simultaneously is growing in popularity (Degryse, 2016; Valenduc & Vendramin, 2016). On the down side, platforms have often been accused of lowering labour standards by promoting contract employment without social guarantees, which is seen as contributing to precarity. Online recruitment satisfies the employers' demand for short-term collaborators who perform only some of the activities related to the process of product preparation or service provision, thus reducing the need for full-time workers. In addition, the vast majority of platforms do not categorise themselves to be employers, even emphasising that they are only intermediaries between two sides of the market. As a result, platform workers do not have a traditional employment relationship with either the platform owners or the principals (Zysman & Kenney, 2018). This hinders organisations that protect workers' rights, such as trade unions.

Innovations that facilitate remote working, including through platforms, also offer a wide range of opportunities related to new forms of outsourcing. These enable companies in highly developed countries to use labour resources from less developed countries quickly and cheaply, without having to relocate or set up subsidiaries onsite. Innovations in digital technologies are increasing the demand for employees performing specialised tasks in a more flexible way, working remotely, outside the office. Decreasing outsourcing costs further encourages businesses to network, as smaller companies can also benefit from new solutions (Yousaf, Radulescu, Sinisi, Serbanescu, & Păunescu, 2021).

The awareness that technological innovations and business models alone are not enough to solve contemporary problems is becoming more and more common (Howaldt & Schwartz, 2010). Proper deployment of human talents is perceived as crucial to the success of innovation by an increasing number of European countries and regions, as well as trade unions and enterprises alike (Pot et al., 2016; Totterdill, Exton, Exton, & Gold, 2016). This is also evidenced by the European Commission's definition that innovation in the workplace can mean many things, such as changing business structure, human resource management, relationships with customers and suppliers or the work environment itself. These innovations improve the motivation and working conditions for employees, leading to increased labour productivity, innovation capacity, market resilience and business competitiveness (Rus et al., 2019).

Employee-driven innovation

Another perspective on the impact of innovation on the labour market and employment relations is the concept of employee-driven innovation (Bäckström & Lindberg, 2019; Echebiri, Engen, & Amundsen, 2021). This concept holds that employees are an important source of innovation. They have great potential to contribute to innovative processes as they gain knowledge and experience-based information from their close contacts with customers and co-workers (Høyrup, 2010). Employee-driven innovation is based not only on a social but also on a humanistic approach to innovation. In this concept, employees are seen as creative individuals who have expert knowledge about the organisation, its operations and external relations. They also have skills that can be used to solve problems and information that management does not have, and which therefore gains the potential to innovate (Tidd & Bessant, 2009). As Bank and Raza (2014) note, encouraging greater employee participation and engaging employees in conversation in order to collaboratively develop innovative solutions supports innovation processes in the organisation.

Smith, Ulhøi and Kesting (2012) identified four factors that are important for employee-driven innovation. The first is the support of a leader, so that employees feel safe when they come up with new ideas that challenge existing practices and differ from management's views. It is also important for motivation and the implementation and allocation of necessary resources. Another factor is autonomy in defining and setting priorities and one's own goals, in expressing social identity and in organising one's own behaviour, which increases creativity and the possibility of introducing unexpected solutions. The third factor is cooperation, which involves acting together and sharing information as well as knowledge. Group interaction and the sharing of ideas with others are important for creativity as they stimulate employees to generate more and more new ideas and facilitate innovative learning. The last factor, management's attitude to change and the internal climate for innovation, is also crucial. The most vital elements are trust, openness, flexibility in the design of work tasks and a climate conducive to learning. Each has a significant impact on employees' creativity and innovative behaviour (Smith et al., 2012).

As Alasoini (2012) notes, an increasing number of innovations will be intangible and service-oriented. Hence, employees' knowledge of the wishes, expectations and needs of users and customers will become increasingly important. Alasoini (2012) recognises three trends that stimulate this change. First, changes on the market will gain momentum, requiring companies to continuously collect information about users and customers. Second, the economy is becoming increasingly networked and innovations will be absorbed through diffusion by smaller players who, in the absence of R&D staff, will have to encourage other employees to participate in the innovation process. Third, problem-solving skills and the ability to spot new opportunities will increase among employees.

In the digital economy, how efficiently organisations share information plays a key role. The mode of production has changed from a model corresponding to the knowledge economy, involving a combination of information, knowledge and innovation, to a model combining human intelligence with new information technologies, information and innovation corresponding to the era of digital economy. Miklosik, Evans, Žák and Lipianska (2019) and Taušer, Žamberský and Čajka (2013) point out that the fourth industrial revolution is seen as the "road to the innovation economy" because the implementation of digital connectivity not only improves efficiency but also accelerates innovation and brings new business models that are implemented much faster. The basis for this is the individual's creativity and the appropriate formation of human capital (Sima, Gheorghe, Subić, & Nancu, 2020).

Limitations of innovation theory for the labour market and employment relations

The concepts presented in the previous section on the impact of innovation on the labour market and employment relations have their limitations. For example, the skills-biased technological change concept and the routine-biased technological change thesis place too much emphasis on technological innovations – after all, companies also employ countless non-technological innovations (Toner, 2011). They do not take into account labour market institutions or the power that mediates the relationship between technological change and job quality. Moreover, the pattern of job quality outcomes is more diverse than these two theories predict (Fernández-Macías, 2012; Muñoz-de-Bustillo et al., 2016). Skill-oriented changes and routine technological changes may also increase inequalities in society because they favour certain groups of workers.

Moreover, the extent to which productivity growth is the result of technological innovation alone is unclear. Other factors affect productivity, including managerial structures and practices as well as organisational arrangements are important (Comin, 2010). Nor does productivity growth immediately translate into higher wages (van Gyes & Schulten, 2015). Some observers (Brynjolfsson & McAfee, 2014; Frey & Osborne, 2017) forecast strong potential for productivity growth and a corresponding decline in employment, primarily in routine activities in manufacturing and services as a result of the use of digital technologies. In contrast, others have suggested innovation will boost employment growth (Greenan & Guellec, 2000; Lachenmaier & Rottmann, 2011). Clearly, empirical studies in this area are not unequivocal.

Despite studies that point to employment growth induced by product innovation, the aforementioned demand effect is quite rarely mentioned in discussions on the digital economy. This may be because our ability to imagine the future is limited. It also includes limitations in imagining the underlying future product innovations, as well as their impact on job creation. Currently, the reduction in employment resulting from the implementation of process innovations seems more evident, as it is more obvious and is associated with changes in products and occupations we are all familiar with.

The concept of employee-driven innovation is a new form of innovation that assumes that employees are an important and effective source of innovation. However, as Høyrup notes, this concept has been little explored, as so far the focus has been more on innovations that have been driven by various types of research, experts, technology, market or users (Høyrup, 2010).

To conclude, new technologies enable innovation in the workplace, but such activities can lead, on the one hand, to a better work-life balance for workers, but, on the other, to greater insecurity and periods of involuntary unemployment, especially as the self-employed often have no legal protection and are not entitled to social benefits. Work carried out in this way will less and less be done in a specific place and at a specific time. As previously indicated, organisational innovation can affect the quality of work. This may include issues related to the way work is organised, the design of workplaces or the formation of organisational relationships. These innovations can improve, or undermine, the quality of work. For example, companies are paying more and more attention to flexible forms of employment, but their impact on the quality of work may vary. While they can lead to greater autonomy and task enrichment, and thus to higher quality of work, they can also bring about higher work pressure, increased stress due to the large number of tasks performed by the employees and uncertainty about the temporary form of employment, which contributes to lower quality work and increasing work-life imbalance (Warhurst, Mathieu, Keune, & Gallie, 2018)

Conclusions and directions for future research

Interest in innovation has evolved over the years, strongly influenced by changes in the global economy, including more recently its digitisation. Initial theoretical considerations primarily emphasised the technical aspects of innovation in connection with the key role of industry and the changes made thanks to technical and technological progress in the economy. The change in the structure of industry became a premise for the development of new concepts in this field and for broadening the focus of innovation to include areas beyond the field of technology.

Innovation brings about creative destruction, which affects the economies of individual countries, including their labour markets and employment relations. They influence the quantity and quality of jobs created in the economy and contribute to the fact that people's work begins to focus on producing, processing and distributing knowledge and information with the use of modern tools. The importance of the knowledge is increasing, especially in highly developed economies, and this brings about innovations that force appropriate adjustments on the labour market.

New technologies emphasise some people's skills while devaluing those of others, leading to their being made redundant. New technologies enable innovations in the workplace, which may one day contribute to the emergence of new occupations with a high proportion of tasks requiring creative and social skills, and a low proportion of routine tasks. To meet these challenges, enterprises should implement a range of innovative workforce strategies, including retraining workers, preparing them for different roles within the enterprise or establishing greater cooperation with the education sector.

The digital economy changes not only the amount of work to be done and the demand for different levels of skills, but also the organisation of work and the ways in which employees are hired. More and more tasks will be carried out outside the company, and the proportion of self-employed people who work on a project basis for different clients will increase. Rather than being rigidly hierarchical, the organisational structures of companies will be more project-oriented. However, the implementation of new technologies may result in growing social inequalities, an important challenge for national policies worldwide. New forms of employment will therefore require new employment regulations and changes in social policy, especially the adjustment of social security institutions.

It is difficult to clearly define the factors that determine the development of flexible relations between the employer and the employee as the links between the theory of innovation and the labour market are very complex. Many different factors should be taken into account, including the type of innovations implemented, the use of existing technologies in new areas, cross-sectoral links or factors related to the creation and diffusion of knowledge. Moreover, the analysis of the impact of innovation on labour market changes is particularly challenging because the links between innovation and employment and the shaping of labour relations rarely have direct and immediate consequences. Their effects appear with varying delays and affect different areas of the economy.

References

Abbott, M., & Ashenfelter, O. (1976). Labour supply, commodity demand and the allocation of time. *The Review of Economic Studies, 43*(3), 389–411.

Alasoini, T. (2012). A new model for workplace development in Finland. Rethinking employee participation and the quality of working life in the context of broad-based innovation policy. *International Journal of Action Research, 8*(3), 245–265.

Bäckström, I., & Lindberg, M. (2019). Varying involvement in digitally enhanced employee-driven innovation. *European Journal of Innovation Management, 22*(3), 524–540.

Balsmeier, B., & Woerter, M. (2019). Is this time different? How digitalization influences job creation and destruction. *Research Policy, 48*(8), 103765.

Bank, J., & Raza, A. (2014). Collaborative idea management: A driver of continuous innovation. *Technology Innovation Management Review, 2*(4), 11–16.

Borowiecki, R., Siuta-Tokarska, B., Maroń, J., Suder, M., Thier, A., & Żmija, K. (2021). Developing digital economy and society in the light of the issue of digital convergence of the markets in the European Union countries. *Energies, 14*, 2717.

Brynjolfsson, E., & McAfee, A. (2014). *The second machine age: Work, progress, and prosperity in a time of brilliant technologies.* New York: Norton Publishers.

Choudary, S.P. (2018). *The architecture of digital labour platforms: Policy recommendations on platform design for worker well-being.* Geneva: ILO.

Cohen, W.M. (2010). Fifty Years of empirical studies of innovative activity and performance. In B.A. Hall & N. Rosenberg (Eds.), *Handbook of the economics of innovation* (pp. 129–213). Amsterdam: Elsevier.

Comin, D. (2010). Total factor productivity. In S.N. Durlauf & L.E. Blume (Eds.), *Economic growth.* London: Palgrave Macmillan. doi:10.1057/9780230280823_32

Dachs, B., Hud, M., Koehler, C., & Peters, B. (2017). Innovation, creative destruction and structural change: Firm-level evidence from European countries. *Industry and Innovation, 24*(4), 346–381.

Degryse, Ch. (2016). Digitalisation of the economy and its impact on labour markets, "ETUI" Working Paper 2016.02.

Dolphin, T., Gottfried, G., Raikes, L., Silim, A., & Thompson, S. (2014). *European jobs and skills: A comprehensive review.* London: IPPR.

Dosi, G., & R. Nelson. (2010). Technical change and industrial dynamics as evolutionary processes. In B.A. Hall & N. Rosenberg (Eds.), *Handbook of the economics of innovation* (pp. 52–126). Amsterdam: Elsevier.

Drucker, P.F. (1985). *Innovation and entrepreneurship practices and principles.* New York: Routledge.

Dykes, F. (2005). Supply and demand: Breastfeeding as labour. *Social Science & Medicine, 60*(10), 2283–2293.

Echebiri, C., Engen, M., & Amundsen, S. (2021). Employee-driven innovation: Conceptualisation, scale development and preliminary validation. *International Journal of Entrepreneurship and Innovation Management, 25*(2–3), 233–255.

Eurofound (2018). *Overview of new forms of employment 2018 update*. Luxembourg: Publications Office of the European Union.

Eurofound and Cedefop (2021), *Innovation in EU companies: Do workplace practices matter?* European Company Survey 2019 series. Luxembourg: Publications Office of the European Union.

European Parliament (2018). The impact of new technologies on the labour market and the social economy. *European Parliamentary Research Service*, February 2018.

Fagerberg, J. (2005). Innovation: A guide to the literature. In J. Fagerberg, D.C. Mowery, & R.R. Nelson (Eds.), *The Oxford Handbook of Innovation* (pp. 1–27). Oxford: Oxford University Press.

Fernández-Macías, E. (2012). Job polarisation in Europe? Changes in the employment structure and job quality, 1997–2005. *Work and Occupations, 39*(2), 157–182.

Frey, C.B., & Osborne, M. (2013). *The future or employment: How susceptible are jobs to computerization?* Oxford: Oxford Martin Programme on Technology and Employment, University of Oxford.

Frey, C.B., & Osborne, M.A. (2017). The future of employment: How susceptible jobs are to computerisation? *Technological Forecasting and Social Change, 114*(1), 254–280.

Goos, M., Manning, A., & Salomons, A. (2014). Explaining job polarization: Routine-biased technological change and offshoring. *American Economic Review, 104*(8), 2509–2526.

Grafström, J., & Lindman, Å. (2017). Invention, innovation and diffusion in the European wind power sector. *Technological Forecasting and Social Change, 114*, 179–191.

Greenan, N., & Guellec, D. (2000). Technological innovation and employment reallocation. *Labour, 14*(4), 547–590.

Hadaya, P., & Cassivi, L. (2009). Collaborative e-product development and product innovation in a demand-driven network: The moderating role of eCRM. *Electronic Markets, 19*(2–3), 71–87.

Harrison, R., Jaumandreu, J., Mairesse, J., & Peters, B. (2014). Does innovation stimulate employment? A firm-level analysis using comparable micro-data from four European countries. *International Journal of Industrial Organization, 36*(C), 29–43.

Hinings, B., Gegenhuber, T., & Greenwood, R. (2018). Digital innovation and transformation: An institutional perspective. *Information and Organization, 28*(1), 52–61.

Howaldt, J., & Schwartz, M. (2010). *Social innovation: Concepts, research fields and international trends*. Aachen: IMA/ZLW.

Høyrup, S. (2010). Employee-driven innovation and workplace learning: Basic concepts, approaches and themes. *Transfer: European Review of Labour and Research, 16*(2), 143–154.

Jasińska-Biliczak, A. (2020). TRIBE 2.0–The microcommunity needs in the frames of the sharing economy concept. *European Research Studies, 23*(2), 75–84.

Jensen, C., & Goldberg, I. (2014). Demand-driven innovation policies in the European Union. CASE Network Studies & Analyses, Research Report No. 468.

Karanović, J., Berends, H., & Engel, Y. (2021). Regulated dependence: Platform workers' responses to new forms of organizing. *Journal of Management Studies, 58*(4), 1070–1106.

Kling, R., & Lamb, R. (2000). IT and organizational change in digital economies. In E. Brynjolfsson & B. Kahin (Eds.), *Understanding the digital economy* (pp. 295–324). Cambridge, MA: MIT Press.

Lachenmaier, S., & Rottmann, H. (2011). Effects of innovation on employment: A dynamic panel analysis. *International Journal of Industrial Organization, 29*(2), 210–220.

Li, Z.Z., Su, C. W., Tao, R., & Hao, L. N. (2019). Enhance or depress? The effect of trade on active females in the labour market. *Economic research-Ekonomska istraživanja, 32*(1), 2680–2698.

Martin, R. (1995). Innovation and industrial relations. In M. Dodgson & R. Rothwell, *The handbook of industrial innovation* (pp. 337–347). Cheltenham: Edward Elgar Publishing.

Miklosik, A., Evans, N., Žák, Š., & Lipianska, J. (2019). A framework for constructing optimisation models to increase the visibility of organizations' information in search engines. *Information Research-An International Electronic Journal, 24*(1), paper 808.

Mohnen, P., & Hall, B.A. (2013). Innovation and productivity: An update. *Eurasian Business Review, 3*(1), 47–65.

Muñoz-de-Bustillo, R., Grande, R., & Fernández-Macías, E. (2016). Innovation and job quality. An initial exploration, QuInnE Working Paper No. 5.

OECD (2020). *A Roadmap toward a common framework for measuring the digital economy, Report for the G20 Digital Economy Task Force.* Saudi Arabia: OECD.

OECD/Eurostat (2018). *Oslo manual 2018: Guidelines for collecting, reporting and using data on innovation, 4th Edition, The measurement of scientific, technological and innovation activities.* Paris: OECD Publishing / Luxembourg: Eurostat.

Pellegrino, G., Piva, M., & Vivarelli, M. (2017). Are robots stealing our jobs?. IZA Discussion Paper No. 10540.

Porter, M.E. (1990). *The competitive advantage of nations.* London: The Macmillan Press.

Pot, F., Totterdill, P., & Dhondt, S. (2016). Workplace innovation: European policy and theoretical foundation. *World Review of Entrepreneurship, Management and Sustainable Development, 12*(1), 13–32.

Rus, D., Oeij, P.R., Pot, F.D., & Totterdill, P. (2019). Workplace innovation: A review and potential future avenues. *International Journal of Technology Transfer and Commercialisation, 16*(3), 208–227.

Rydvalova, P., & Skala, M. (2021). Innovation and innovation partnership. In M. Zizka & P. Rydvalova (Eds.), *Innovation and performance drivers of business clusters* (pp. 47–57). Cham: Springer.

Schumpeter, J.A. (1934). *The theory of economic development: An inquiry into profits, capital, credit, interest and the business cycle.* Harvard College, Cambridge, MA: Harvard University Press.

Sima, V., Gheorghe, I.G., Subić, J., & Nancu, D. (2020). Influences of the industry 4.0 revolution on the human capital development and consumer behavior: A systematic review. *Sustainability, 12*, 4035.

Sørensen, E., & Torfing J. (2013). Enhancing social innovation by rethinking collaboration, leadership and public governance, social frontiers. Paper presented at NESTA Social Frontiers, London, 1–13.

Smith P., Ulhöi J. P., & Kesting, P. (2012). Mapping key antecedents of employee-driven innovations. *International Journal of Human Resources Development and Management, 12*(3), 224–236.

Spencer, A.S., & Kirchhoff, B.A. (2006). Schumpeter and new technology based firms: Towards a framework for how NTBFs cause creative destruction. *International Entrepreneurship and Management Journal, 2*(2), 145–156.

Taušer, J., Žamberský P., & Čajka R. (2013). Comparative price levels of new EU member countries. *International Journal of Management and Economics, 39*, 9–17.

Tidd, J., & Bessant, J. (2009). *Managing innovation. Integrating technological, market and organizational change.* Chichester: Wiley and Sons.

Todolí-Signes, A. (2019). Algorithms, artificial intelligence and automated decisions concerning workers and the risks of discrimination: The necessary collective governance of data protection. *Transfer: European Review of Labour and Research, 25*(4), 465–481.

Toner, P. (2011), Workforce skills and innovation. OECD Education Working Papers No. 55, Paris: OECD.

Totterdill, P., Exton, O., Exton, R., & Gold, M. (2016). High-performance work practices in Europe: Challenges of diffusion. *European Journal of Workplace Innovation, 2*(1), 63–81.

Valenduc, G., &Vendramin, P. (2016). Work in the digital economy: Sorting the old from the new, "ETUI" Working Paper 2016.03.

Van Gyes, G., & Schulten, T. (2015). *Wage bargaining under the new European Economic Governance.* Brussels: European Trade Union Institute.

Viotti, E.B. (2002). National learning systems: A new approach on technological change in late industrializing economies and evidences from the cases of Brazil and South Korea. *Technological Forecasting and Social Change, 69*(7), 653–680.

Warhurst, Ch., Mathieu, Ch., Keune M., & Gallie, D. (2018). Linking innovation and job quality: Challenges and opportunities for policy and research. QuInnE Working Paper No. 11.

Węgrzyn, G. (2013). Innowacje jako determinanta zmian strukturalnych rynku pracy. *Studia Ekonomiczne, 145*, 209–219.

West, M.A., & Farr, J.L. (1990). *Innovation and creativity at work: Psychological and organisational strategies.* Chichester: John Wiley.

Yousaf, Z., Radulescu, M., Sinisi, C.I., Serbanescu, L., & Păunescu, L.M. (2021). Towards sustainable digital innovation of SMEs from the developing countries in the context of the digital economy and frugal environment. *Sustainability, 2021*(13), 5715.

Zysman, J., & Kenney, M. (2018). The next phase in the digital revolution: Intelligent tools, platforms, growth, employment. *Communications of the ACM*, 2018, *61*(2), 54–63.

8 Agency theory and the digital economy

Agnieszka Żur

Introduction

The focus of this chapter is on high-tech industries, the playground for engineers, programmers, inventors, developers and other high-tech jobs. These groups hold the knowledge and brainpower that make or break innovative firms, from risky start-ups to oligopolistic market leaders. At the same time, these professions need high-tech firms to put their ideas, expertise, creativity and brainpower to work; to be productive, gain new experience and advance their professional careers. Both parties need each other to grow and deliver results. They connect through work relationships, which are increasingly not limited to traditional long-term employment contracts.

Recent years have brought a more diverse constellation of work relationships to high-tech industry. The new forms of work include temporary work contracts, interim management, freelance work, casual work or mobile work. High-tech employees may be employed by the firm and may choose to deliver their expert services through self-employment. This trend is coupled with labour market disequilibrium: the demand for skilled and experienced high-tech professionals far exceeds the supply. The digital economy has increased the share of IT work in almost all sectors of the economy. In traditional manufacturing industries, the majority of the workforce performs IT-based tasks requiring people to increasingly engage in advanced digital technologies (Malecki & Moriset, 2007). This demand for tech talent has grown exceedingly throughout the COVID-19 pandemic months as tech adoption and digitalisation surged across all industries. In June 2021, Forbes magazine referred to the shortage of workers with tech skills and attendant search for such workers as the "tech talent wars" (English, 2021). Additionally, the COVID-19 pandemic gave rise to widespread mobile work, making employers less dependent on local constraints, enabling many high-tech companies to take advantage of global talent pools, extending the scope of these talent wars.

The digital economy is in fact enabled and shaped by high-tech firms and the technologies they create. Galloping innovations are changing how consumers, employees, markets, enterprises and other organisations function.

DOI: 10.4324/9781003254638-11

Digital transformations form the basis of a hectic ecosystem in which ever more efficient and user-friendly inventions and innovations are rapidly accumulating (Śledziewska & Włoch, 2021). These innovations are evolving faster than ever, and high-tech firms are engaged in a race for innovation. Innovation is what distinguishes industry leaders from followers.

This combination of technology, opportunity, talent shortage and new forms of work has shifted the dynamics of workplace relations. These trends present a new research space for scholars from a range of fields and provoke us to ask new questions. What is the market power of high-tech professionals versus the bargaining power of the firms they work for? How do they work together in a collaborative and mutually beneficial way, sharing both risks and rewards? How do these people and organisations establish optimal levels of collaborations on the labour market that is satisfactory, fair and risk minimal for both sides? This chapter attempts to unpack the contractual nature of new labour relations in innovation driven industries through the prism of agency theory. Agency refers to any situation where authority is delegated and risk is involved. Risk is involved whenever the principal's and agents' interests and goals are unaligned and when the agent might not act in the best interest of the principal. In this chapter, we look at the interests of high-tech professionals and high-tech firms to evaluate scenarios of potential alignment and misalignment.

The relevance of agency theory for the labour market in the digital economy

Agency theory originated in economic models of risk and decision-sharing arrangements in the first half of 20th century. "Agency relationships occur whenever one partner in a transaction (the principal) delegates authority to another (agent) and the welfare of the principal is affected by the choices of the agent" (Arrow, 1985, p. 303). As a contractual agreement, agency refers to the conditions of authority delegation that are more optimal than no contract between agent and principal or full control of the agent by the principal (Rogers, 2001). Hence the unit of analysis is the contract between principal and agent. Agency theory focuses on resolving two common problems that can occur in agency relationships: (1) conflicts of interest between the principal and agents and (2) difficulties with establishing what the agent is actually doing (Eisenhardt, 1989).

The agency lens is applicable in a variety of settings whenever a principal and an agent are involved in cooperative behaviour, but may have different goals and different attitudes toward risk (Bendickson, Muldoon, Liguori, & Davis, 2016; Eisenhardt, 1989), including settings relative to innovation and high-tech industries (Colombo, Croce, & Murtinu, 2014). Authors agree that agency theory can be applied to employer-employee relationships, supplier-buyer or lawyer-client relations (Maestrini, Luzzini, Caniato, & Ronchi, 2014). In the quickly growing diversity of work arrangements and new types of work contracts, agency theory seems applicable to identify various contract alternatives under varying levels of outcome uncertainty, risk taking and information asymmetry between the two parties involved.

The premise of this theory is that principals delegate duties to agents who are expected to act in the principal's best interest. Yet one of the strengths of agency theory is that it is realistic and assumes that agents may prefer to pursue their own interests over the principal's. The focus of this theory is on determining an optimal contract governing principal-agent relations given realistic and possible assumptions about the nature of people, organisations and information. Such a contract would include agency controls, i.e. mechanisms eliminating the agency problems mentioned above.

Today, agency theory is promising in the context of new work arrangements in high-tech industries because its models include two variables critical for these industries: information and risk. Agency theory treats information/knowledge as a commodity that has a cost and can be purchased. Risk is a central concept in agency theory as the alignment of interests is not always evident between principal and agent, particularly, in the high-tech industries, as I explain below. One of the primary reasons why conflict emerges is that work contracts are imperfect – not only can every single contingency not be accounted for, but monitoring is difficult and costly. These factors make the outcome of agency relations uncertain (Bendickson et al., 2016). Outcome uncertainty is embedded in all agency relations and it is viewed in terms of a risk/reward trade-off, not just in terms of the inability to plan (Eisenhardt, 1989). Outcome uncertainty coupled with different attitudes toward risk between the principal and agent influence the shape of the contract. Hence, the potential value of the agency lens may lie in determining the optimal and most efficient contracts, agency control mechanism and incentives adapted to new work arrangements.

Factors determining employment relations in high-tech industries from an agency theory perspective

Development of flexible employment forms in high-tech industries

High-tech industries are characterised by volatile and non-stationary demand, very complex production processes and extremely high resource acquisition costs (Smirnov, van Jaarsveld, Atan, & de Kok, 2021). Rapid technological advancement shortens product life cycles, which, in turn, bring about high resource utilisation costs and cause these resources to quickly become obsolete. In addition, the demand for resources in high-tech industries often exceeds the available supply.

This complex and unpredictable market situation poses severe management risks. The pace of change has made expanding the capacity of critical resource groups, particularly talent resources, much more challenging. Hammering out a sourcing strategy is a difficult managerial challenge, often with far-reaching consequences. To cope with the rising demand as well as the race for innovation high-tech firms must find ways to hedge against market uncertainty. One of the ways can include new talent acquisition strategies.

Long-term work contracts may no longer fit the needs of fast-paced project-based firm operations. Resource planning is therefore increasingly limited to shorter time periods with relative certainty about demand and resource availability (Lee, Chen, & Kang, 2020; Nguyen & Wang, 2019; Smirnov et al., 2021). Timing has become a much more important issue in human resource management, as firms must constantly adapt the optimal resource level to match a given new technology, new products/services being introduced and/or new customer groups addressed (Nguyen & Wang, 2019). Thanks to these trends, new forms of employment relationships have emerged to suit the needs of the high-tech sector better than traditional long-term employment contracts. These include:

- interim management, in which highly skilled experts are hired temporarily for a specific project or to solve a specific problem, thereby integrating external management capacities in the work organisation;
- freelance work, where a person is self-employed and performs work based on a limited time contract without committing to a particular employer long-term;
- casual work, where an employer is not obliged to provide work regularly to the employee, but has the flexibility of calling them in on demand;
- ICT-based mobile work, where workers can do their job from any place at any time, supported by modern technologies;
- portfolio work, where a self-employed individual works for a large number of clients, doing small-scale jobs for each of them.

These forms of employment are not confined to a contract that specifies terms of employment and a corresponding wage or salary, but instead are geared to flexibility and individualisation (Degryse, 2016). Within this wide range of new forms of employment, the labour contract, wage standards, working time regulations, workplace training and access to trade unions may vary significantly and is most often subject to individual negotiations between the high-tech professional and the firm.

These new work arrangements are often preferred by high-tech professionals themselves for at least a couple of reasons. First, research suggests that high-tech professionals can be characterised by three aspects: excellent education, a strong preference for independence and a strong professional growth orientation rather than an organisational focus (Al-Ghazali & Afsar, 2021). High-tech professionals identify themselves more with high-tech culture rather than with a specific firm or industry (Yitshaki & Kropp, 2016) looking to develop their career, knowledge assets and future earnings power. Second, their driving motivational factors are knowledge growth, skills development and autonomy (Saether, 2019). Autonomy is highly valued by high-tech professionals and this why they might not be keen to engage in long-term work relationships. High-tech professionals focus primarily on the availability of learning and development opportunities when deciding whether or not to join an organisation (Gebauer, 2006). This is why they might prefer to work for more than one employer and thus gain access to multiple knowledge pools.

Contractual relationships

Given this new landscape, and the new employment forms and work relationships flourishing within it, new questions emerge about the power relationships between high-tech expert professionals and high-tech firms. High-tech firms are constantly seeking ways to leverage innovation as means to disrupting markets. They seek top talent and top market expertise to deliver breakthrough innovation and create competitive advantage for the firm. Knowledge intensive high-tech industries are characterised by rich growth prospects and a high level of intellectual work and hence a large proportion of their assets are tied to the intellectual capital of high-tech professionals (Shaikh, O'Brien, & Peters, 2018). A company may be looking to apply current knowledge to develop profit yearning innovation. High-tech professionals are looking for autonomy, new challenges and the opportunity to learn. Their goals may collide with those of high-tech firms in two likely scenarios: (i) firms may not be willing to grant the expected level of autonomy due to the high risks involved, and (ii) firms may prefer to hire individuals who have proven they can perform, leaving them unchallenged with new areas to learn.

This situation provokes agency problems that typify contemporary high-tech firms, especially those where payoffs are very high for both the firm and the professional. In effect, in some industries and in certain contexts, high-tech employees are rewarded at levels that bring their marginal utility into question (Baumann & Stieglitz, 2014). Organisations with big budgets are driving up wages, paying more for high-tech talent. This has precipitated wage inflation and fierce competition for high-tech professionals worldwide (English, 2021). In a race for innovation and market leadership, high-tech employees are faced with multiple options, which may appear more satisfying than further organisational commitment. Today, experienced and trained employees are faced with multiple opportunities for alternative career options, including setting up their own venture (Yitshaki & Kropp, 2016). As a result, firms experience retention problems and enormous turnover among high-tech professionals (English, 2021).

Research suggests that the contractual nature of the work relationship between high-tech firms and high-tech professionals primarily concerns the knowledge sharing that occurs between these two agents (Dong, Karhade, Rai, & Xu, 2021). Ownership of knowledge, which could provide the organisation with competitive advantages, may not be owned or even controlled by the firm. In the high-tech world, knowledge is the central issue and the object of exchange/transaction between the principal and agent. The agent's and principal's knowledge do not overlap. Principals (owners/managers) hold inside information about the firm to which agents have no access or limited access. Agents will not gain access to the inside information regardless of whether their contracts are short- or long-term; particularly to tacit knowledge about the firm, such as the culture, values, mind-set, informal relationships or informal leaders. Agents working as contract experts might not be interested in this type of information. They join a certain company to gain new knowledge and experience from the company in favour of future earnings and/or because they are passionate about high-tech and about the firm's projects/developments. So, agents expect to gain new knowledge from the principal (firm/employer) and principals expect to gain a great deal from the expert knowledge of the agent. In today's high-tech industry, agents are more likely to hold greater information/knowledge than the firm, especially when expert professionals work on a freelance basis and have access to several knowledge pools in their work.

Risk of agents' behaviour

According to agency theory, when there is information asymmetry and the agent possesses more knowledge/information than the principal, the agent is more likely to misrepresent the principal (Zajac & Westphal, 1994). In agency theory, this is known as moral hazard, and it is likely to grow in situations when agents, who exhibit a high tolerance for risk and are driven by learning and experimentation, have extended access to financial resources, large operating budgets and extended decision-making power (Shaikh et al., 2018). This, in turn, can lead to overinvesting and/or poor innovation outcomes for the firm, yet positive learning effects for the agent. This is a huge risk inherent to high-tech industry work arrangements today.

Early works on agency theory focused on the key issues of the time, one of which concerned how to separate risk and decision-making. Agency was an issue for senior managers, who were supposed to act in the best interest of the owner(s)/stakeholders. They were the decision-makers, while the business risk fell to the owner(s). Principals delegated the decision-making power to agents who were supposed perform services on their behalf, but this was not always the case. Principals were and still are unable to control the behaviour of agents and need to bear the risk of what representing the firm's and/or owners' best interests. To bring about some degree of risk sharing, with time, senior managers were offered bonuses in the form of stock options. In the 1980s, most software firms had stock ownership plans for their employees. While many firms still offer these plans, expert high-tech professionals working on a freelance or limited contract basis do not qualify.

Yet the risk of agents pursuing their own self-interest still exists. In high-tech firms, this risk can take various forms, such as by agents prioritising their sub-units or their projects, even though this may have negative implications for the company as a whole. As high-tech professionals, agents are highly invested in the projects they work on, driven by curiosity and novelty while possessing high risk tolerance (Saether, 2019). Hence in contemporary innovation-driven industries and work environments with a high saturation of high-tech professionals, agency costs are high. The performance of high-tech firms depends largely on the knowledge, skills and behaviours of the high-tech professionals hired.

Risk mitigation – agency controls

The solution to separating risk from decision-making and unwanted agent behaviour is agency controls, including monitoring and incentives. Early agency theory assumed that the employment of well-adapted monitoring and incentivisation methods and instruments would reduce agent opportunism and improve performance (Fama, 1980). Studies in this area are rather inconclusive and boil down to a single finding: it depends. Monitoring of agents to reduce the risk for owner(s) involves organisational procedures and processes that limit the agent's autonomy. Agency theory scholars established that firms pursue employee monitoring only up the point when the monitoring costs are lower than the losses due to agency problems (Coase, 1937; Eisenhardt, 1985). However, organisational control mechanisms are totally incompatible with the free and open exchange of ideas, room for experimentation and mistakes, all of which are indispensible for radical innovation. The cost of monitoring can therefore include a high turnover rate. In fact, a meta-analysis of the literature on monitoring showed no direct relationship between traditional monitoring and performance, but rather indicated that certain conditions may moderate this relationship (Dalton, Daily, Ellstrand, & Johnson, 1998). Additionally, a study from 2007 found that monitoring does not increase task performance, but may sometimes hinder it (Fong & Tosi Jr, 2007). All of this suggests the need to revisit the notion of monitoring methods in the context of work relations in the high-tech industry.

In the late 1990s, agency theory scholars introduced the concept of horizontal agency or peer monitoring as means of agency control. Mutual monitoring coupled with frequent communication within the team and with superiors can be used to collect information unavailable to superiors through other means (Mosakowski, 1998). Informal monitoring mechanisms like day-to-day interactions of colleagues are not seen as limiting autonomy. Horizontal monitoring may also align individuals' interests with the those of the organisation. Therefore, higher investment in practices that encourage open communication, sharing information and exchanging ideas may result in effective agency controls.

The second form of risk mitigation is incentives. To be effective, they must be aligned with the agent's expectations and preferences (Eisenhardt, 1989). As mentioned above, high-tech professionals are characterised by a strong need for professional growth, self-determination and autonomy. Additionally, existing studies provide evidence that these needs often require new non-traditional incentives and reward systems to keep employee motivation high. In creative and complex jobs such as one finds in high-tech industries, professionals are often driven by autonomous motivation, which is associated with higher self-determination and fosters performance more effectively than extrinsic motivation (Gagné & Deci, 2005). Intrinsic motivation is a fully autonomous (self-determined) type of motivation, and means that one is motivated by the task out of interest and enjoyment. There is empirical support for a positive relationship between employees' intrinsic motivation and their innovative behaviour (Yuan & Woodman, 2010), and that intrinsic motivation is a stronger predictor of performance quality than external motivation (Cerasoli, Nicklin, & Ford, 2014). These two studies provide useful information regarding the alignment of agents' incentives. Research also suggests that a person-organisation fit plays a pivotal role in reinforcing intrinsic motivation and raises the probability that the agent will act in the firm's best interests. Person-organisation fit concerns the correspondence between an individual's characteristics and the organisation, a high degree of congruity between personal attributes and contextual factors (Deci, Olafsen, & Ryan, 2017).

Finally, existing research studies suggest that traditional monetary incentives may not always be effective, especially in complex and creative jobs. It can be argued that in the high-tech industry keeping employees educated and developing them for future challenges has become an effective incentive for professionals (Kennedy & Daim, 2010).

Applications and limitations of agency theory for the labour market

Thus far, I have discussed the core elements underpinning agency theory in the context of new work relations in the high-tech industry. I will now turn to where those underpinnings may now lead the theory and why it may be useful or fall short in explaining current shifts in work relations. What are the boundary conditions and implications of agency theory that are misaligned with issues in today's business environment? Is there empirical evidence to suggest agency theory can explain contemporary work arrangements and complex principal-agent relationships? This theory has been subject to much criticism and claims have been made that it is "hardly subject to any empirical test since it rarely tries to explain actual events" (Perrow, 1986, p. 24). So how useful is agency theory and in which situations does it provide merely theoretical explanations for real life phenomena?

First and foremost, agency theory provides a useful lens to map out and understand the basic elements of work relations – the principal, the agent, the agency contract and agency controls. Looking through this lens sheds light on these basic elements and their shape in today's business reality. This is important as it provides a framework of cognition to comprehend the essential elements that relate to an agency-based employment contract. Agency theory distinguishes two basic contract types: behaviour-based and outcome-based, which differ in how they compile agency controls. Behaviour-based contracts focus on controlling agent behaviour and involve salary-based compensation and hierarchical control. Outcome oriented contracts focus on evaluating and rewarding the outcomes of the work performed and involve commissions, stock options and market governance.

Additionally, agency theory can help determine the optimal contract for regulating principal-agent relations, behaviour versus outcome or a balanced mix of the two types. Agency theory studies have established that when the principal is buying the agent's behaviour, a contract based on behaviour is more effective (Ekanayake, 2004). This is based on the assumption that the agent is self-interested, risk-averse, rational and attempting to exert the least acceptable effort, while the principal is able to evaluate the agent's behaviour. An outcome-based contract is more applicable when the principal cannot evaluate the agent's behaviour (due to information asymmetry, knowledge gaps or greater expertise on the part of the agent) or cannot fully verify the agent's skills at the time of hiring. In this case, the theory claims, the only viable option is to align the goals and preferences of the principal and agent by transferring a portion of the risk to the agent through outcome-based contracts (Harris & Raviv, 1979).

Looking at these claims, two important observations must be made. First, high-tech professionals do not fall into the model agent category, as they tend to have a high tolerance for risk. At the same time, the opposite may hold for high-tech firms today – the principal is more risk-averse than the agent. This assumption accords with the premise that agents are self-interested and driven by their own goals. High-tech professionals are driven by the will to experiment, learn and grow their own market advantage (Saether, 2019). This is why they are more willing to take risk and not afraid to test various solutions and experiment. They are most likely more afraid to miss an opportunity than to make a mistake. An outcome-based contract would here seem a better fit, as it would provide shared responsibility for risk-taking. Second, high-tech expert professionals tend to be short-term partners/employees hired through a variety of contracts. In short-term agency relationships, the information asymmetry between principal and agent tends to be greater (Eisenhardt, 1989), while the principal's ability to learn of and evaluate the agent's behaviour is far more difficult. This argument also suggests that outcome-based contracts would suit new work arrangement better, as the principal can assess the outcomes much more accurately than the behaviour of agents.

Researchers suggest that these two types of contracts – behaviour-based and outcome-based – can be associated with different industries. Meanwhile, managerial ownership applies to new economy industries which operate in more uncertain environments than old-economy firms (Tebourbi, 2016). Interestingly, the results of this study indicate that the positive relationship between pay-performance sensitivity and risk does not hold for small new-economy firms, but does remain valid for medium and large ones. This could be explained by the fact that information asymmetry is lower in smaller high-tech firms and the principal can monitor the agent in closer settings (Tebourbi, 2016).

Traditionally, both non-compete contracts and stock options have been used to align interests and protect the firm. However, these seem to be out of the question for self-employed or short-term employees in the high-tech industry, as they are likely to work with several firms at once. Therefore, in the light of agency theory, the challenge nowadays is to align a monitoring mechanism, incentives and work contracts with the needs and expectations of high-tech professionals. This calls for far more flexibility and possibly completely new types of contracts.

Researchers have pointed to several limitations of agency theory when it is applied to present day work settings. High-tech firms capitalise on their agents' opportunity-seeking behaviours. This strategic approach requires a different way of thinking and acting, but also poses different agency issues. Bendickson et al. (2016) claim that rather than focusing on agency controls, innovative firms should focus on building partnerships and achieving compromise between principals and agents: "Compromise is the glue that will allow organisations to continue to be innovative while growing and addressing the interests of principals and agents alike, yet in its current form, agency theory is inadequate in its discussion of compromise" (p. 184). While agency theory plays an important role in explaining how organisations gain control and use resources, partnerships and compromise are a somewhat marginal issue. Ever since the development of the human relations school of thought in management theory, agency theory has come in for criticism, as it focuses on controlling conflict rather than reaching common ground or consensus. This critique is all the more valid in view of the fact that agents are not subject to long-term traditional contracts and often perform work as self-employed. Common ground is not often defined in typical principal-agent contracts, even though the outcome of a compromise may lead to several different variations of principal-agent contracts. Therefore the contribution of the human relations approach can be an important component in reducing agency conflicts and potentially advancing agency theory to include the notion of cooperation and partnerships between the principal and agent.

Another line of critique mirrors the growing role of stakeholders in modern businesses, which is not embraced by traditional agency problems. In addition to dealing with principal's goals, agents working for any modern business must also balance the interests of multiple stakeholders (Ferrell et al., 2014). Agents spend time and energy dealing with stakeholders, who are better educated than ever about their power and businesses' responsibilities toward the community and about enforcing their rights. Agency theory must consider these influences, especially since it may no longer be the principal to whom the agent answers. This debt to stakeholders is strongly reinforced by business education; most ethics books and scholars argue that managers should be more beholden to stakeholders than to shareholders (Ferrell et al., 2014). Furthermore, social media has shifted more power to stakeholders than ever before. Twenty years ago, local problems, such as an upset worker or customer, for the most part remained local. Today they can "go viral" as shareholder groups have a greater ability to mobilise. Hence agents need to pay even greater attention to other stakeholders, perhaps causing more conflict with shareholders (Bendickson et al., 2016).

Conclusions and future research directions

Further exploration of the boundary conditions of agency theory should provide scholars with fertile ground for numerous strands of future research. Such research should aim to develop extensions to agency theory, including contributions from other theories, that help explain new phenomena that arise with the changing landscape of work relations.

One promising avenue could be engaging contributions from employee engagement theory.

> Employee engagement is a concept that is generally viewed as managing discretionary effort, that is, when employees have choices, they will act in a way that furthers their organisation's interests. An engaged employee is a person who is fully involved in, and enthusiastic about, his or her work.
> (Kennedy & Daim, 2010)

Engaged employees feel passion about their work, provide drive and innovation and feel that their contribution helps in moving the company forward. Towers Perrin defines employee engagement as "workers' willingness and ability to contribute to a company's success, the extent to which employees put discretionary effort into their work" (Gebauer, 2006, p. 96). This perspective seems very useful in crafting incentives and creating a work environment that would ensure work engagement among high-tech professionals within the firm.

Another potential contribution could stem from contemporary motivation theories. The notions of intrinsic motivation and person-organisation fit make a useful contribution to soft agency controls.

Undoubtedly, agency theory provides a useful lens for analysing work relations and power dynamics in the digital economy. This chapter has employed agency theory to the high-tech industry. But agency theory presents a framework to analyse other work relations such as platform work. Recently, new labour relations have induced labour agency to expand agency theory and consider the geographies of non-unionised workers, the influence of horizontal factors across and within various locations, scales and industries and the many intersections, contradictions and conflicts which emerge as a result of new forms of work.

References

Al-Ghazali, B.M., & Afsar, B. (2021). Narcissism and entrepreneurial intentions: The roles of entrepreneurial self-efficacy and environmental complexity. *The Journal of High Technology Management Research, 32*(1), 100395.

Arrow, K.J. (1985). Informational structure of the firm. *The American Economic Review, 75*(2), 303–307.

Baumann, O., & Stieglitz, N. (2014). Rewarding value-creating ideas in organizations: The power of low-powered incentives. *Strategic Management Journal, 35*(3), 358–375.

Bendickson, J., Muldoon, J., Liguori, E., & Davis, P.E. (2016). Agency theory: The times, they are a-changin'. *Management Decision, 54*(1), 174–193.

Cerasoli, C.P., Nicklin, J.M., & Ford, M.T. (2014). Intrinsic motivation and extrinsic incentives jointly predict performance: A 40-year meta-analysis. *Psychological Bulletin, 140*(4), 980–1008.

Coase, R.H. (1937). The nature of the firm. *Economica, 4*(16), 386–405. doi:10.1111/j.1468-0335.1937.tb00002.x

Colombo, M.G., Croce, A., & Murtinu, S. (2014). Ownership structure, horizontal agency costs and the performance of high-tech entrepreneurial firms. *Small Business Economics, 42*(2), 265–282.

Dalton, D.R., Daily, C.M., Ellstrand, A.E., & Johnson, J.L. (1998). Meta-analytic reviews of board composition, leadership structure, and financial performance. *Strategic Management Journal, 19*, 269–290.

Deci, E.L., Olafsen, A.H., & Ryan, R.M. (2017). Self-determination theory in work organizations: The state of a science. *Annual Review of Organizational Psychology and Organizational Behavior, 4*, 19–43.

Degryse, C. (2016). Digitalisation of the economy and its impact on labour markets. ETUI research paper-working paper. Working Paper 2016.02.

Dong, J.Q., Karhade, P.P., Rai, A., & Xu, S.X. (2021). How firms make information technology investment decisions: Toward a behavioral agency theory. *Journal of Management Information Systems, 38*(1), 29–58.

Eisenhardt, K.M. (1985). Control: Organizational and economic approaches. *Management Science, 31*(2), 134–149.

Eisenhardt, K.M. (1989). Agency theory: An assessment and review. *Academy of Management Review, 14*(1), 57–74.

Ekanayake, S. (2004). Agency theory, national culture and management control systems. *Journal of American Academy of Business, 4*(1/2), 49–54.

English, L. (2021). The Tech Talent War Has No End In Sight. Here's What You Need To Know. Available at: https://www.forbes.com/sites/larryenglish/2021/06/01/the-tech-talent-war-has-no-end-in-sight-heres-what-you-need-to-know/?sh=515f1e905f2d (accessed 7 September 2021).

Fama, E.F. (1980). Agency problems and the theory of the firm. *Journal of Political Economy, 88*(2), 288–307.

Fong, E.A., & Tosi Jr, H.L. (2007). Effort, performance, and conscientiousness: An agency theory perspective. *Journal of Management, 33*(2), 161–179.

Gagné, M., & Deci, E.L. (2005). Self-determination theory and work motivation. *Journal of Organizational Behavior, 26*(4), 331–362.

Gebauer, J. (2006). Workforce engagement. *Training and Development*, November, 28–30.

Harris, M., & Raviv, A. (1979) Optimal incentive contracts with imperfect information. *Journal of Economic Theory, 20*, 231–259.

Kennedy, E., & Daim, T.U. (2010). A strategy to assist management in workforce engagement and employee retention in the high tech engineering environment. *Evaluation and Program Planning, 33*(4), 468–476.

Lee, A.H., Chen, S.C., & Kang, H.Y. (2020). A decision-making framework for evaluating enterprise resource planning systems in a high-tech industry. *Quality Technology & Quantitative Management, 17*(3), 319–336.

Maestrini, V., Luzzini, D., Caniato, F., & Ronchi, S. (2018). Effects of monitoring and incentives on supplier performance: An agency theory perspective. *International Journal of Production Economics, 203*, 322–332.

Malecki, E.J., & Moriset, B. (2007). *The digital economy: Business organization, production processes and regional developments*. London: Routledge.

Mosakowski, E. (1998). Entrepreneurial resources, organizational choices, and competitive outcomes. *Organization Science, 9*(6), 625–643.

Nguyen, P.H., & Wang, K.J. (2019). Strategic capacity portfolio planning under demand uncertainty and technological change. *Flexible Services and Manufacturing Journal, 31*(4), 926–944.

Perrow, C. (1986). Economic theories of organization. *Theory and Society, 15*(1–2), 11–45.

Rogers, E.W. (2001). A theoretical look at firm performance in high-tech organizations: What does existing theory tell us? *The Journal of High Technology Management Research, 12*(1), 39–61.

Saether, E.A. (2019). Motivational antecedents to high-tech R&D employees' innovative work behavior: Self-determined motivation, person-organization fit, organization support of creativity, and pay justice. *The Journal of High Technology Management Research, 30*(2), 100350.

Shaikh, I.A., O'Brien, J.P., & Peters, L. (2018). Inside directors and the underinvestment of financial slack towards R&D-intensity in high-technology firms. *Journal of Business Research, 82*, 192–201.

Śledziewska, K., & Włoch, R. (2021). *The economics of digital transformation: The disruption of markets, production, consumption, and work*. London: Routledge.

Smirnov, D., van Jaarsveld, W., Atan, Z., & de Kok, T. (2021). Long-term resource planning in the high-tech industry: Capacity or inventory? *European Journal of Operational Research, 293*(3), 926–940.

Tebourbi, I. (2016). Trade-off between risk and incentives: Evidence from new-and old-economy firms. *Journal of Corporate Accounting & Finance, 27*(2), 53–71.

Yitshaki, R., & Kropp, F. (2016). Entrepreneurial passions and identities in different contexts: A comparison between high-tech and social entrepreneurs. *Entrepreneurship & Regional Development, 28*(3–4), 206–233.

Yuan, F., & Woodman, R.W. (2010). Innovative behavior in the workplace: The role of performance and image outcome expectations. *Academy of Management Journal, 53*(2), 323–342.

Zajac, E.J., & Westphal, J.D. (1994). The costs and benefits of managerial incentives and monitoring in large US corporations: When is more not better? *Strategic Management Journal, 15*(S1), 121–142.

9 Regional economic theories and the digital economy

Joanna Kudełko

Introduction

Stimulating socioeconomic development and improving inhabitants' quality of life is a major challenge for regional economies. The socioeconomic development of a region can be defined as irreversible quantitative and qualitative changes aimed at achieving a sustainable increase in its socioeconomic and cultural potential (Stöhr & Tödtling, 2017). The ultimate measure and objective of development is improving living conditions and ensuring the population's prosperity. The development process takes place in changing conditions, affected by endogenous factors related to the effective use of a region's internal economic and social potential as well as by exogenous factors in its external environment. The impact of these factors varies in terms of its intensity in particular locations and changeability over time.

Over the years, a number of theories have been developed for explaining the processes and mechanisms of regional development. Views on these issues have changed in response to particular periods and socioeconomic conditions. They have been reflected in various theories and concepts of regional and local development including the theory of localisation, classical development theories, the concepts of unsustainable development, endogenous development and more recent concepts such as that of a learning region (Higgins & Savoie, 2017).

Regional development theories do not refer directly to labour market relations, but they are correlated with them. They identify the conditions of the entire regional ecosystem which constitutes a framework for economic activities. They point to the determinants of employment and job creation, the structure of employment, unemployment rates, compensation levels and labour market inequalities (Benner, 2003).

Among the numerous regional development theories, the concept of regional resilience to cyclical macroeconomic shocks originating in regions' external environments plays an increasingly important role (Christopherson, Michie, & Tyler, 2010). It stresses the fact that socioeconomic development plans are affected by a number of variables which are not desirable, expected or predictable. Exogenous shocks, which disturb regional development,

DOI: 10.4324/9781003254638-12

include random factors and conditions – natural phenomena, natural disasters, weather anomalies, as well as crises, external economic shocks or changes in global business cycles. Significant changes in the conditions of regional economies also include such factors as rapid technological advancement and the development of the digital economy.

This chapter presents the importance of the concept of regional resilience in explaining changes in regional labour markets. From a wide range of regional theories, the concept of resilience was chosen for the following reasons:

- it refers to development factors that make economies more resilient to various disturbances, thereby helping better prepare them to function in changing conditions;
- it facilitates identification of the determinants of changes on the labour market;
- it is up-to-date and relevant to the contemporary conditions of regional development as one of the newest concepts explaining the mechanisms of regional economies.

The first part of the chapter outlines the concept of regional resilience. It then discusses the role of this economic concept in explaining changes in regional labour markets. It shows how regional resilience affects labour markets, paying particular attention to employment and its structure and the adopted forms of employment. It identifies the determinants of changes, which forms the basis for formulating recommendations for entities implementing regional policies with the express goal of improving labour markets. The application and limitations of the concept of regional resilience in explaining changes in labour markets are also examined. The chapter ends with conclusions and proposals for new research. The regions/territories under consideration are referred to as NUTS II in the nomenclature used by Eurostat.

The concept of regional resilience in regional development in the digital economy

The word "resilience" originates from physics. It refers to the reaction of an object to the action of an external force, and it assumes that as a result of this action the significant characteristics of this object remain unchanged. Debates on measuring regional and national economic resilience to external factors started in the 1970s within the framework of the natural sciences (Holling, 1973). Later studies also included macroeconomic aspects (Hamilton, 1983; Jones & Leiby, 1996; Tobin, 1980). The concept of regional resilience refers to a region's ability to predict threats and take measures to mitigate the negative effects of shocks and to reconstruct a regional economy. Resilience is a specific measure of regional development and competitiveness (Bristow, 2010; Hudson, 2009; Peng, Yuan, Gu, Peng, & Ming, 2017).

Interest in the concept of economic resilience increased after the 2008 financial crisis, a major external shock in most European regions. The crisis drew the attention of researchers and public policymakers to the resilience of territorial entities. This resilience was defined as their ability to absorb and counteract shocks and to return to their development path. Since that time, regional economic resilience and the reconstruction of economies after crises have represented a new and widely discussed area of research and scientific debate (Boschma, 2015; Christopherson et al., 2010; Foster, 2007; Hill, Wial, & Wolman, 2008; Martin, 2012; Yicheol & Stephan, 2015). The global financial crisis stimulated a popular debate on the reconstruction of regional economies after the crisis and accelerated the development of research into this new economic concept.

Regional resilience relates to regions' response to various external disturbances (Dawley, Pike, & Tomaney, 2010; Hassink, 2010; Pendall, Foster, & Cowell, 2010; Stanickova & Melecký, 2018). Resilience indicates a region's response to exogenous shocks resulting from economic recession (Breathnach, van Egeraat, & Curran, 2015), or other market, competition-related and environmental phenomena (Martin, Sunley, & Tyler, 2015). In another approach, economic resilience indicates a system's ability to adapt to changes as well as the ability of individuals and communities to adopt an appropriate strategy, allowing them to handle the adverse effects of external impacts or avoid potential losses (Rose & Lim, 2002).

A region's resilience is characterised on the basis of three factors: stability, self-organisation and innovation (Peng et al., 2017). Stability indicates the ability to anticipate threats, prepare to counteract external shocks and retain one's main functions during a crisis (Foster, 2007; Xiaohui, 2012). Self-organisation relates to quick, effective and reasonable responses to crisis situations (Wilbanks, 2008). Finally, innovation determines a region's ability to learn and adapt to new conditions affected by external factors, and, consequently, to find opportunities to gain strength and develop further. Thanks to innovation, a region is able to return to its original state or change its original trajectory and achieve a new state through changes in the structure and functions of its economy (Hill et al., 2008). In this approach, a region's resilience is defined as its ability to anticipate problems and prepare for them in the face of external shocks, which enables the region to retain its existing potential, or even strengthen it, thanks to the resources it has available (Peng et al., 2017). Foster (2007, p. 14) offered a general definition of regional resilience as "an ability of a region to anticipate, prepare for, respond to, and recover from a disturbance".

In light of the above, regional resilience can be viewed from two perspectives. On the one hand, it can be treated as an ability to retain an existing equilibrium or to return to the levels of production and employment that had been in place before an exogenous shock occurred. At the same time, resilience can involve more than a return to an original state. It can be an ability to benefit from opportunities resulting from changes. In this context, evolutionary concepts are developed which identify a region's economic adaptability with the process of constant change and adapting to new conditions – not only maintaining stability.

The concepts at work within evolutionary resilience have been widely discussed in research studies (Davoudi & Porter, 2012; Folke, 2006; Holling, & Gunderson, 2002; Walker, Holling, Carpenter, & Kinzig, 2004). The concept of evolution considers dynamic correlations related to continuance, adaptation and structural changes in various spatial and temporal frameworks in a process aimed at achieving a unique state of equilibrium.

A good understanding and analysis of resilience in the regional context mainly concerns regions' response to negative exogenous shocks such as economic crises. However, this issue can be seen in a broader perspective, particularly in connection with Briguglio's definition of resilience as a region's ability to respond to and effectively cope with changes. This means an ability to adapt to the impact of external factors and benefit from possible positive effects of shocks and to mitigate possible negative effects (Briguglio, Cordina, Farrugia, & Vella, 2009). In this broader perspective, external shocks affecting an economy may refer to all changes in the external environment, which influence economic activities and enforce adaptation measures. Such changes are not always negative in character, as is the case with economic crises and natural disasters. Regional environments also experience positive changes, for example those resulting from technological advancement or the development of the digital economy. It is necessary to adapt to such changes in order to be successful in an increasingly competitive global economy. Therefore, we suggest that a traditional understanding of the concept of regional resilience should be extended by incorporating regions' ability to adapt to all socioeconomic changes – both negative and positive ones. In this context, the development of the digital economy is a challenge for regional economies because it forces them to take adaptation measures which are necessary to maintain a competitive position in the global economy.

The importance of regional resilience in explaining changes in regional labour markets

The determinants of labour market changes from the perspective of regional resilience

Unlike microeconomic theories, the concept of regional resilience does not directly refer to employer-employee labour market relationships, but rather to the entire regional economy, a complex system of numerous elements which represent various connections, interactions and interdependencies. Successfully achieving economic targets requires efforts to be made by various entities as well as their joint undertakings. However, solving labour market problems is not always vested in the hands of the economic entities that face them, but requires the action and intervention of public entities engaged in regional development policies as well as the cooperation of many regional stakeholders.

With regard to labour markets, the concept of regional resilience allows for an overall picture of their conditions and determinants of changes to be drawn (Bigos et al., 2013). Labour market interactions are affected not only by market mechanisms and the rules of the game market participants must follow, but also by the institutional environment enterprises function in and the socioeconomic policies that are implemented. Nor does the situation of employers and employees on a regional market depend exclusively on their independent activities and decisions – they operate in specific socioeconomic conditions that partially guide their market activities. In this light, the concept of regional resilience concerns not enterprises themselves but the public authorities that create conditions for corporate development in a region.

Research on regional resilience focuses on identifying the factors that strengthen the entire economy, prepare it to function more effectively in a changing environment, and, consequently, facilitate its further development despite external disturbances (Yamamoto, 2011). Well-developed regions have strong labour markets, while low regional resilience to crises and shocks has a negative impact on the labour market. Regions' vulnerability to crises is of key significance to their long-term economic activities, as it measures their investment attractiveness.

Resilient regional economies find it easier to maintain sustained socio-economic development. Resilience stimulates corporate development and, consequently, job creation and higher compensation levels for employees (Chapple & Lester, 2010). Highly developed regions which respond effectively to digital economy requirements offer high-quality jobs. Their employment structures are transformed, with modern industries characterised by innovation and advanced technologies playing a more important role. Resilient regions offer more high-quality, higher paying jobs.

Low-resilience regions are more affected by economic crises, resulting in a radical deterioration in the prevailing labour market conditions (Reggiani, De Graaff, & Nijkamp, 2002). Adverse effects are felt in various spheres of economic activity, leading to periodical reductions in business activities. Recession, which results from low resilience, leads to negative economic phenomena including reduced production output, higher unemployment rates and a decrease in GDP and inhabitants' income. These factors, in turn, balloon the scale of recessions. Economic crises lead to economic downturns on a global scale, reflected in lower investment, difficult access to credit, corporate failures, higher unemployment rates and decreased international trade. Low resilience makes regions more vulnerable to economic slow-downs, reduced production output, lower income levels and unemployment. The concept of regional resilience is important because it allows the factors that increase resilience to be identified, which, in turn, boost labour markets. Analyses of the 2008 crisis and the recent crisis caused by the COVID-19 pandemic have allowed researchers to reach a number of conclusions.

Regional economic adaptability in response to exogenous shocks is determined by the originally adopted development path (Hassink, 2010; Martin, 2010), based on economic structures and socioeconomic and institutional relations. Another significant characteristic of resilient regions is their economic diversification, which allows them to maintain employment stability at the time of crisis (Deller & Watson, 2016). Industry diversification and diversified economic structures can prevent regional economic downturns and facilitate the process of economic reconstruction (Martin, 2010). Areas with diversified activities tend to be more resilient than specialised regions (Dawley et al., 2010; Xiaohui, 2012). Another significant factor in regional economic development is human capital. The results of research studies point to the key role played by the share of young population and the quality of human capital in increasing regional resilience (Rios & Gianmoena, 2020).

Other important factors which influence economic conditions and regional labour markets include the quality of institutions and the policies that are implemented. Regional resilience theory stresses the importance of government institutions and agencies being able to respond to political, economic and social crises (Cho, Willis, & Stewart-Weeks, 2011). Research on crisis response indicates that regional resilience can be greatly increased by the quality of public administration. Regions characterised by high-quality administration were less damaged by the effects of crises (Ezcurra & Rios, 2019). Lastly, promoting cooperation in local communities is important in facilitating and developing innovation processes.

Walker and Salt (2006) stress that greater resilience is demonstrated by regional economies characterised by high-quality institutions and human and social capital, advanced technologies, sufficient capital resources in enterprises and local governments, high financial leverage levels, economic diversification, innovativeness and well-developed ecosystem services.

Some researchers consider resilience in a broader perspective, approaching it through exposure as a factor determining regional vulnerability to crisis situations (Turner et al., 2003). Exposure determines the degree of vulnerability to external factors, and is greater in regions which participate in the global economy and which are characterised by more sensitive economic structures. Exposure is correlated with the volume of foreign direct investment, the openness of an economy measured by export and import volumes (Briguglio et al. 2009), and the employment structure. Greater exposure to crises occurs in the periods of increased global economic integration and results from the openness and interdependence of economies (Hudson, 2010). The effect of greater exposure manifests itself in the first phase of a crisis.

The highest levels of exposure are found in the most developed regions due to their extensive global relations. This leaves them more exposed to the negative effects of crises than their less-developed counterparts. At the same time, best-developed regions are more resilient – they have the ability to respond to shocks, and they perform better in dealing with crisis situations in the long run. The results of research studies show that in the initial phase of the COVID-19 crisis, highly developed regions were hit harder, which was reflected in higher unemployment rates than less developed areas suffered (Kudełko & Rynio, 2020). Their ability to return to the development path will be verified with time.

Other interesting studies related to the crisis caused by the pandemic look at its impact on labour market conditions. The crisis led to more flexible forms of employment. It also caused higher unemployment rates, accompanied by a larger number of part-time jobs and employment limited contracts (Green & Livanos, 2017). The structure of employment (the share of steady and temporary jobs) was mainly affected by regional production structures (Gialis, Gourzis, & Underthun, 2018).

Recommendations for entities implementing regional policies

As established earlier, regional economic resilience is determined by modern economic structures, diversified business activities in a region, high-quality human capital, technological advancement and companies' innovativeness, institutional quality and policies, and the availability of financial resources. The analysis of factors which increase regional resilience and improve working conditions leads to practical conclusions entities implementing regional policies may find worth considering. These guidelines and recommendations are intended to strengthen economic resilience and, ultimately, to sustain job retention or even create high-quality jobs while lowering unemployment resulting from external shocks.

It is recommended that entities implementing regional policies strive to strengthen regions' endogenous potential (Adamowicz, 2016). The modernisation of economic structures is an important area to improve in this regards. Public authorities can use various incentives to improve economic structures. Priority should be given to supporting high technology sectors, which are characterised by high value added and create high-quality jobs. The support offered to economic entities should focus on creating diversified economic structures with industry-diversified entities. Local and regional economies which rely on one sector are vulnerable to downturns or when new technologies are introduced. The public sector should focus on creating favourable conditions for business development, launching information campaigns and adjusting priorities to the needs of the most innovative economic sectors.

In the long-run, measures should be taken to increase employment. Proactive labour market policies should be based on a set of instruments in support of enterprises, particularly SMEs, the main source of employment and household incomes (Ingold & Stuart, 2015). Such instruments include a system of concessions and financial incentives, as well as advisory assistance in carrying out business activities, legal regulations and organisational techniques. The unemployed should also be helped to find jobs. Public investment projects jointly implemented with private entities is a standard but effective method of activating companies and creating jobs.

Clearly, the possibility of finding and retaining employment is conditioned by people's employability and mobility. Better educated and highly skilled workers have an advantage on the labour market. Activities aimed at increasing employability include education services understood in a broad sense (Nicea, Andreea-Gabriela, & Romeo, 2017). Education programmes at all levels should be constantly modified and adjusted to changes in labour markets, especially those resulting from rapid changes in technologies. It is essential that a regional's education offerings be adjusted to the needs of local and regional labour markets and enterprises. Adults should be offered a wide range of courses and training to promote constant learning and its benefits. Acquiring new competences and skills is indispensable in the face of scientific and technological progress.

The flexibility and resilience of institutions and services cannot be achieved without flexible and effective administration, which enables entire sectors to function effectively. As such, administrative staff should also receive education and training. Strengthening the network of social and economic relations is another essential area to be addressed. In economies today, networks made up of numerous cooperating entities are responsible for creating the greatest value added (Charykova & Markova, 2019). Public sector activities should therefore focus on supporting cluster initiatives and integrating local manufacturing potential. Cooperation between similar companies stimulates the learning process and promotes the dissemination of knowledge and competences. Crises and other challenges should be treated as the drivers of changes that can increase resilience to potential external shocks. Interventions should look to exceed pre-crisis states. Measures undertaken should result in economic transformation and, ultimately, more competitive and resilient economies.

The applications and limitations of regional resilience in explaining labour market phenomena

The concept of regional resilience can be useful in analysing changes in employment and its structure as well as unemployment rates. It also helps observers identify the determinants of labour market changes as they relate to the characteristics of regions which are resilient to changes in an economy – negative economic shocks, crises and natural disasters as well as structural changes resulting from the development of modern technologies and the digital economy. The concept not only describes labour market phenomena, but also identifies the causes of changes. It describes labour market problems in a broad perspective, giving consideration to the environments companies function in, policies and changing socioeconomic conditions. It explains the correlations between labour markets and the economy's ability to effectively respond to changing conditions. The notion of regional resilience is also useful in contextualising the main tasks and directions of regional policies performed by public authorities. One of the strengths of this concept is that it addresses today's world, gaining relevance by addressing the challenges of the contemporary economy.

At the same time, the concept of regional resilience has its limitations. It does not focus directly on labour market issues. Accordingly, it does not examine labour relations and employer-employee interactions, considering such matters too detailed. These issues are better explained by microeconomic theories.

Conclusions and future directions

This chapter has explained the importance of regional resilience in explaining changes in regional labour markets. A region's resilience indicates its ability to respond to changes caused by various exogenous shocks – to adapt to external impacts, benefit from possible opportunities, mitigate possible damage and solve emerging problems. Economic crises and other global challenges, e.g., the development of the digital economy, should be treated as the drivers of changes aimed at accelerating a region's development and increasing its competitiveness, which, in turn, increases resilience to various types of disturbances in the development process. Regions' resilience to crises is a basis for their long-term functioning and helps make them more attractive. Resilience mechanisms determine regions' ability to embark on a development path in changing and turbulent conditions.

Regional resilience is strongly correlated with labour market conditions, affecting the size and structure of the employment and unemployment rates as well as compensation levels. Regional economic resilience, which guarantees high employment levels and the creation of new high-quality jobs, is mainly dependent on a region's economic structure, the quality of its human capital, companies' technological advancement and innovativeness, institutional quality, the effectiveness of the development policies it adopts and the availability of financial resources for regional economic entities. Such characteristics of a resilient economy are prerequisite to effective development-oriented policies implemented by a region's public authorities.

The conclusions of this paper set the directions for further in-depth analyses. It would be advisable to supplement scientific debates in this area with new empirical research studies exploring correlations between the level of regional resilience and labour market changes, making reference to international comparisons of European countries and other continents. Another area of future studies could explore is regional resilience in the context of solving problems caused by the COVID-19 pandemic and its long-term effects on labour markets and employment relationships.

References

Adamowicz, M. (2016). Smart specialization as a way of strengthening the innovation potential of a region. *Acta Scientiarum Polonorum. Oeconomia, 15*(4), 5–15.

Benner, C. (2003). Labour flexibility and regional development: The role of labour market intermediaries. *Regional Studies, 37*(6–7), 621–633.

Bigos, M., Qaran, W., Fenger, M., Koster, F., Mascini, P., & Van der Veen, R. (2013). *Review essay on labour market resilience.* Working paper series 2013 no. 1.

Boschma, R. (2015). Towards an evolutionary perspective on regional resilience. *Regional Studies, 49*(5), 733–751.

Breathnach, P., van Egeraat, Ch., & Curran, D. (2015). Regional economic resilience in Ireland: The roles of industrial structure and foreign inward investment. *Regional Studies, Regional Science, 2*(1), 496–516.

Briguglio, L., Cordina, G., Farrugia, N., & Vella, S. (2009), Economic vulnerability and resilience: Concepts and measurements. *Oxford Development Studies, 37*(3), 229–247.

Bristow, G. (2010). Resilient regions: Re-'place'ing regional competitiveness. *Cambridge Journal of Regions. Economy and Society, 3*(1), 153–167.

Chapple, K., & Lester, T.W. (2010). The resilient regional labour market? The US case. *Cambridge Journal of Regions, Economy and Society, 3*(1), 85–104.

Charykova, O.G., & Markova, E.S. (2019). Regional clustering in the digital economy. *Ekonomika regiona, 15*(2), 409.

Cho, A., Willis, S., & Stewart-Weeks, M. (2011). CISCO white Paper: The resilient society-innovation, productivity, and the art and practice of connectedness. CiscoInternet Business Solutions Group (IBSG). Available at: https://www.cisco.com/web/about/ac79/docs/ps/The-Resilient-Society IBSG.pdf (accessed 30 August 2021).

Christopherson, S., Michie, J., & Tyler, P. (2010). Regional resilience: Theoretical and empirical perspectives. *Cambridge Journal of Regions, Economy and Society, 3*(1), 3–10.

Davoudi, S., & Porter, L. (2012), Resilience: A bridging concept or a dead end? *Planning Theory and Practice, 13*(2), 299–333.

Dawley, S., Pike, A., & Tomaney, J., 2010. Towards the resilient region? *Local Economy, 25*(8), 650–667.

Deller, S., & Watson, P. (2016). Did regional economic diversity influence the effects of the great recession? *Economic Inquiry, 54*(4), 1824–1838.

Ezcurra, R., & Rios, V. (2019). Quality of government and regional resilience in the European Union. Evidence from the Great Recession. *Papers in Regional Science, 98*(3), 1267–1290.

Folke, C. (2006). Resilience: The emergence of a perspective for social–ecological systems analyses. *Global Environmental Change, 16*(3), 253–267.

Foster, K.A. (2007). A case study approach to understanding regional resilience. Berkeley: Institute of Urban and Regional Development, University of California. Available at: http://iurd.berkeley.edu/wp/2007-08.pdf (accessed 3 September 2021).

Gialis, S., Gourzis, K., &, Underthun, A. (2018). Going under-employed': Industrial and regional effects, specialization and part-time work across recession-hit Southern European Union regions. *European Urban and Regional Studies, 25*(3), 300–319.

Green, A., & Ilias Livanos, I. (2017). Involuntary non-standard employment in Europe. *European Urban and Regional Studies, 24*(2), 175–192.

Hamilton, J.D. (1983). Oil and the macroeconomy since World War II. *Journal of Political Economy, 91*(2), 228–248.

Hassink, R. (2010). Regional resilience: A promising concept to explain differences in regional economic adaptability? *Cambridge Journal of Regions, Economy and Society, 3*, 45–58.

Higgins, B., & Savoie, D.J. (2017). *Regional development theories & their application*. Boca Raton, FL: Routledge.

Hill, E., Wial, H., & Wolman, H. (2008). *Exploring regional economic resilience*. California: University of California, Institute of Urban and Regional Development.

Holling, C.S. (1973). Resilience and stability of ecological systems. *Annual Review of Ecology and Systematics, 4*, 1–23.

Holling, C.S., & Gunderson L.H. (2002), Resilience and adaptive cycles. In L.H. Gunderson, C.S. Holling, & S. Panarchy (Eds.), *Understanding transformations in human and natural systems* (pp. 25–62). Washington, DC: Island Press.

Hudson, R. (2009). Resilient regions in an uncertain world: Wishful thinking or practical reality? *Cambridge Journal of Regions, Economy and Society, 9*, 26–41.

Hudson, R. (2010). Resilient regions in an uncertain world: Wishful thinking or practical reality. *Cambridge Journal of Regions, Economy and Society, 3*(1), 11–25.

Ingold, J., & Stuart, M. (2015). The demand-side of active labour market policies: A regional study of employer engagement in the Work Programme. *Journal of Social Policy, 44*(3), 443–462.

Jones, D.W., & Leiby, P.N. (1996), *The macroeconomic impacts of oil price shocks: A review of literature and issues*. Oak Ridge, TN: Oak Ridge National Laboratory.

Kudełko, J., & Rynio, D. (2020). Level of regional development and the dynamics of unemployment during the COVID-19 crisis, based on observations of German and polish regions. In K.S. Soliman (Ed.), *Sustainable economic development and advancing education excellence in the era of global pandemic*: Proceedings of the 36th International Business Information Management Association Conference (IBIMA), 4–5 November 2020, Granada, Spain. International Business Information Management Association, 1890–1904.

Martin, R. (2010). Roepke lecture in economic geography—Rethinking regional path dependence: Beyond lock-in to evolution. *Economic Geography, 86*, 1–27.

Martin, R. (2012). Regional economic resilience, hysteresis and recessionary shocks. *Journal of Economic Geography, 12*(1), 1–32.

Martin, R., Sunley, P., & Tyler, P. (2015). Local growth evolutions: Recession, resilience and recovery. *Cambridge Journal of Regions, Economy and Society, 8*(2), 141–148.

Nicea, M., Andreea-Gabriela, D., & Romeo, D. (2017). Continuous education and training of adults–Purpose of an active life on the labour market. *Junior Scientific Researcher, 3*(2), 9–18.

Pendall, R., Foster, K., & Cowell, M. (2010). Resilience and regions: Building understanding of the metaphor. *Cambridge Journal of Regions Economy and Society, 3*(1), 71–84.

Peng, C., Yuan, M., Gu, C., Peng, Z., & Ming, T. (2017). A review of the theory and practice of regional resilience. *Sustainable Cities and Society, 29*(1), 86–96.

Reggiani, A., De Graaff, T., & Nijkamp, P. (2002). Resilience: An evolutionary approach to spatial economic systems. *Networks and Spatial Economics, 2*(2), 211–229.

Rios, V., & Gianmoena, L. (2020). The link between quality of government and regional resilience in Europe. *Journal of Policy Modeling, 42*(5), 1064–1084.

Rose, A., & Lim, D. (2002). Business interruption losses from natural hazards: Conceptual and methodological issues in the case of the Northridge earthquake. *Global Environmental Change Part B: Environmental Hazards, 4*(1), 1–14.

Stanickova, M., & Melecký, L. (2018). Understanding of resilience in the context of regional development using composite index approach: The case of European Union NUTS-2 regions. *Regional Studies, Regional Science, 5*(1), 231–254.

Stöhr, W., & Tödtling, F. (2017). Quantitative, qualitative, and structural variables in the evaluation of regional development policies in Western Europe. In G. Demko (Ed.), *Regional Development* (pp. 157–173). London: Routledge.

Tobin, J. (1980), Stabilization policy: Ten years after. Brookings Papers on Economic Activity nr 1, Washington.

Turner, II B.L., Kasperson, R.E., Matson, P.A., McCarthy, J.J., Corell, R.W., Christensen, L., … Schiller, A. (2003). A framework for vulnerability analysis in sustainability science. *Proceedings of the National Academy of Sciences of the United States of America, 100*(14), 8074–8079.

Xiaohui, H. (2012). Regional economy resilience research review and prospects. *Foreign Economics & Management, 34*(8), 64–72.

Yamamoto, D. (2011). Regional resilience: Prospects for regional development research. *Geography Compass, 5*(10), 723–736.

Yicheol, H., & Stephan, J. (2015). The economic resilience of U.S. counties during the great recession. *The Review of Regional Studies, 45*(2), 131–149.

Walker, B.H., & Salt, D. (2006). *Resilience thinking. Sustaining ecosystems and people in a changing world.* Washington, DC, Covelo and London: ISLANDPRESS.

Walker, B.R., Holling, C.S., Carpenter, S.R., & Kinzig A. (2004). Resilience, adaptability and transformability in social-ecological systems. *Ecology and Society, 9*(2). doi: 10.5751/ES-00650-090205

Wilbanks, T.J. (2008). Enhancing the resilience of communities to natural and other hazards: What we know and what we can do. *Natural Hazards Observer, 32*(5), 10–11.

Part III

Flexible forms of employment in the digital economy

Exploratory research

10 Overview of non-standard work arrangements

Agnieszka Postepska

Introduction

There is no official definition of *non-standard employment*, and different classifications are present in the literature. According to the International Labour Organization (ILO), *non-standard forms of employment* is an umbrella term encompassing various forms of employment relations that deviate from permanent, full-time employment arrangements with a clear subordinate relationship with the end-user (ILO, 2016). Temporary employment, part-time and on-call work, remote work, temporary agency work and other multi-party employment relationships, as well as disguised employment and dependent self-employment, all fall under the non-standard employment category.

The prevalence of non-standard work arrangements has been on the rise throughout the European Union, and non-standard work arrangements appear across all occupations at all skill levels. The changing of the labour market brought about by the digital economy, the demographic changes, the decline in agricultural jobs and the economic recession that followed the financial crisis call for a revision of the definition of workers and employment relationships. Technological progress is among the main drivers of increasing variety and the prevalence of non-standard forms of employment (Chinoracký & Čorejová, 2019; Huws, Spencer, & Syrdal, 2018; Reljic, Cetrulo, Cirillo, & Coveri, 2021). The rise of digital labour platforms is an excellent example of a technological improvement that allowed for more flexible employment arrangements. In addition, demographic changes and governments' efforts to ease the restrictions on conditions of employment other than through a standard permanent contract contributed to the popularity of non-standard forms of employment (ILO, 2016). In some instances, the new employment arrangements allow for more flexibility and freedom for workers (Leighton, 2016; Van Gelderen & Jansen, 2006) and prove to be effective cost-saving measures for employers (Ackers, 2014; Burke & Cowling, 2020; Seth & Sethi, 2011). In many cases, though, the non-standard work arrangements are associated with significant insecurity, wage penalties, variable schedules and significant occupational safety and health risks (ILO,

DOI: 10.4324/9781003254638-14

2016). This chapter provides a comprehensive overview of the non-standard work arrangements, their prevalence and their consequences for employees and employers in the EU labour markets in the age of digital transformation.

Research methodology

We will follow the ILO classification and group the non-standard forms of employment into four broad categories: *temporary employment*, *part-time and on-call work*, *multipart employment relationship* and *disguised employment*, noting that this classification is not clear-cut and some forms of non-standard employment relationships could very well be classified in different groups (ILO, 2016). This classification focuses on employees, so genuinely self-employed workers are excluded. However, dependent self-employed workers are captured under the disguised employment category. We will employ the most recent data from Eurostat (2021) and provide an overview of the prevalence and trends in non-standard work arrangements in the EU labour markets (excluding the UK), keeping in mind that individual-level data on non-standard employment remains scarce.

Types and prevalence of non-standard forms of employment in the European Union

Temporary employment

Temporary employment comprises employment arrangements with a predictable end date and includes fixed-term workers (including precarious workers,[1] interim management and project or task-based work) and casual workers (including daily workers). In most countries, the maximum duration of temporary contracts and the number of renewals are strictly regulated (ILO, 2016). A particular type of temporary employment is *casual work*, which involves engaging workers for a short time or on an occasional basis in exchange for a specified daily or periodic wage. The growth of the service sector and the rise of the on-demand economy in the age of digital transformation have enabled such work arrangements to boom in the developed world in recent years (Van Doorn, 2017). Most casual workers are employed on a part-time basis, and therefore, casual work is sometimes classified under part-time employment.

The incidence of precarious work remains fairly low across the European Union (Figure 10.1) and it declined in 18 member states between 2011 and 2020. The overall average has also decreased by about half a percentage point – from 2.6% in 2011 to 2.2 in 2020. The highest shares of employees in precarious jobs can be found in Belgium, France, Croatia, Finland, Spain, Italy and Sweden (over 3%), while in Bulgaria, Czechia, Germany, Cyprus, Latvia, Lithuania, Malta, the Netherlands and Romania, less than 1% of employees are bounded by a contract that does not exceed three months.

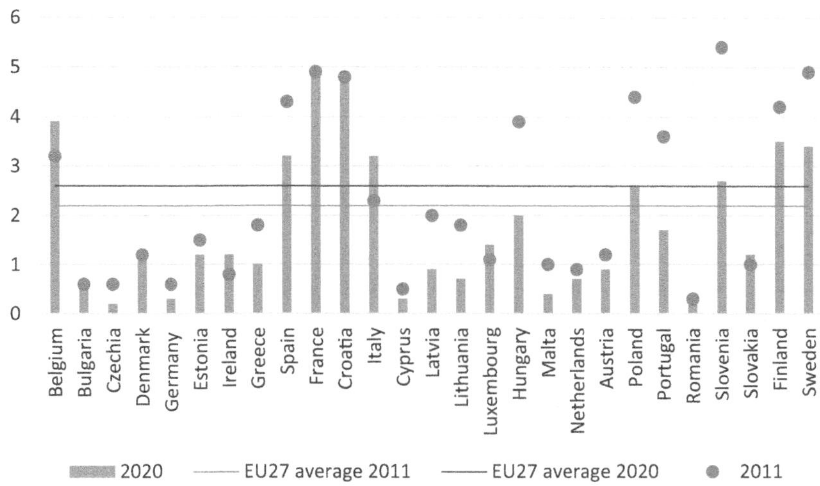

Figure 10.1 Precarious workers as a percentage of all employees in the EU 27
Source: the authors' own research based on Eurostat (2021).

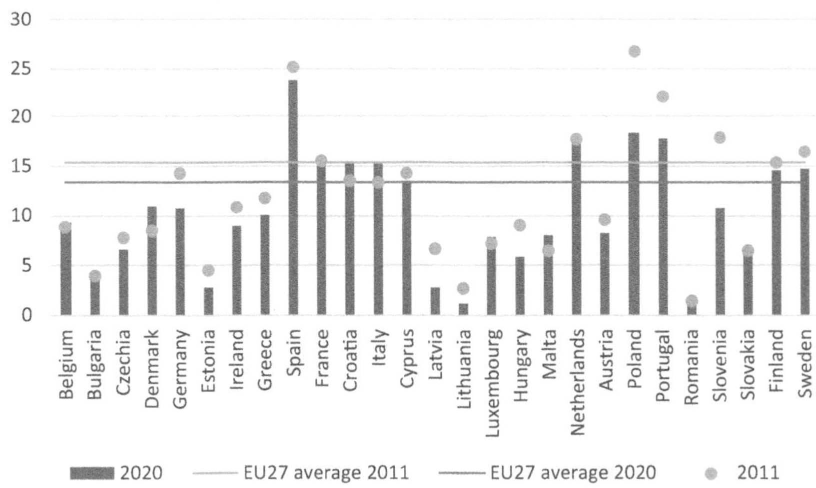

Figure 10.2 Temporary workers as a percentage of all employees in the EU 27
Source: the authors' own research based on Eurostat (2021).

Temporary employment is much more prevalent in many Member States (Figure 10.2). The share of workers in temporary jobs varies greatly by country, but the general decreasing trend seems to be present in much of the EU. With the exception of Denmark, Croatia, Italy and Malta, the incidence of temporary employment in the EU 27 decreased or remained almost unchanged between 2011 and 2020.

Part-time and on-call work

Part-time and on-call work refers to non-full-time employment arrangements. The definition of full-time work differs between countries, but usually there is a legal distinction between part-time and full-time employees with the threshold set at 30 or 35 hours a week.[2] As Figure 10.3 shows, the share of part-time workers in the EU remained fairly stable between 2011 and 2020. About one in five workers in the EU works part-time, with the Netherlands having the highest share of part-time workers. Over 50% of Dutch employees in 2020 were engaged in part-time work, compared to just 2% of Bulgarian employees. However, not all part-time work is the form of work desired. While the share of involuntary part-time workers has declined, still one in four workers worked part-time in 2020 because they could not find a full-time job (Figure 10.3).

Part-time employment has been popular among many governments in the EU to promote labour market access for certain groups, such as women, students, people with family responsibilities and older workers. It offers flexibility that allows such workers to combine the non-labour market responsibilities with paid employment (Kjeldstad & Nymoen, 2012), and therefore it is much more popular among women. For example, in the Netherlands, while about 17% of men work part-time (still quite a high number relative to other Member States), a full 60% of women are employed in such jobs (ILO, 2016).

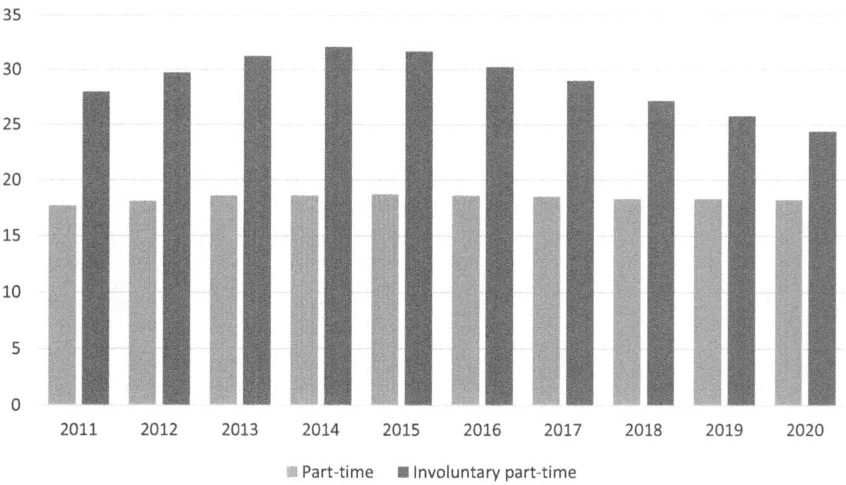

Figure 10.3 Overview of the part-time employment in the EU 27

Source: the authors' own research based on Eurostat (2021).

"Part-time" series refers to the percentage of part-time workers out of all employees "Involuntary part-time" refers to the percentage of part-time workers that cannot find a full-time job out of all part-time employees.

Figure 10.4 shows significant differences between the countries in the prevalence of part-time employment. Alongside the Netherlands, Belgium, Austria, Germany and Sweden have over 25% of all employees in part-time jobs, while in Bulgaria, Croatia, Slovakia and Hungary, the share of part-time workers did not exceed 5%. Also, there is no general increasing or decreasing trend visible over the period considered: between 2011 and 2020, in about half of the Member States, the share of part-time workers increased, while in the other half it decreased.

The variation in involuntary part-time work is even more considerable among Member States. As Figure 10.5 shows, even though there was a slight decline (four percentage points) between 2011 and 2020, the decreasing trend is not present in all Member States, and in some countries, the shares of involuntary part-time workers remain very high. In Bulgaria, Greece, Spain, Italy, Cyprus and Romania, about half of the part-time workers cannot find a full-time job. Furthermore, in countries where more workers hold part-time jobs, fewer workers are employed in such employment involuntarily (Boeri & Van Ours, 2013). The Netherlands, Denmark, Germany, Austria and Belgium all have high shares of part-time workers (over 25%), and less than 10% of those workers hold part-time jobs involuntarily.

Specific forms of part-time employment include *job-sharing* (a situation when two employees share a full-time position and divide the hours between

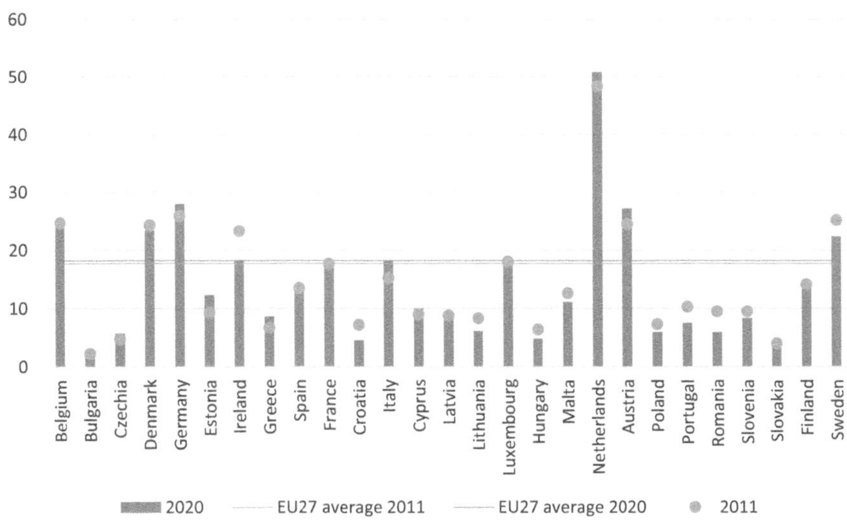

Figure 10.4 Part-time workers as a percentage of all employees in the EU 27
Source: the authors' own research based on Eurostat (2021).

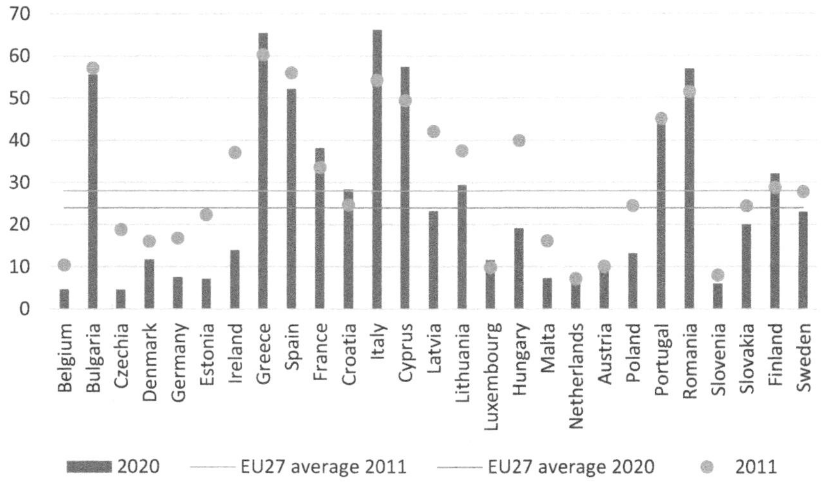

Figure 10.5 Involuntary part-time workers as a percentage of all part-time employees in the EU 27

Source: the authors' own research based on Eurostat (2021).

them in agreement with the employer) (ILO, 2004), *progressive retirement* (incremental reduction of working hours of employees close to retirement age) and *part-time parental leave* (reduced work schedule for parents of your children). *On-call* workers usually follow a highly variable work schedule and have little to no control over their working hours. About 2.5% of employees in the EU worked "on-call" in 2004 (ILO, 2016). Examples of on-call workers include *zero-hours contracts*, wherein workers have no guarantee of working hours or earnings and agree to work only when their services are required.[3]

Multipart employment relationship

A multipart employment relationship exists when workers are not directly employed by the firm for which they provide services. Multipart employment arrangements include temporary agency work (TAW) and subcontracted labour and on-demand managers and executives. An employment agency usually employs TAW workers, and their services are sold to third parties, which are bound by an agreement with the employment agency. There is no direct contractual agreement between the workers and the entity contracting the services provided by the worker. However, starting from 2008 in the EU, the same primary working and employment conditions apply to a TAW worker on assignment as to a worker hired directly by the user firm.

Figure 10.6 summarises the trends concerning TAW workers across the EU Member States during the period 2011–2020. While there was a slight

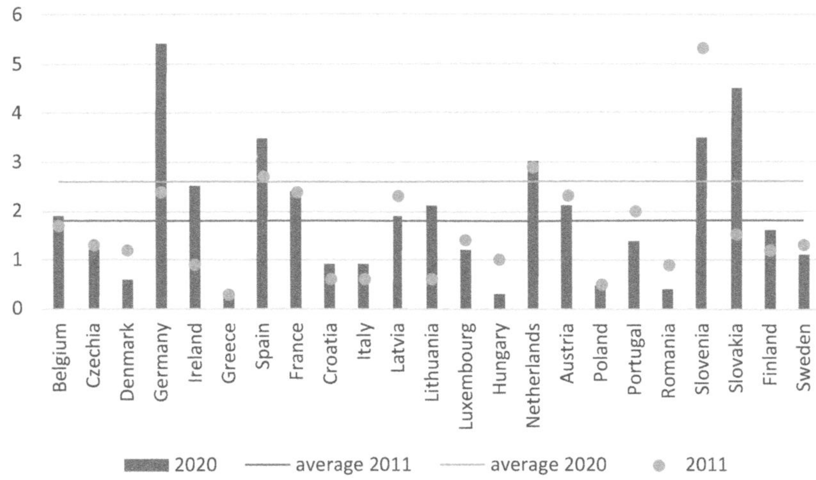

Figure 10.6 Temporary Agency workers as a percentage of all employees in the EU 27
Source: the authors' own research based on Eurostat (2021).

increase (about 1%) in the share of workers employed by TAW agencies in the EU, the prevalence of TAW workers varies greatly by country. In most Member States, the percentage of TAW workers remained below 2% between 2011 and 2020. In Germany, it increased from 2.5% to 5.5%. In Spain, Slovenia and Slovakia, the share of TAW workers was also above the EU average, with 3.5, 3.5 and 4.5% employed by temporary employment agencies, respectively. Across all Member States, the incidence of TAW is highest among younger and less-educated workers (ILO, 2016).

Disguised employment and dependent self-employment

Both terms describe work arrangements that operate in the grey area between employment and self-employment (Thörnquist, 2019; Williams & Horodnic, 2018). *Disguised employment* comprises any work arrangements that are not part of an employment relationship, i.e., when an employer treats an individual as other than an employee even though that individual should be treated as a regular employee. *Dependent self-employed* refers to self-employed individuals providing their services to one or a very small number of buyers. Many Member States have introduced laws to protect the rights of and ensure more secure work arrangements for such workers. Since both types of employment are in the legal grey zone of labour law, labour surveys do not include a separate category for such workers.

Two very specific types of workers in this category emerged with the rise of the gig economy: *platform* and *work on-demand via app. Platform work* (or *crowdworking*), a new form of employment growing rapidly in the digital economy, is defined as "employment that uses an online platform to enable organisations and individuals to access an indefinite and unknown group of other organisations or individuals to solve specific problems or to provide specific services or products in exchange for payment" (Eurofound, 2015). The use of online platforms is essential as it facilitates the matching between the clients and workers and task execution.

Work on-demand via app is also on the rise in the digital economy. The term describes relatively traditional working activities such as cleaning or transport being arranged via mobile app and executed locally (as opposed to being executed via the app as in the case of *platform work*). This category comprises ride-sharing companies such as Uber or Lyft.

Conclusions and implications

There are many contributors to the changes in the labour market in the age of digital transformation: technological progress, demographic, social changes, changes in the business cycle. The new forms of employment evolve in response to these changes and often offer a preferable working arrangement for both workers and employers. Non-standard employment comprises many different work arrangements with diverse consequences for the employers and employees (Kiersztyn, 2017; Schmid & Wagner, 2017). The emergence of the new employment arrangements facilitated previously unknown levels of flexibility, both to employers and workers. It has the potential to fight unemployment growth during recessions, engage working-age individuals who cannot or do not want to participate in the labour market (such as women, migrants, students or people close to retirement age). However, the prevalence of non-standard employment has not always been beneficial to organisations and workers. Without a proper legal framework, it can lead to a dualism of the labour markets. This led many countries to introduce regulations to hinder the growth of non-standard employment and protect workers and promote more traditional working arrangements (ILO, 2016).

Impact on employers

Firms today use non-standard forms of employment as it allows them to absorb fluctuations in short-term labour demand due to seasonality of the demand for their goods or services, changes in the business cycles (Bentolila & Dolado, 1994), or to test new employees before offering them a full-time position (Bauer & Truxillo, 2000). Increasingly though, firms rely on non-standard employment on a more regular basis. This allows them to focus on their core competencies (ILO, 2016) while saving costs related to hiring full-time employees (Bryson, 2013).

Using non-standard work arrangements has multiple consequences for organisations (George & Chattopadhyay, 2015). As non-standard employees are usually involved in the organisation's non-core tasks (Shi, 2007), the recruitment and selection strategies are not as precise as those for permanent full-time workers. Similarly, some evidence suggests that non-standard workers are less attached to the organisation (Battisti & Vallanti, 2013). Management can use practices to decrease the social distance between the non-standard workers and the permanent full-time employees to facilitate better involvement of non-standard workers (Benson & Brown, 2007). The evidence for the effect of non-standard workers on productivity is mixed. Some studies find that non-standard workers initially improve productivity, for example by lowering labour costs (Bryson, 2013; Hirsch & Mueller, 2012), but after a certain point, the negative effect of the lack of firm-specific human capital outweighs the benefits in cost savings (Hirsch, & Mueller, 2012; Nielen & Schiersch, 2014).

Impact on employees

The consequences for workers are even more complex as many aspects of non-standard employment need to be considered to assess their effects in the digital economy. Numerous factors need to be taken into account including the type of non-standard employment, the duration of the non-standard employment spells, whether the non-standard employment is voluntary, whether it improves (or hinders) the chance of transitioning to standard employment (or is a dead-end job), the degree of social protection and the job stability it offers (ILO, 2016).

For many workers, non-standard employment, if voluntary, provides an attractive alternative to permanent, full-time employment. It often creates opportunities for young people and less-skilled workers who would not get standard employment contracts (due to high hiring costs). Temporary contracts create opportunities to develop job-specific skills and build up a network (ILO, 2016; Muja, Blommaert, Gesthuizen, & Wolbers, 2019). The availability of part-time jobs is also attractive to parents as it eases the pressure on the work-life balance. Students and older workers might also prefer part-time jobs over full-time employment to free up time for school or ease the transition into retirement. The literature on happiness points to job flexibility as an essential determinant of life satisfaction among voluntary non-standard workers (Álvarez & Miles-Touya, 2016; Booth & Van Ours, 2008; Minnotte, Minnotte, & Thompson, 2016; Pollmann-Schult, 2018; Yu & Postepska, 2020)

However, involuntary non-standard employees do not seem to enjoy similar benefits. In addition to a lack of job security and stability, many non-standard jobs do not result in transitions to standard employment (European Commission, 2015). In addition, non-standard workers suffer a significant wage penalty as compared to standard workers (ILO, 2016), and typically have substandard access to social security coverage (Spasova, Bouget, Ghailani, & Vanhercke, 2017), even if legally they are eligible for such benefits (as is the case in most EU Member States) due to longer unemployment and shorter employment spells. To summarise, the non-standard forms of employment are increasing in popularity both among employers and employees in the digital economy. Governments therefore need to improve the legal framework to ensure a safe and secure work environment as specified among the Sustainable Development Goals (Frey, 2017; Rai, Brown, & Ruwanpura, 2019; Venkatesan & Luongo, 2019).

Notes

1 We follow the definition of precarious work used by Eurostat. Precarious employment means that the work contract did not exceed three months.
2 OECD defines part-time workers as employees who work less than 30 hours a week (OECD, 2016).
3 In recognition of the vulnerability of the workers with zero-hour contracts, in 2019 the European Parliament approved new rules to guarantee minimum workers' rights including requiring all employers to inform all workers on their first day of employment about their typical working day or hours. Source: European Parliament (2019).

References

Ackers, P. (2014). Rethinking the employment relationship: A neo-pluralist critique of British industrial relations orthodoxy. *The International Journal of Human Resource Management, 25*(18), 2608–2625.

Álvarez, B., & Miles-Touya, D. (2016). Time allocation and women's life satisfaction: Evidence from Spain. *Social Indicators Research, 129*(3), 1207–1230.

Battisti, M., & Vallanti, G. (2013). Flexible wage contracts, temporary jobs, and firm performance: Evidence from Italian firms. *Industrial Relations: A Journal of Economy and Society, 52*(3), 737–764.

Bauer, T.N., & Truxillo, D.M. (2000). Temp-to-permanent employees: A longitudinal study of stress and selection success. *Journal of Occupational Health Psychology, 5*(3), 337.

Benson, J., & Brown, M. (2007). Knowledge workers: What keeps them committed; what turns them away. *Work, Employment and Society, 21*(1), 121–141.

Bentolila, S., & Dolado, J.J. (1994). Labour flexibility and wages: Lessons from Spain. *Economic Policy, 9*(18), 53–99.

Boeri, T., & Van Ours, J. (2013). *The economics of imperfect labour markets.* Princeton, NJ: Princeton University Press.

Booth, A.L., & Van Ours, J.C. (2008). Job satisfaction and family happiness: The part-time work puzzle. *The Economic Journal, 118*(526), F77–F99.

Bryson, A. (2013). Do temporary agency workers affect workplace performance? *Journal of Productivity Analysis, 39*(2), 131–138.

Burke, A., & Cowling, M. (2020). The role of freelancers in entrepreneurship and small business. *Small Business Economics, 55*(2), 389–392.

Chinoracký, R., & Čorejová, T. (2019). Impact of digital technologies on labour market and the transport sector. *Transportation Research Procedia, 40*, 994–1001.

Eurofound (2015). *New forms of employment.* Luxembourg: Publications Office of the European Union.

European Commission. Directorate-General of Employment, Social Affairs and Inclusion. (2015). *Labour market and wage developments in Europe 2015*. Brussels: European Commission.

Eurostat (2021). *Database*. Available at: https://ec.europa.eu/eurostat/data/database (accessed 26 August 2021).

Frey, D.F. (2017). Economic growth, full employment and decent work: The means and ends in SDG 8. *The International Journal of Human Rights, 21*(8), 1164–1184.

George, E., & Chattopadhyay, P. (2015). *Non-standard work and workers: Organizational implications*. Geneva: International Labour Office.

Hirsch, B., & Mueller, S. (2012). The productivity effect of temporary agency work: Evidence from German panel data. *The Economic Journal, 122*(562), F216–F235.

Huws, U., Spencer, N.H., & Syrdal, D.S. (2018). Online, on call: The spread of digitally organised just-in-time working and its implications for standard employment models. *New Technology, Work and Employment, 33*(2), 113–129.

ILO (2004). *Work-sharing and job-sharing*. Information Sheet No. WT-17, Conditions of Work and Employment Programme (Geneva).

ILO (2016). *Non-standard employment around the world: Understanding challenges, shaping prospects*. Geneva: International Labour Office.

Kiersztyn, A. (2017). Non-standard employment and subjective insecurity: How can we capture job precarity using survey data? In A. Kalleberg & S. Vallas (Eds.), *Precarious work* (pp. 91–122). Bingley: Emerald Publishing Limited.

Kjeldstad, R., & Nymoen, E.H. (2012). Part-time work and gender: Worker versus job explanations. *International Labour Review, 151*(1–2), 85–107.

Leighton, P. (2016). Professional self-employment, new power, and the sharing economy: Some cautionary tales from Uber. *Journal of Management & Organization, 22*(6), 859–874.

Minnotte, K.L., Minnotte, M.C., & Thompson, K. (2016). The life satisfaction of dual-earner mothers and fathers: Does flexible scheduling matter? *Journal of Happiness Studies, 17*(6), 2365–2388.

Muja, A., Blommaert, L., Gesthuizen, M., & Wolbers, M.H. (2019). The role of different types of skills and signals in youth labor market integration. *Empirical Research in Vocational Education and Training, 11*(1), 1–23.

Nielen, S., & Schiersch, A. (2014). Temporary agency work and firm competitiveness: Evidence from German manufacturing firms. *Industrial Relations: A Journal of Economy and Society, 53*(3), 365–393.

Pollmann-Schult, M. (2018). Parenthood and life satisfaction in Europe: The role of family policies and working time flexibility. *European Journal of Population, 34*(3), 387–411.

Rai, S.M., Brown, B.D., & Ruwanpura, K.N. (2019). SDG 8: Decent work and economic growth–A gendered analysis. *World Development, 113*, 368–380.

Reljic, J., Cetrulo, A., Cirillo, V., & Coveri, A. (2021). Non-standard work and innovation: Evidence from European industries. *Economics of Innovation and New Technology*, 1–29. https://doi.org/10.1080/10438599.2021.1893139

Schmid, G., & Wagner, J. (2017). Managing social risks of non-standard employment in Europe. ILO Working Paper, Conditions of Work and Employment Series, (91).

Seth, M., & Sethi, D. (2011). Human resource outsourcing: Analysis based on literature review. *International Journal of Innovation, Management and Technology, 2*(2), 127.

Shi, Y. (2007). Today's solution and tomorrow's problem: The business process outsourcing risk management puzzle. *California Management Review, 49*(3), 27–44.

Spasova, S., Bouget, D., Ghailani, D., & Vanhercke, B. (2017). Access to social protection for people working on non-standard contracts and as self-employed in Europe. *A study of national policies, European Social Policy Network (ESPN).* Brussels: European Commission.

Thörnquist, A. (2019). Truck drivers in the grey area between employment and self-employment: Swedish experiences. *Nordic Journal of Working Life Studies, 9*(S6), 33–52. doi:10.18291/njwls.v9iS6.114690

Van Doorn, N. (2017). Platform labour: On the gendered and racialized exploitation of low-income service work in the 'on-demand'economy. *Information, Communication & Society, 20*(6), 898–914.

Van Gelderen, M., & Jansen, P. (2006). Autonomy as a start-up motive. *Journal of Small Business and Enterprise Development, 13*(1), 23–32. doi:10.1108/14626000610645289

Venkatesan, M., & Luongo, G. (2019). Sustainable development Goal 8 in context. In M. Venkatesan & G. Luongo (Eds.), *SDG8 – Sustainable economic growth and decent work for all (Concise guides to the United Nations sustainable development goals)* (pp. 5–38). Bingley: Emerald Publishing Limited. doi:10.1108/9781789730913

Williams, C.C., & Horodnic, I.A. (2018). Evaluating the prevalence and distribution of dependent self-employment: Some lessons from the European working conditions survey. *Industrial Relations Journal, 49*(2), 109–127.

Yu, S., & Postepska, A. (2020). Flexible jobs make parents happier: Evidence from Australia. IZA Discussion Paper No. 13700.

11 Highly skilled solo self-employed individuals in the digital economy

Ondřej Dvouletý and Agnieszka Postepska

Introduction

Technological advances, widespread high-speed internet and economic growth are continuously reshaping labour markets and opening up new opportunities. The digital labour revolution has gathered pace with the emergence of the COVID-19 crisis (Śledziewska & Włoch, 2022). The emergence of new digital business models reorganises labour relationships on all skill levels (Śledziewska & Włoch, 2022). Over time, it has led to a sharp increase in non-agricultural self-employment and increased the heterogeneity of self-employed workers (Burke, 2015; van Stel & van der Swan, 2020; Vermeylen, Wilkens, Biletta, & Fromm 2017).

This chapter focuses on modern *freelancers,* a specific type of self-employed individuals often overlooked in the academic literature. While freelancers once comprised low-skilled shadow workers (Burke & Van Stel, 2011), new evidence suggests that today's freelancers in highly developed economies are predominantly highly skilled (Burke, 2015; van Stel & van der Swan, 2020). In this chapter, we employ an established definition of freelancers, capturing them statistically as solo self-employed individuals, working as Managers, Professionals or Technicians and Associate Professionals (Burke, & Cowling, 2020a, 2020b; Dvouletý, 2020). Stable own-account workers account for about 26% of the self-employed workers in the EU. According to the European Foundation for the Improvement of Living and Working Conditions (Eurofound, 2017), a great majority of those workers are voluntarily self-employed, and 93% work for more than one client. These individuals are sometimes referred to as iPros (Nye & Jenkins, 2016), e-workers (Pink, 2001), information workers (Florida, 2014) or lattepreneurs (Dunstan, 2015).

As a mode of labour contracting, freelancing has been on the rise in the EU (van Stel & van der Swan, 2020). Over the last ten years (2011–2020), the absolute number of freelancers increased by about 15% (see the left panel of Figure 11.1), while the share of freelancers in all self-employed workers increased by five percentage points (from 22 to 27%; see the right panel of Figure 11.1).

DOI: 10.4324/9781003254638-15

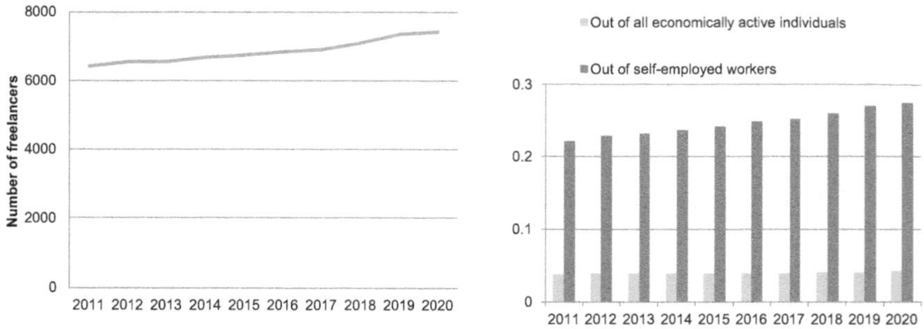

Figure 11.1 Freelancing in the EU

Source: the authors' own research based on Eurostat (2021).

Notes: The left panel presents the number of freelancers in all EU 2011–2020. The right panel presents the changes in shares of freelancers in the entire economically active populations and among self-employed workers.

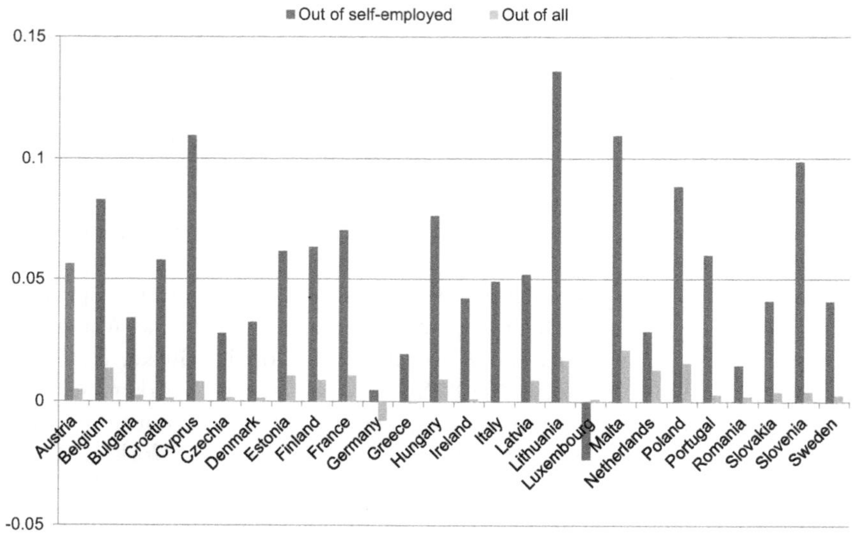

Figure 11.2 Growth of freelancing in the EU

Source: the authors' own research based on Eurostat (2021).

Notes: Changes in the shares of high-skilled own-account workers in the EU between 2011 and 2020. A positive value indicates an increase over time.

However, these overall patterns still hide significant inter-country differences, as illustrated in Figure 11.2, which reveals that while all countries (with the exception of Germany) experienced an increasing trend, the speed of growth varies across countries.

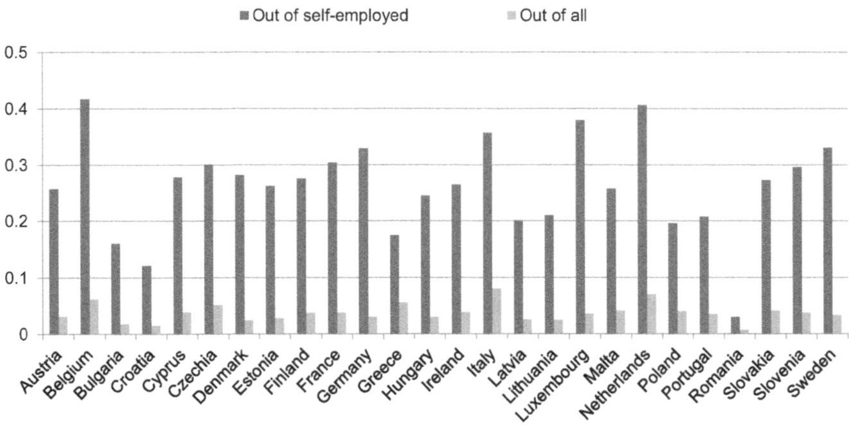

Figure 11.3 Shares of high-skilled own account workers in the EU member states in 2020

Source: the authors' own research based on Eurostat (2021).

As Figure 11.3 shows, in 2020 Belgium, the Netherlands, Luxembourg, Germany and Italy were among the frontrunners among countries with the highest share (over 35%) of own-account self-employed workers in professional high-skilled occupations (Managers, Professionals, Technicians and Associate Professionals). These figures clearly illustrate that freelancing is on the rise across the EU, and that the process differs by country. Thus, it is a valid research question to explore institutional and economic factors that have influenced the rise of freelancing.

The rapid growth in the frequency of self-employment among professionals stems from the emergence of the digital economy (Bögenhold, 2019). The presence of online platforms increases the probability and decreases the cost of finding potential customers (Clifton, Füzi, & Loudon, 2022). With the higher levels of freedom, work flexibility and work autonomy, own-account self-employment has become an attractive form of employment among highly skilled professionals and managers (Leighton, 2016; Van Gelderen & Jansen, 2006). On the demand side, the desire to reduce costs of hiring full-time staff as well as to become more dynamic and innovative as a company is driving the increasing trend, making freelancing an increasingly attractive substitute to hiring full-time staff among employers (Ackers, 2014; Burke, 2012; Burke, & Cowling, 2020a, 2020b; Seth & Sethi, 2011). The increasing trend also contributes to job creation, enables entrepreneurship (Burke & Van Stel, 2011; Burke et al., 2020a) and facilitates market entry (Burke et al., 2020).

While the literature on entrepreneurship determinants is vast (Urbano, Aparicio, & Audretsch, 2019 for an excellent review of the literature), it rarely distinguishes self-employed workers who create jobs and own-account workers without employees (Dvouletý, 2018). Similarly, little is still known about the macro-level determinants of freelancing. This chapter strives to fill this gap in the literature and analyse the determinants of freelancing in the EU over the last ten years. More specifically, we are interested in drilling down into the effects of local labour-market conditions and the country's institutional settings for freelancing at a country level in the digital economy.

The next section of this chapter presents the research methodology, followed by a discussion of the results and conclusions.

Research methodology

Using the Eurostat (2021) database, we collected data on highly skilled solo self-employed persons classified according to the International Standard Classification of Occupations (ISCO) as levels 3 and 4 and calculated their proportions in the total number of self-employed persons. Data were available for the years 2011–2020 for 26 European Union member countries[1]: Austria, Belgium, Bulgaria, Croatia, Cyprus, Czech Republic, Germany, Denmark, Estonia, Finland, France, Greece, Hungary, Ireland, Italy, Latvia, Lithuania, Luxembourg, Malta, Netherlands, Poland, Portugal, Romania, Slovakia, Slovenia and Sweden. To investigate the institutional and economic factors that influenced the rise of freelancing in the age of digital transformation, we have included additional variables collected from the World Bank Database (2021) and Heritage Foundation (2021) presented in Table 11.1.

The literature on determinants of entrepreneurial activity, such as the review article by Urbano et al. (2019), inspired the selection of the variables. The country's economic development is operationalised by the *Unemployment rate*, which is often associated with being a push factor for joining independent business activity (Krasniqi, 2014). As our research examines the role of digitisation and the gig economy, we expect the share of freelancers to be positively associated with the spread of the internet (Lehdonvirta, 2018); thus, we include variable *Individuals using the internet* to test this assumption. The institutional factors shaping the business environment might significantly influence an individual's decisions on whether to join self-employment or not (Dvouletý, 2017); and thus we consider it essential to check for the quality of the business environment by including the variable *Business Freedom Index*.

Opting for solo self-employment may be significantly associated with the country's tax and social security policies, as high-income taxes and social security payments can discourage some individuals from bearing the risks of becoming more entrepreneurial (Bruce & Deskins, 2012). This led us to consider in our analysis the following two variables: Taxes *on income* and *Social contributions*. The literature on the determinants of self-employment also acknowledges the role of *Foreign direct investments* (FDIs), which may crowd out domestic self-employment activity (Barbosa & Eiriz, 2009), and thus we

Table 11.1 Definition of variables

Variable	Description
Share of freelancers in total self-employed	Percentage share of highly skilled professionals (Managers, Professionals, Technicians and Associate Professionals) working on their own account in total self-employed.
Unemployment rate	Unemployment, total (% of total labour force, national estimate)
Population ages 15–64	"Total population between the ages of 15 and 64 as a percentage of the total population."
Individuals using the internet	Percentage share of the total population using the internet.
Business freedom index	Heritage Foundation's index "measuring the efficiency of government regulation of business, ranging between 0 and 100, when 100 corresponds to the highest business freedom."
Foreign direct investments, net inflows	"Foreign direct investment is the net inflows of investment to acquire a lasting management interest (10 percent or more of voting stock) in an enterprise operating in an economy other than that of the investor."
Taxes on income	Percentage share of revenues paid to governments from income, profits and capital gains.
Social contributions	"Percentage share of revenues, including social security contributions by employees, employers, and self-employed individuals and contributions to social insurance schemes operated by governments."

Source: the authors' own research based on World Bank Database (2021), Heritage Foundation (2021) and Eurostat (2021).

include this variable in our analysis. We have also used a control variable representing the share of the economically active population (*Population ages 15–64*), which was also used in the previously published studies (Roman, Bilan, & Ciumaş, 2018). The summary statistics (mean, standard error, minimum, maximum) of all variables can be found in Table 11.2. Our final sample size ranges between 233 and 260, depending on the availability of particular variables in respective years.

We proceeded by checking the panel unit roots of our variables with the help of panel unit root tests and concluded that our variables were stationary. Therefore, the obtained results will not be biased from the non-stationarity issues (Pesaran, 2007). As a next step, we employed multivariate panel regression analysis, where our dependent variable represents the share of freelancers, and the independent ones are their determinants. Following Wooldridge (2010), we estimate the least-squares dummy variables (LSDV) model with robust standard errors, allowing us to control for the country- and year-specific heterogeneity and to focus on the role of the factors under analysis.

Table 11.2 Summary statistics

Variable	*Mean*	*Standard error*	*Minimum*	*Maximum*	*Observations (N)*
Share of freelancers in total self-employed	23.3	9.2	1.5	47.7	260
Unemployment rate	8.5	4.3	2.0	27.5	260
Population ages 15–64	66.0	2.2	61.6	72.0	260
Individuals using the internet	77.4	11.9	40.0	98.1	229
Business freedom index	77.1	9.7	53.6	99.7	260
Foreign direct investments, net inflows	10.2	31.2	−40.3	280.1	234
Taxes on income	21.7	9.5	4.7	48.0	233
Social contributions	30.9	10.8	2.0	55.6	233

Source: the authors' own research.

Research findings

The estimated model, presented in Table 11.3, was found to be statistically significant and meets the standard econometric assumptions. Despite the fact that not all included variables were statistically significant, we kept them in our model because they improved the model's explanatory power (Wooldridge, 2010).

Our findings support the hypothesis that freelancing is positively related to the spread of internet users. We also observe the importance of tax and social security policies. The results show a statistically significant and negative impact of the proportions of social contributions paid from revenues. The estimated model also suggests the tax rate had a negative effect, though this was not statistically proved. There is also evidence that net foreign direct investments exerted a crowding-out effect on freelancing, documented by a negative and statistically significant coefficient. The level of business freedom was found to have a positive impact. Nevertheless, this variable was not found to be statistically significant. Beyond these, we see a negative association between the proportions of freelancers and the share of the economically active population. Finally, our results propose a positive but statistically insignificant effect of the country's unemployment rate on the percentage of freelancers in the economy.

Conclusions and practical implications

This study sought to determine the role local labour market conditions play in the prevalence of freelancing in EU Member States in the age of digital transformation. Our findings are suggestive of two important trends. First, the spread and use of the internet are significant determinants of the

Table 11.3 Determinants of highly skilled solo self-employed individuals

Independent variables/dependent variable	*(1)* *Share of freelancers in total self-employed*
Unemployment rate	0.0334
	(0.0973)
Population ages 15–64	−1.317***
	(0.332)
Individuals using the internet	0.117**
	(0.0358)
Business freedom index	0.0292
	(0.0407)
Foreign direct investments, net inflows	−0.00857+
	(0.00503)
Taxes on income	−0.104
	(0.0993)
Social contributions	−0.360***
	(0.0940)
Constant	123.0***
	(23.57)
Country dummies included	Yes
Year dummies included	Yes
Observations	228
Wald chi2 (40)	16,359.07
Prob > chi2	0.000
R^2	0.975
Adjusted R^2	0.970
Akaike information criterion (AIC)	892.9
Bayesian information criterion (BIC)	1033.5

Source: the authors' own research.

Notes: Robust regression estimates. A pooled sample of 26 European countries. Countries included: Austria, Belgium, Bulgaria, Cyprus, Czech Republic, Germany, Denmark, Estonia, Finland, France, Greece, Croatia, Hungary, Ireland, Italy, Latvia, Lithuania, Luxembourg, Malta, Netherlands, Poland, Portugal, Romania, Slovakia, Slovenia and Sweden. Robust standard errors are in parentheses, statistical significance is reported as follows: + $p < 0.10$, * $p < 0.05$, ** $p < 0.01$, *** $p < 0.001$.

share of highly skilled solo professionals. This finding is not surprising given the importance of technological progress in facilitating the matching of entrepreneurs and end-users and the product or service being delivered (both firms and individual customers) as has been emphasised by Popiel (2017), Lehdonvirta (2018) or Tudy (2021). Second, the social contributions potential freelancers would have to pay appear to deter them from entering the labour market. High contributions to the social security system may prevent some individuals from bearing risks of entrepreneurship (Bruce & Deskins, 2012; Buschoff & Protsch, 2008; Nawaz, Zhang, Mansoor, & Ilmudeen, 2019). Future research should focus on the mechanisms responsible for these correlations, especially on the role of social security policies and the legal definition of freelancing. To what extent do governmental agencies monitor freelancers, tax freelancers' incomes, and control their social security payments? Can research on cross-country differences in determinants of highly skilled professionals contribute to a better understanding of the state of digital economies?

Answering these research questions will help researchers to shed further light on these issues and policymakers to better grapple with the issues freelancers face as their mode of labour becomes an equal career choice, not only among youth (Burke & Cowling, 2020a, 2020b). Policymakers need to make a greater effort to properly understand freelancing as the business activities conducted by freelancers often extend beyond the home-country's borders and are not subject to any geographical constraints. Thus, freelancing provides individuals with a unique opportunity to pursue fully independent business activity in the area of their choice. It is up to the individual whether to expand their self-employment activity and employ other people in the future or continuously pursue their solo ride (Cieślik & Dvouletý, 2019).

Note

1 Spain was excluded from the analysis due to many missing values.

References

Ackers, P. (2014). Rethinking the employment relationship: A neo-pluralist critique of British industrial relations orthodoxy. *The International Journal of Human Resource Management, 25*(18), 2608–2625.

Barbosa, N., & Eiriz, V. (2009). The role of inward foreign direct investment on entrepreneurship. *International Entrepreneurship and Management Journal, 5*(3), 319–339.

Bögenhold, D. (2019). From hybrid entrepreneurs to entrepreneurial billionaires: Observations on the socioeconomic heterogeneity of self-employment. *American Behavioral Scientist, 63*(2), 129–146.

Bruce, D., & Deskins, J. (2012). Can state tax policies be used to promote entrepreneurial activity?. *Small Business Economics, 38*(4), 375–397.

Burke, A. (2012). *The role of freelancers in the 21st-century British economy.* London: PCG. Available at: https://www.ipse.co.uk/resource/the-role-of-freelancers-in-the-21st-century-british-economy-report.html (accessed 26 August 2021).

Burke, A. (2015). Introduction: A freelancing and self-employment research agenda. In A. Burke (Ed.), *The handbook of research on freelancing and self-employment* (pp. iii–viii). Dublin: Senate Hall Academic Publishing.

Burke, A., & Cowling, M. (2020a). The relationship between freelance workforce intensity, business performance, and job creation. *Small Business Economics, 55*(2), 399–413.

Burke, A., & Cowling, M. (2020b). The role of freelancers in entrepreneurship and small business. *Small Business Economics, 55*(2), 389–392.

Burke, A., & Van Stel, A. (2011). The entrepreneurship enabling role of freelancers: Theory with evidence from the construction industry. *International Review of Entrepreneurship, 9*(3), 131–158.

Buschoff, K.S., & Protsch, P. (2008). (A-)typical and (in-) secure? Social protection and "non-standard" forms of employment in Europe. *International Social Security Review, 61*(4), 51–73.

Cieślik, J., & Dvouletý, O. (2019). Segmentation of the population of the solo self-employed. *International Review of Entrepreneurship, 17*(3), 281–304.

Clifton, N., Füzi, A., & Loudon, G. (2022). Coworking in the digital economy: Context, motivations, and outcomes. *Futures*, 135, 102439.

Dunstan, M. (2015). *The coworking revolution: Four secrets to successfully working for yourself.* London: Rising Tide Publishing.

Dvouletý, O. (2017). Determinants of Nordic entrepreneurship. *Journal of Small Business and Enterprise Development, 24*(1), 12–33.

Dvouletý, O. (2018). Determinants of self-employment with and without employees: Empirical findings from Europe. *International Review of Entrepreneurship, 16*(3), 405–426.

Dvouletý, O. (2020). Classifying self-employed persons using segmentation criteria available in the Labour Force Survey (LFS) data. *Journal of Business Venturing Insights, 14*, e00199.

Eurofound (2017). *The many faces of self-employment in Europe*. European Foundation for the Improvement of Living and Working Conditions: Dublin. Available at: https://www.eurofound.europa.eu/publications/blog/the-many-faces-of-self-employment-in-europe (accessed 26 August 2021).

Eurostat (2021). *Database*. Available at: https://ec.europa.eu/eurostat/data/database (accessed 26 August 2021).

Florida, R. (2014). The creative class and economic development. *Economic Development Quarterly, 28*(3), 196–205.

Heritage Foundation (2021). *Business freedom index*. Available at: https://www.heritage.org/index/business-freedom (accessed 26 August 2021).

Krasniqi, B.A. (2014). Characteristics of self-employment: A refuge from unemployment or road to entrepreneurship. *Small Enterprise Research, 21*(1), 33–53.

Lehdonvirta, V. (2018). Flexibility in the gig economy: Managing time on three online piecework platforms. *New Technology, Work and Employment, 33*(1), 13–29.

Leighton, P. (2016). Professional self-employment, new power, and the sharing economy: Some cautionary tales from Uber. *Journal of Management & Organization, 22*(6), 859–874.

Nawaz, Z., Zhang, J., Mansoor, R., & Ilmudeen, A. (2019). Gig workers in sharing economy: Conceptualizing Freelancer Value Proposition (FVP) in e-lancing platforms. *Advances in Management and Applied Economics, 9*(6), 51–75.

Nye, L., & Jenkins, K. (2016). *'Report – Understanding independent professionals in the EU'*. IPSE: London. Available at: https://www.ipse.co.uk/resource/understanding-independent-professionals-in-the-eu-2015.html (accessed 26 August 2021).

Pesaran, M.H. (2007). A simple panel unit root test in the presence of cross-section dependence. *Journal of Applied Econometrics, 22*(2), 265–312.

Pink, D. (2001). *Free agent nation: The future of working for yourself.* New York: Business Plus.

Popiel, P. (2017). "Boundaryless" in the creative economy: Assessing freelancing on Upwork. *Critical Studies in Media Communication, 34*(3), 220–233.

Roman, A., Bilan, I., & Ciumaş, C. (2018). What drives the creation of new businesses? A panel-data analysis for EU countries. *Emerging Markets Finance and Trade, 54*(3), 508–536.

Seth, M., & Sethi, D. (2011). Human resource outsourcing: Analysis based on literature review. *International Journal of Innovation, Management and Technology, 2*(2), 127.

Śledziewska, K., & Włoch, R. (2022). *The economics of digital transformation: The disruption of markets, production, consumption, and work*. London: Routledge.

Tudy, R.A. (2021). From the corporate world to freelancing: The phenomenon of working from home in the Philippines. *Community, Work & Family, 24*(1), 77–92.

Urbano, D., Aparicio, S., & Audretsch, D. (2019). Twenty-five years of research on institutions, entrepreneurship, and economic growth: What has been learned? *Small Business Economics, 53*(1), 21–49.

Van Gelderen, M., & Jansen, P. (2006). Autonomy as a start-up motive. *Journal of Small Business and Enterprise Development, 13*(1), 23–32.

van Stel, A., & van der Zwan, P. (2020). Analyzing the changing education distributions of solo self-employed workers and employer entrepreneurs in Europe. *Small Business Economics, 55*(2), 429–445.

Vermeylen, G., Wilkens, M., Biletta, I., & Fromm, A. (2017). *Exploring self-employment in the European Union*. Luxembourg: Publications Office of the European Union.

Wooldridge, J.M. (2010). *Econometric analysis of cross-section and panel data*. Cambridge: Massachusetts Institute of Technology.

World Bank Database (2021). *Statistical database*. Available at: https://data.worldbank.org (accessed 26 August 2021).

12 Platform work in the digital economy

Michał Głuszak and Agnieszka Małkowska

Introduction

The digital transformation has enabled the emergence of the digital platform work, which has recently gained in popularity particularly for household maintenance, food delivery and personal transport work, as well as in IT services. It is arguably one of the most important phenomena related to the digital economy and industry 4.0 on the labour market (Urzì Brancati, Pesole, & Fernández-Macías, 2019). Platform work has been only vaguely defined, thus several alternative terms are used simultaneously to describe it. In the literature, labour mediation through different types of digital platforms is referred to as gig work, platform work, platform labour, digital labour, on-demand work or crowdsourcing (Florisson & Mandl, 2018). According to the Eurofound report, platform work can be defined as an employment form "matching of the supply of and demand for paid work through an online platform" (Eurofound, 2018b, p. 1). Work platforms are an outgrowth of the platform economy, but are distinct from capital platforms (providing access to accommodation like Airbnb, or financial resources or sales platforms such as eBay).

The features of platform work include temporary, task-driven assignments, online coordination and optimisation, as well as flexibility and lack of formal employment contracts typical to traditional labour relations. The digital labour platforms that act as intermediaries rather than employers are "digital networks that coordinate labour service transactions in an algorithmic way" (Eurofound, 2018a, p. 19). The category of digital labour platform is not homogenous. Most studies distinguish between location-based platforms coordinating services delivered physically in a given place and online platforms where virtual services are provided globally. There are more elaborate classifications; however, Pesole et al. (2018) categorise digital labour platforms based on (1) the skills level required, (2) whether the service is delivered on-location or online, (3) the scale of the tasks, (4) the selection process and (5) the form of matching and distinguish between 120 potential categories of work platforms. The empirical data suggest that only a few categories have gained significant popularity. For practical reasons, another categorisation is provided by Eurofound and consists of ten distinct groups of work platforms

DOI: 10.4324/9781003254638-16

(Eurofound, 2018b), but in this research, as did Fabo, Beblavý, Kilhoffer and Lenaerts (2017), we have focused on a simplified version and identify four types of work platforms:

- on-location routine low-skilled work: where simple and routine tasks are performed in a specific geographic location, but matching is done online. This popular format is typical to transportation and delivery services such as Delivery Hero, Glovo and Uber;
- on-location moderately/high skilled work: where more demanding services are done in a specific location, but clients and workers are matched online. This type of platform work is typical form activities requiring some level of expertise, such as house maintenance and massage therapy. Examples include Helpling, Werkspot and TakeLessons;
- online low/moderately skilled work: where simple and unified tasks are delivered online. This type of platform work involves automation tasks (classification and classification or acquiring survey participants). Examples include Amazon Mechanical Turk;
- online specialist high-skilled work: where the clients are matched with high-skilled workers typically but not necessarily based on contest setting. This particular type of platform typically applies to unique, creative tasks (design, IT solution, data analytics). Examples include 99 Designs, Freelancer and Upwork.

According to an International Labour Organization survey (International Labour Office, 2021), the distribution of on-site delivery digital labour platforms that receive funding from venture capital and other investors has not been uniform. Most of the platforms originated in North America (44 surveyed platforms; approximately 27% of the sample) and Western Europe (33 platforms). A considerable number of platforms operate in South Asia (21), East Asia (16), Latin America and the Caribbean (15) and Eastern Europe (10) (Table 12.1).

The geography behind digital labour platforms specialising in transport services was somewhat different. The largest concentration of transportation platforms that received funding was observed in North America (19 platforms, 31%), Western Europe (10 platforms) and Africa (8 platforms). Compared to delivery and transport web-based digital labour platforms, the distribution of online web-based digital labour platforms that received funding was far more concentrated in the Western Hemisphere. Here too most platforms were from North America (66 platforms, 46,5% of the sample) or Europe (36 platforms, 25,4%).

A European study (Fabo et al., 2017) identified 200 work platforms operating in European countries. The vast majority of the labour platforms (85%) originated in European countries (mainly France, UK, Germany and the Netherlands), but several important platforms were created outside Europe, with 9% coming from US and 6% from other regions (Figure 12.1). Notably, the study revealed a significant concentration of platform activity,

Table 12.1 Total funding received by delivery digital labour platforms across regions of the world in 1999–2020

Country	*On-location delivery services*		*On-location transportation services*		*Online web-based services*	
Number of platforms						
	Number	%	Number	%	Number	%
Africa	5	3.05	8	13.11		
Arab States	6	3.66	1	1.64	1	0.01
Central and Western Asia	6	3.66	2	3.28	4	4.20
East Asia	16	9.76	4	6.56	11	21.52
Latin America and the Caribbean	15	9.15	6	9.84	4	0.07
North America	44	26.83	19	31.15	66	59.51
South Asia	21	12.80	5	8.20	6	0.26
South-East Asia and the Pacific	8	4.88	4	6.56	9	2.86
Eastern Europe	**10**	**6.10**	**2**	**3.28**	**5**	**0.45**
Western Europe	**33**	**20.12**	**10**	**16.39**	**36**	**11.11**
Total	164	100.00	61	100.00	142	100.00
Total funding from venture capital and other investors						
	Funds (mln USD)	%	Fund (mln USD)	%	Fund USD)	%
Africa	13	0.03	45	0.07		
Arab States	48	0.13	772	1.23	0,3	0.01
Central and Western Asia	51	0.14	929	1.48	113	4.20
East Asia	8915	23.78	21581	34.37	579	21.52
Latin America and the Caribbean	3019	8.05	337	0.54	2	0.07
North America	11116	29.65	33032	52.61	1601	59.51
South Asia	4199	11.20	3850	6.13	7	0.26
South-East Asia and the Pacific	222	0.59	26	0.04	77	2.86
Eastern Europe	**110**	**0.29**	**1001**	**1.59**	**12**	**0.45**
Western Europe	**9803**	**26.14**	**1211**	**1.93**	**299**	**11.11**
Total	37496	100.00	62784	100.00	2690,3	100.00

Source: the authors' own research based on International Labour Office (2021).
Note: Western and Eastern European values are highlighted.

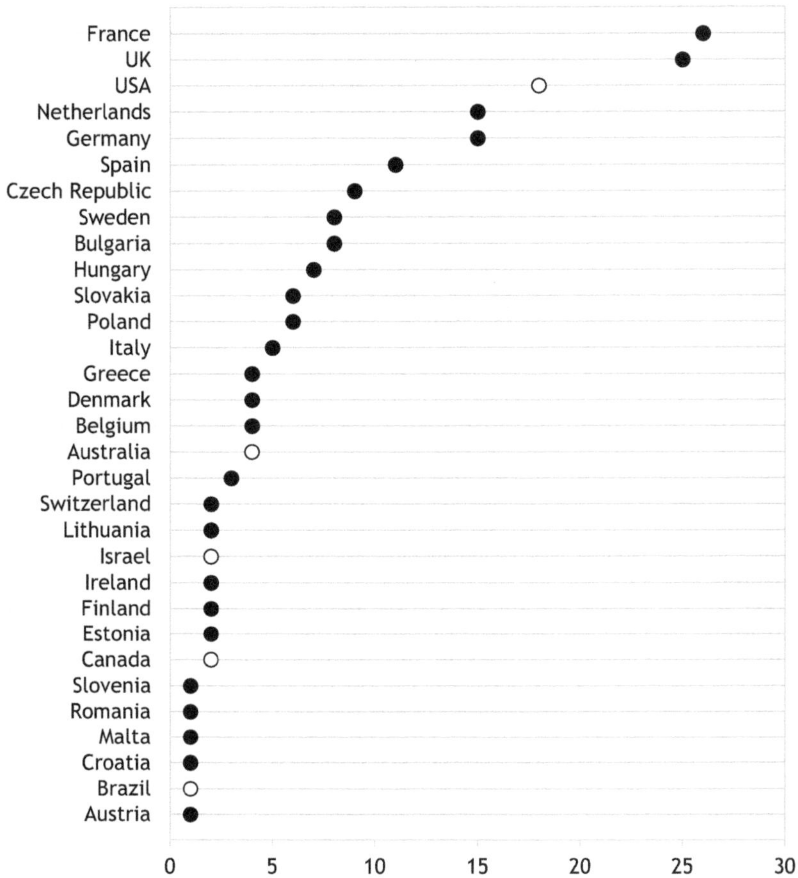

Figure 12.1 The geography of work platforms operating in Europe by country of origin in 2017

Source: the authors' own research based on Fabo et al. (2017).

Note: European countries are highlighted by full circle.

as most of the funding, mediation and revenues were absorbed by a few platforms. 'Zombie platforms,' or those with negligible activity, are another interesting presence on the market. The study investigated the spatial patterns of work platform activity and spatial diffusion processes. The findings suggest that language and culture may facilitate platform adoption, as German work platforms are easily adopted in other German speaking countries, while Latin-American work platforms are popular in Spain.

Empirical evidence suggests that platform work in Europe is considerably less common than in developing countries, most notably BRICS. A BCG survey (2019) of workers (with the exception of highly qualified specialists) in 2018 revealed that 33% of China's workforce used the gig economy as a secondary source of income (and 12% as a primary source). The digital economy was a secondary source of income for 31% of workers in India and 13% in Brazil (primary for 8% and 5% of workers, respectively). Digital labour was less popular in Europe, with only 7% of workers reporting the gig economy as a secondary source of income in the UK, 6% in Germany and Spain and 3% in France and Sweden. Similar shares of the working age population using work platforms are reported in other studies. The most comprehensive and robust estimate of the digital platform workforce in European countries was done by Pesole et al. (2018) based on COLLEEM survey in 14 EU Member States. The report distinguishes competitive indicators of the adoption of digital labour in European countries: (1) ever performing platform work, (2) frequently performing platform work, (3) significant income from platform work or (4) platform work as main occupation. According to estimates, the share of platform workers in Europe ("defined as those who earn 50% or more of their income via platforms and/or work via platforms more than 20 hours a week") is approximately 2% of the adult population. The share is the highest in the UK, the Netherlands and Germany, and the lowest in Hungary, Slovakia and Finland.

The objective of the chapter is to identify the benefits and challenges related to the platform work for both companies and workers offering their services through online platforms. Additionally, we assess the consequences of growing platformisation for the labour market.

It is organised as follows. In the following section we examine some key elements of the methods used in the empirical part. We then discuss the benefits and drawbacks of the platform work considering different types of digital labour platforms from the perspective of the various actors involved. The chapter concludes with a look at policy implications and future scenarios.

Research methodology

Platform work is a relatively new phenomenon, thus the statistical data is scarce and covers a relatively short period of time. The existing empirical evidence has largely been collected by International Labour Office and European Foundation for the Improvement of Living and Working Conditions. Additionally, several papers offering empirical evidence on the narrow topics related to platform work include: on job satisfaction (Hartono, Raharjo, & Ronyastra, 2021), and on ethical concerns related to exploitation and job precarity (Tan et al., 2021). Platformisation and the problems arising from it were examined by Spurk and Straub in 2020.

The aim of the chapter is to identify the benefits and challenges associated with platform work. Additionally, we examine the differences between several types of platform work. In the empirical section we use a modified and simplified typology of work platforms, accounting for two salient characteristics: location where the service is delivered (online vs on-location) and scale of operations (domestic vs international). We synthesise the available

Table 12.2 Examples of work platforms used in case study analysis

Platforms	*On-site delivery*	*On-site transportation*	*Online*
Small-scale (regional)	Pyszne.pl (Poland)	LeCab (France)	Talent Alpha (Poland)
Large-scale (global)	Delivery Hero	Uber	Upwork

Source: the authors' own research.

statistical data on work platforms in Europe based on a growing number of reports and studies that provide empirical evidence on various facets of digital platform labour (qualifications required, salaries, stability and security, flexibility and job satisfaction). Where feasible, we supplement the conclusions using a qualitative approach. For more in-depth insights into the operations of work platforms, a case study approach is used to examine different categories of work platforms that are active in Europe: global, multi-country and single-country (Table 12.2).

Eurofound has identified platform work as one of the fastest growing forms of employment in Europe. The emerging market for digital labour platforms is highly competitive, and subject to rapid and turbulent changes. While the competitive position of platforms changes over time, global leaders can be identified based on profits generated, funds gathered, number of clients and number of users providing services. The literature (Wach, 2014) distinguishes four platform types: dominant platforms (active globally, leaders on the market), strong platforms (major players especially at regional scale), average platforms (smaller, operating more locally) and finally poor platforms (with limited potential for effective competition). Unfortunately, their different sizes and scopes make comparison of these platforms difficult.

Reports on the contemporary landscape of platforms operating in Europe suggest that several leading platforms are global entities originating outside of Europe (mainly in the US). The number of work platforms has changed rapidly due to the growing number of new platforms and substantial number of platforms ceasing to operate. M&A activity within the sector has also been robust. One example is Delivery Hero, a German origin platform offering food ordering and delivery services. According to the tracxn database, as of September 2021 the company has spent 6.26 billion USD on 24 acquisitions and 14 investments in multiple sectors (Food Tech, Logistics Tech, Online Grocery). Foodpanda, Woowa Brothers and InstaShop have been among it notable acquisitions (Figure 12.2).

Delivery Hero's acquisition history suggests that the sector witnessed pronounced global competition and turbulent changes over the last decade.

Four categories of consequences of platform work for the labour force can be identified: behavioural (job performance, absenteeism, turnover), attitudinal (job satisfaction, involvement, commitment), role perception (ambiguity and conflict), well-being (anxiety, stress, work-life balance) (Schroeder,

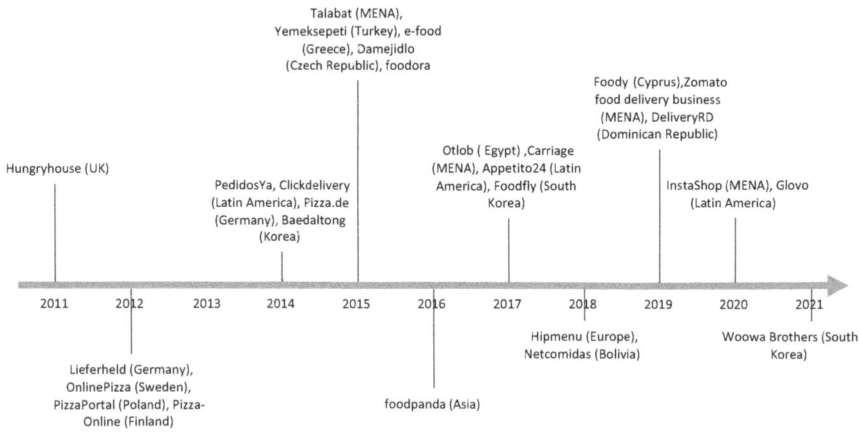

Figure 12.2 Delivery Hero's acquisitions and mergers in 2011–2021
Source: the authors' own research based on Tracxn Technologies (2021).

Bricka, & Whitaker, 2021). The following section examines the benefits and risks of platform work in greater detail.

Research findings

The benefits of platform work

According to the subject literature, full-time or part-time platform work offers several benefits that at least partially explain its meteoric rise in popularity (Table 12.3).

As Table 12.3 shows, leading benefits of platform work include: relatively easy access to the labour market (especially when tasks do not involve skilled work); source of extra income; a path to self-employment, flexibility in task-related work, reasonable, market-aligned pay, opportunity to develop new skills and the promotion of universal and transparent health and safety measures.

More insights come from case studies based on evidence coming from work platforms themselves. According to a survey conducted online in the US in 2020 of people who worked for Uber as drivers or delivery persons, the most satisfactory facet of this particular work platform was the independence and flexibility it afforded (evaluated as good by 76% of respondents). Respondents were also satisfied with Uber's protection policy measures in response to COVID-19 (60%) and its physical protection programme (55%) (Table 12.4).

The Uber case study reveals that satisfaction with platform work is based on unique, platform-specific factors as well as the universal component shared by a given type of platform work in general. In the former case, mostly related to Uber's policy, the responses could not be fully generalised to other delivery/transportation work platforms. In the latter case, the overwhelming appraisal

Table 12.3 The benefits of different categories of platform work

Specification of benefits	*On-location routine work*	*On-location moderately skilled work*	*Online moderately skilled work*	*Online specialised work*
Easy labour market access	+		+	
Source of extra income	+	+	+	
A path to self-employment		+		+
Flexibility at work		+		+
Adequate pay	+	+		
Skill development		+		+
Occupational health and safety	+	+	+	+

Source: the authors' own research based on Eurofound (2019).

Table 12.4 The benefits related to platform work based on survey of Uber drivers/delivery persons in US in 2020

Platform work benefits	*Good*	*Okay*	*Poor*
Your flexibility and independence when driving/delivering (like working when and where you want)	76%	19%	5%
Uber's efforts to protect your health and well-being during COVID-19	60%	32%	8%
Uber's efforts to protect your physical safety (unrelated to COVID-19)	55%	35%	10%
Uber's efforts to ensure that riders, Uber Eats customers and restaurant partners treat you with respect	54%	35%	11%

Source: the authors' own research based on Statista (2020).

for flexibility and independence expressed by drivers and delivery persons using Uber's platform is quite universal to platform work in general. On the other hand, empirical evidence based on the online piecework platforms (Mechanical Turk, MobileWorks and CloudFactory) suggests that there are several structural and socio-cognitive constraints limiting this flexibility (Lehdonvirta, 2018). Satisfaction derived from work is to some extent also mediated by cultural and social factors specific to a given country – had the Uber surveys been conducted elsewhere, the results may well have differed significantly.

The challenges associated with platform work

There are also several challenges and caveats associated with the increasing role of digital labour. The report on digital labour markets identified several possible threats related to platformisation (Table 12.5).

Table 12.5 Risks related to different categories of platform work

Risks	*On-location routine work*	*On-location moderately skilled work*	*Online moderately skilled work*	*Online specialised work*
Labour market segmentation	+		+	
Vague employment status	+		+	
Deskilling	+		+	
Problematic rating systems	+		+	+
Lack of autonomy	+		+	
Short notice	+		+	
High work intensity		+		+
Problematic career opportunities	+	+	+	+
unstable earnings	+	+	+	+
Vague health and safety responsibility	+			

Source: the authors' own research based on Eurofound (2019).

There are several risks related to the diffusion of platform work. Among the most important described in the literature are: labour market segmentation and deskilling (especially in applications requiring low to medium qualifications), and vague employment status (are workers self-employed, employees or service providers?). There are also universal concerns about whether platform work enables career planning and stable earnings. Having flexibility also may mean the need to work on short notice and intensively. Additional evidence comes from various reports on work platforms, ones typically based on case study methodology.

A survey conducted in the Netherlands by Robert Half on a sample of managers in the financial, administrative and accounting sectors revealed that increased flexibilisation presents important challenges on the job market (Statista, 2018). The most notable among them for the digital labour market include: the difficulty in evaluating of temporary employees competences (39% mentions), the difficulty in adapting company structures and operations (38%), the difficulty in sustaining the company mission (32%), talent management and performance evaluation (30%), complying with the evolving temporary work legislation (27%) and the rising complexity of human resources of organisations (26%). See Table 12.6 for the results of the survey.

According to another online survey conducted in 2020 in the US on a sample of Uber drivers and delivery persons, a number of factors adversely affect user satisfaction with two issues: using the platform and delivering on-site services. In general, although most of the respondents expressed general satisfaction with the platform work at Uber, a number of negative issues

Table 12.6 Challenges of increased flexibility on the labour market in the Netherlands in 2017

Challenges of increased flexibility	*Share*
There are no challenges	3%
Handling payments and invoices	19%
Adapting the company structure in terms of work places and technology	23%
Employers taking advantage of decreasing personnel costs of temporary employees	23%
Increasing complexity of workforce	26%
Complying with the changing legislation regarding temporary work	27%
Managing the talents and performances of employees	30%
Maintaining the company mission and values among the personnel	32%
Adapting company structures and management styles	38%
Checking and validating the qualities of temporary employees	39%

Source: the authors' own research based on Statista (2018).

Table 12.7 The challenges related to platform work based on a survey of Uber drivers/delivery persons in the US in 2020

Challenges related to platform work	*Good*	*Okay*	*Poor*
Dependability of earnings	32%	41%	27%
Quality of customer support	43%	37%	20%
Responsiveness to feedback	41%	40%	19%
App performance and features	42%	43%	15%

Source: the authors' own research based on Statista (2020).

came to light in answers to the general question: "Overall, how would you rate your driving or delivery experience with Uber in the following areas?" The aspects of the work that came in for the most criticism included earnings dependability (27% rated it as poor) and the quality of customer support (20% rated it as poor). A considerable share of respondents were also dissatisfied with the company's responsiveness to feedback (19%) and app performance and features (15%) (Table 12.7).

Dissatisfaction with platform work using Uber is based on unique, platform-specific factors (such as web application features and customer service) and universal components shared by a given type of platform work in general – for example, income dependability. The income dependability as the latter challenge is reported in other studies on platform work, and to some extent depends on the type of platform work at issue. On-site platform work related to delivery and transportation fall in the middle of the earnings scale compared to other types of digital labour. According to an appjobs.com report on the gig economy, average per hour earnings of delivery person in the US in 2020 (Statista, 2021) were $17.10, while drivers brought in $14.36. The lowest paid platform work were low-skills jobs like cleaning ($11.29 per hour) and pet sitting or walking ($13.17). At the opposite end of the scale were teaching (on average $20.81), freelancers including editors, translators, designers and consultants ($25.33) and massage therapy ($27.84). All of those jobs generally required high qualifications.

Transport platforms raise new regulatory issues. As with other digital platforms like Airbnb, labour platforms have a profound impact on traditional service providers. Transportation platforms like Uber and Blablacar help shape the way people commute in cities and are at least partially used as a substitute for public transportation including trams, railways and buses (Montero, 2019).

Last but not least, digital work platforms have fostered the division of labour activity into simple tasks and activities that can be performed by workers with low qualifications – and potentially be easily replaced by algorithms (job taskification). Indeed, platform work may be one factor that leads humans to be replaced by machines in a growing number of industrial sectors and services (Poutanen, Kovalainen, & Rouvinen, 2019)

Conclusions and practical implications

The rise of the platform economy has changed the landscape of the labour market, not only for employees and their clients (organisations and individuals that use their services), but also for traditional players in the field (service providers, unions). The biggest benefits of platform work – improved access to the labour market (including in rural areas and less-developed countries) and job flexibility – are offset by the rising risk of workforce precarity, career uncertainty and exploitation.

The sector is growing, but its size is not fully represented in the official statistics. A recent study done in the US revealed that gig work contributes to approximately 3.8 million full-time jobs, and if accounted for the real employment rate would be 4 pp higher (Bracha & Burke, 2021). The digital revolution poses several challenges and has several policy implications. A new regulatory framework is needed to ensure that labour platforms thanks to their economic efficiency and relative lack of legal burdens, do not crowd out traditional service providers. As noted in the case of on-line transportation platforms, the process has already started, and created substantial tensions in several European countries (Montero, 2019). The ongoing platformisation has significant consequences for the future of cities as it may transform the modes of mass transportation, commuting behaviours and the urban landscape itself (Stevens & Shearmur, 2020).

Digital platforms and the work they enable require more research for three reasons. First, based on the growth dynamics, it is safe to say that until the 2030s platformisation will dominate in several industries that currently rely on traditional employment. Companies are willing to rely on platform work thanks to the lack of regulatory measures in place, financial and organisational benefits, especially in case of standard assignments and routine works (Schroeder et al., 2021). Second, digital platforms are understudied in emerging economies, where digital transformation of the labour market is even faster and challenges related to inequality, exploitation of workforce and job precarity pose even more of a threaten. Finally, platform work is in constant flux due to market mechanisms, competition between platform providers and technological advancement.

References

Bracha, A., & Burke, M.A. (2021). How big is the gig? The extensive margin, the intensive margin, and the hidden margin. *Labour Economics, 69*, 101974. doi:10.1016/j.labeco.2021.101974

Eurofound (2018a). *Automation, digitisation and platforms: Implications for work and employment. Publications Office of the European Union, Luxembourg.* Available at from http://eurofound.link/ef18002%0Ahttps://digitalcommons.ilr.cornell.edu/intl/636%0Ahttp://eurofound.link/ef18002 (accessed 15 September 2021).

Eurofound (2018b). *Employment and working conditions of selected types of platform work. Employment and working conditions of selected types of platform work.* Available at: https://www.eurofound.europa.eu/sites/default/files/wpef18053en.pdf (accessed 16 September 2021).

Eurofound (2019). *Platform work: Maximising the potential while safeguarding standards?* Luxembourg: Publications Office of the European Union. doi:10.2806/212968

Fabo, B., Beblavý, M., Kilhoffer, Z., & Lenaerts, K. (2017). *An overview of European platforms: Scope and business models* (No. JRC109190). *JRC Working Papers.* doi:10.2760/762447

Florisson, R., & Mandl, I. (2018). *Platform work: Types and implications for work and employment – Literature review* (No. WPEF18004). *Digital age – Eurofound.* Available at: https://www.eurofound.europa.eu/sites/default/files/wpef18004.pdf (accessed 15 September 2021).

Hartono, M., Raharjo, H., & Ronyastra, I.M. (2021). What difference does the gig mobility service make in the workers' human needs structure? *International Journal of Industrial Ergonomics, 82*, 103100. doi:10.1016/j.ergon.2021.103100

International Labour Office (2021). The role of digital labour platforms in transforming the world of work. World Employment and Social Outlook. Available at: https://www.ilo.org/wcmsp5/groups/public/---dgreports/---dcomm/---publ/documents/publication/wcms_771749.pdf (accessed 15 September 2021).

Lehdonvirta, V. (2018). Flexibility in the gig economy: Managing time on three online piecework platforms. *New Technology, Work and Employment, 33*(1), 13–29. doi:10.1111/ntwe.12102

Montero, J.J. (2019). *Regulating transport platforms: The case of carpooling in Europe.* Springer International Publishing. doi:10.1007/978-3-319–96526-0_2

Pesole, A., Biagi, F., Fernández-Macías, Brancati, E., Urzí, M. C., & González Vázquez, I. (2018). *Platform workers in Europe – Publications Office of the EU.* Luxembourg: Publications Office of the European Union. doi:10.2760/742789

Poutanen, S., Kovalainen, A., & Rouvinen, P. (2019). *Digital work in the platform economy. Digital work and the platform economy.* doi:10.4324/9780429467929-1

Schroeder, A.N., Bricka, T.M., & Whitaker, J.H. (2021). Work design in a digitized gig economy. *Human Resource Management Review, 31*(1), 100692. doi:10.1016/j.hrmr.2019.100692

Spurk, D., & Straub, C. (2020). Flexible employment relationships and careers in times of the COVID-19 pandemic. *Journal of Vocational Behavior, 119*, 103435. doi:10.1016/j.jvb.2020.103435

Statista (2018). Robert Half Salarisgids 2018. Available at: statista.com (accessed 15 September 2021).

Statista (2020). 2020 Uber experience survey. Available at: statista.com (accessed 15 September 2021).

Stevens, L., & Shearmur, R.G. (2020). The end of location theory? Some implications of micro-work, work trajectories and gig-work for conceptualizing the urban space economy. *Geoforum, 111*, 155–164. doi:10.1016/j.geoforum.2020.02.010

Tan, Z.M., Aggarwal, N., Cowls, J., Morley, J., Taddeo, M., & Floridi, L. (2021). The ethical debate about the gig economy: A review and critical analysis. *Technology in Society, 65*, 101594. doi:10.1016/j.techsoc.2021.101594

Tracxn Technologies (2021). Acquisitions by delivery hero. Available at: https://tracxn.com/d/acquisitions/acquisitionsbyDelivery-Hero (accessed 15 September 2021).

Urzì Brancati, C., Pesole, A., & Fernández-Macías, E. (2019). *Digital labour platforms in Europe : Numbers, profiles, and employment status of platform workers. JRC Technical Reports.* doi:10.2760/16653

Wach, K. (2014). The theoretical modelling of the firm-level international competitiveness in business studies (Chapter 5), In D. Kiendl-Wendner & K. Wach (Eds.), *International competitiveness in Visegrad countries: Macro and micro perspective* (pp. 33–43). Graz: Fachhochschule Joanneum.

13 Casual work in the digital economy

Joanna Kudełko and Dariusz Żmija

Introduction

The digital transformation affects all areas of social and economic life. One of the effects of on-going changes is that flexible forms of employment and non-standard job contracts, which differ from traditional employment systems based on long-term employment agreements, have become more widely used (Degryse, 2016; Małkowska, Urbaniec, & Kosała, 2021). The flexible character of work concerns the forms of employment, the type of tasks done and the time and place at which they are performed (Brenner, 2004). Employment flexibility enables both the number and competencies of employees to be adapted to changing conditions and needs (Piątkowski, 2020).

Traditional employer–employee relations are changing. In Europe, new forms of employment supplement long-term employment contracts: employee sharing, job sharing, voucher-based work, interim management, casual work, ICT-based mobile work, platform work, portfolio work and collaborative employment (Eurofound, 2020).

New forms of employment include casual work, characterised by the lack of permanence and regularity. According to the definition proposed by the European Parliament (2000), casual work is irregular or intermittent work in which permanent employment is not expected. It can involve irregular working hours and work schedules. Such work is not stable and does not guarantee the continuous employment, benefits or the protection enjoyed by permanent staff. Employers are not obligated to provide permanent work opportunities – workers are employed on a flexible (on-call) basis (Eurofound, 2015). Casual workers are hired on temporary work contracts. They do not have long-term relationships with employers, which implies a lack of job security and limited access to social benefits (Eurofound, 2007).

Casual work is usually performed by young people or low-skilled workers. The most common reason for accepting this form of work is the lack of standard full-time work opportunities, though earning additional income to complement one's earnings from full-time employment may also be a factor (Eurofound, 2019). This form of work is mainly used in agriculture, tourism, gastronomy and entertainment – sectors characterised by seasonality and up

DOI: 10.4324/9781003254638-17

and down demand for workers. Casual work is strongly affected by changes in business cycles. In worsened economic circumstances, employers are more inclined to hire casual workers (Eurofound, 2020). According to Eurofound, there are two types of casual work (Eurofound, 2017):

- intermittent work – hiring a worker for a limited period of time, a specific number of working days, or a period required to perform a specific task (implementing a project or seasonal work). Employers hire workers on a regular or irregular basis. Such solutions are more common in Belgium, Croatia, France, Hungary, Italy, Romania, Slovakia and Slovenia.
- on-call work – is based on an employment contract but isn't permanent; so, an employer can hire people on an on-call basis. Work schedules are based on a specific number of working hours during a week or a month. This solution is commonly used in Ireland, Italy, the Netherlands, Sweden and the UK.

Some countries do not differentiate between these two types of work (e.g., Czechia, Malta, Poland and Portugal). Despite the increasing use of flexible forms of employment, EU countries differ considerably in how they see legislation, work relationships, the concept of a "worker" and the application of labour regulations (Dockès, 2019). Also, with regard to casual work, European countries lack clear-cut regulations or standards. This form of work is regulated by each individual company.

For example, legal regulations set forth a maximum number of working hours or a maximum period that a temporary work contract can be used. In Czechia, intermittent workers work not more than 300 hours during a calendar year. Italy limits temp workers to 400 hours in a three-year period. If work is performed for longer than that, the contract is transformed into an unlimited full-time agreement. In Italy, this regulation does not apply to workers below the age of 24 and above the age of 55 in tourism, gastronomy and entertainment. In some countries, employers must notify workers in advance of the date of work (in the case of intermittent work). Portugal, where employers must give workers a 20-day notice (Eurofound, 2020), is one such country.

The scale of casual work cannot be precisely determined, as most European countries do not keep relevant statistical data. Casual workers are included in statistics on temporary work or part-time work (Eurofound, 2020). Poland is among the countries that do not treat casual work as a separate form of employment, and its legal regulations do not recognise the term "casual work". Temporary workers are hired on the basis of civil law contracts. The Polish civil code describes two types of such contracts (Ustawa, 2021):

- contract of mandate – covers the performance of tasks in a specified period of time;
- contract for specific work – concerns the performance of a specific task.

Official statistical data on the labour market indicate that, in Poland in 2018, the total number of workers hired by temporary work agencies amounted to 102,000, accounting for 0.64% of Poland's working population. At the same time, 998,900 workers, or 6.26% of the working population, worked on the basis of a contract of mandate and did not have other employment contracts, while 105,700 workers (who did not have other employment contracts) were contracted for specific work (0.66%) (Yearbook of Labour Statistics, 2019). These data indicate that a small percentage of workers are employed under non-standard employment contracts. The aim of this chapter is to analyse casual work as a new form of employment using a selected example. The case study presents workers employed by a Polish temporary work agency, delegated to work abroad for German courier companies as warehouse keepers-sorters.

The benefits and threats of casual work

New forms of employment generate benefits as well as threats for employers and employees, especially in the case of casual work. One benefit for employers is the flexibility to adapt the number of staff to current needs. It is a convenient solution in the face of uncertain demand for products and services. Entrepreneurs can effectively respond to market conditions, hiring more people in favourable market circumstances and vice versa. Casual work is also effective in seasonal business activities. The labour costs generated by temporary workers are lower than those generated by long-term contracts. Employers do not incur costs in periods of decreased economic activity and lower profitability. Those offering work can better adapt labour resources to specific activities and demand for their products or services, and hire workers on a call-on basis depending on company needs. As necessary, reliable employees can be hired quickly, with labour costs resulting from recruitment and onboarding processes kept in check (Eurofound, 2020).

Of course, hiring casual workers can also have negative effects for the employer. Workers tend not to become attached to their jobs or to identify themselves with a company because they lack stability and job security (Tremblay, 2008). For this reason, casual work is characterised by high employee turnover. Employees leave a company when they find a better paid job or employment closer to their residence. Casual work is often not stable, so those doing it often quit even if other employers offer longer job opportunities. High employee turnover can decrease a company's stability and necessitates continuous recruitment and, sometimes, training. However, given that casual workers usually perform simple and routine tasks and are easily replaceable, the training aspect may be less of a problem. Moreover, the companies need not invest a lot in time-consuming training as temporary workers most often perform low-skilled and simple tasks.

A more serious problem is posed by casual workers' lower productivity. Temporary workers have no prospects for long-term employment and promotions, so they are not motivated to increase their productivity. It seems that greater work flexibility should enable companies to effectively allocate resources and, consequently, increase innovativeness (Bartelsman, Gautier, & Wind, 2016). However, as the results of many studies indicate, the trend is the opposite. Greater work flexibility deteriorates the quality of workstations, hindering companies' technological changes, innovativeness and competitiveness. Reljic, Cetrulo, Cirillo and Coveri (2021) conducted research studies of temporary and part-time work in Germany, France, Italy, the Netherlands and the UK in 18 industrial sectors and 23 service sectors. They pointed to a clearly negative correlation between the share of workers hired on the basis of non-standard employment contracts and product- and process-related innovation. Reliance on casual workers does not encourage businesses to introduce technological changes and product and process innovation, which constitutes a major barrier to technological advancement, particularly for high-tech industries.

Similar findings were presented by Cetrulo, Cirillo and Guarascio (2019), who analysed industrial sectors. They found a negative correlation between temporary work and companies' inclination to introduce product innovation. This mainly applies to companies in which silent knowledge about a given activity plays a key role. The results of studies also indicate that hiring temporary and part-time workers as well as those with limited employment contracts considerably decreases companies' productivity, resulting in reduced R&D investments for the purpose of increased innovativeness (Cappellari, Dell'Aringa, & Leonardi, 2012; Grinza & Quatraro, 2019). High turnover among casual workers and their lack of motivation can have a negative impact on the quality of products and services, and, consequently, a company's image and its long-term competitive position (Eurofound, 2019).

Casual workers' low productivity results from, among others things, insufficient investment in the development of human capital. High employee turnover does not justify the costs of increasing workers' qualifications, and the lack of training opportunities lowers the level of their competencies (Ortega & Marchante, 2010). Also, employees themselves, without good prospects for developing professional careers, are not motivated, so their productivity is lowered. Moreover, they are not inclined to gain a company's silent knowledge, but prefer to acquire general skills that may prove useful in looking for other jobs (Bassanini, Nunziata, & Venn 2009).

Another reason for casual workers' low productivity is the lack of trust between employers and employees, which results from uncertainty and low motivation on the part of the latter to contribute to the company's development. Yet another barrier is that people in workplaces are not integrated and are often not inclined to cooperate and share acquired silent knowledge that they could disseminate, thereby increasing a company's knowledge potential (Svensson, 2011).

In conclusion, casual work generates benefits and threats both for employers and employees. People have individual attitudes to casual work, depending on their preferences and life situation. This form of employment is beneficial for those who cannot work full time, including people who are not available for full-time jobs, like mothers with small children, students or retired people who take on casual work to increase their income.

Part-time work and flexible working hours make it possible to balance one's career and household duties (Beauregard & Henry, 2009). Such solutions are beneficial for childcare providers or persons who are dependent on others, such as the elderly. Casual work enables them to combine professional and other responsibilities and to earn additional income. It can also be an additional source of income for low earners.

Therefore, flexible forms of employment increase some people's personal satisfaction and improve their wellbeing as workers (ter Hoeven & Van Zoonen, 2015; Wang, Lawler, & Shi, 2011). Moreover, people often take up casual employment not because of their preferences but due to the lack of other job opportunities – full-time jobs offering stability and security that they would choose if they had a chance to do so. Casual work does not satisfy the needs of people who intend to become dedicated workers concerned with their self-development. The main problems include low wages, the lack of job security and stable income, inappropriate working conditions and no promotion opportunities (Kalleberg, 2011). Casual workers do not have good prospects for professional development and higher earnings, particularly at the beginning of their careers when entering the labour market (de Lange, Gesthuizen, & Wolbers, 2014). In addition to that, unlike ongoing employment arrangements, casual work does not provide social security benefits. According to labour codes, the loss of one's job is not compensated (de Stefano, 2016). Other drawbacks of flexible forms of employment include the lack of job security and limited prospects for professional development and promotion (Bone, 2006; Leslie, Park, & Mehng, 2012; Whittle & Mueller, 2009), irregular and unpredictable earnings, limited access to trainings and social security benefits.

Therefore, as with other alternative forms of employment, casual work increases the risk of precarity, workers' poverty and labour market segmentation (European Parliament, 2016). Moreover, casual workers belong to the groups of employees most vulnerable to job loss in the periods of economic crisis, when employers are forced to cut jobs (Eurofound, 2020). The lack of stability and job security, low earnings and limited prospects for professional development can have a negative impact on workers' health and wellbeing. The resulting stress also affects life choices, such as young people make when deciding whether to start a family.

Research methodology

The empirical part of this chapter is based on a case study. The method explores single objects and draws general conclusions for entire populations. It analyses one case in detail for the purpose of gaining a full understanding of the population. The selected case does not confirm universal phenomena.

The analysis is based on the case of a temporary work agency based in Krakow, Poland, the capital of Małopolska voivodeship. To protect personal data and classified information, the name of the agency is not disclosed. The agency recruits casual and temporary workers who are posted to work in Germany. Recruited individuals are males seeking employment in the sorting warehouses of courier companies, mainly GLS in Neuenstein, and several smaller GLS depots near Munich and Augsburg. Some employees are transferred to DPD in Chemnitz and Morsdorf, DHL in Ludwigsau and HERMES in Ohrdruf. The recruits perform manual tasks as warehouse workers.

The study covers the period from November 2019 to September 2021 and answers the following research questions: (1) to what extent were the 964 casual workers employed during the period under review? and (2) what are the main features of these casual workers? Answers to these questions are based on an analysis of data obtained from the temporary work agency. The relevant data were statistically analysed using stratified weighting. The results allowed for formulating conclusions.

Research findings

The youngest workers of the 964 males recruited during the 23 months were aged 18, while the oldest person was 58 years old. Most workers were young – 70% were below the age of 35. The majority of casual workers (400) were aged 18–24, accounting for 42% of all workers (Table 13.1). Another large group was represented by males aged 25–35 (271 workers –28%). Slightly older workers, aged 35–44 (175), represented 18% of those recruited, and 107 individuals, 11%, were aged 45–54. Only 11, or 1%, were aged above 55 years.

The results of the study show that it was mainly young people that applied for temporary jobs. This is likely due to two reasons. First, young people are more inclined to do manual work, which requires physical effort and good health. Second, this particular work involved being seconded from Poland to Germany. Young people are more mobile, and many have yet to start

Table 13.1 Number of workers by age groups

Age of workers	Number of workers
18–24	400
25–34	271
35–44	175
45–54	107
55 and above	11
Total	*964*

Source: the author's own research.

Table 13.2 Number of workers by duration of employment

Total duration of work (months)	Number of workers
below 1	412
[1,3)	361
[3,6)	96
[6,12)	53
above 12	42
Total	*964*

Source: the author's own research.

families, making them more inclined to work away from their permanent residence.

An important metric with casual work is the duration of work expressed in days or months. Because of the nature of the work, the number of working days is usually relatively small, a fact reflected in the present case. Of the 964 workers, as many as 773, or 80%, worked for not longer than three months (Table 13.2). The largest group was made up of workers who worked for less than one month (412 individuals, 43%). A relatively large group worked from one to three months (361, 37%). A small group worked from three to six months (96, 10%). There were rare cases of work from 6 to 12 months (53 people, 6%) and longer than 12 months (42 males, 4%).

The results of the study point to a high employee turnover rate among casual workers in courier company sorting warehouses. It can be assumed that employees were not attached to their positions: They were inclined to leave when they found employment closer to their permanent residence or when offered higher pay elsewhere. Work far from permanent residence proved problematic because workers had to leave their families. From the perspective of the courier companies, hiring casual workers is beneficial because their labour costs less than that of German workers. However, employers cannot expect casual workers to remain in their employ for longer periods of time. This is not a major problem – workers who quit are quickly replaced by new recruits. High turnover rates do not involve high costs as the work does not require specific qualifications or time and funds to be spent on training.

Looking at the age of workers relative to the duration of their employment provides interesting insights into the analysis and allows correlations between these two factors to be determined. The study compares the number of workdays by age groups based on the average of workdays in particular age groups. The average number of workdays for all employees came in at 73 (Table 13.3), with some differences recorded in particular age groups. The youngest workers (aged 18–24) stood out from the remaining groups, with an average of 56 workdays.

Differences in the older age groups were not significant. The average number of workdays ranged from 77 (workers aged 45–54) to 89 (35–44).

Table 13.3 Average workdays by age groups

Total duration of work (months)	**Number of workers**
below 1	412
[1,3)	361
[3,6)	96
[6,12)	53
above 12	42
Total	*964*

Source: the author's own research.

Table 13.4 The share of workers in different age groups who take casual employment multiple times (in %)

Age of workers	**Share in the total number of workers**
18–24	15%
25–34	25%
35–44	26%
45–54	21%
55 and above	36%
Total	*20%*

Source: the author's own research.

Interestingly, the oldest employees (55+) worked for a relatively long period of time (83 days). The results of the study lead to the conclusion that the youngest workers, aged 18–24, were least determined to take up employment abroad as manual workers despite being regarded as the most mobile group. Older workers demonstrated more perseverance, especially those aged 25–34 and 35–44, perhaps because the individuals that make up these groups are determined to increase their income to support their families. Another reason may be that older people do not have a strong position on the labour market, so they are less inclined to give up temporary jobs.

As the data show, some casual workers are hired by the temporary work agency more than once in the same workplace. Of the 964 individuals in the group, 198 (20%) have taken up employment several times intermittently, while most have taken up such jobs twice, and there are cases where employment repeated four or five times. The oldest workers (aged 55 and above) are the most inclined to be hired again in the same place (Table 13.4), with as many as 36% taking on the same numerous times. The youngest workers (aged 18–24) are least inclined to do so (15%).

It is difficult to explicitly explain the motivation of workers who take on casual jobs in the same place twice or many times. It can be assumed that it is mainly low-skilled older workers with no other job prospects. Young workers show less determination to continue their jobs. They may also be more focused on looking for other jobs which offer better prospects for professional development.

Conclusions and future directions

Casual work is a flexible form of employment. Its main feature is irregular employment for a specified period of time. As such, it does not guarantee ongoing employment. Employers use workers' services when they find it necessary. Employers can benefit from this arrangement thanks to the possibility of adapting the number of staff to a company's changing situation and reducing labour costs as compared with the system of full-time employment. At the same time, casual work is characterised by high employee turnover, which obviously does not increase a company's stability, forcing it to instead continuously supplement staff. Moreover, hiring casual workers hinders the introduction of technological changes and innovation, decreasing market competitiveness. From the perspective of workers, casual work is attractive for people who are not available for full-time employment. Unfortunately, it distorts employment stability and does not offer high wages and development opportunities, nor does it provide employees with social security benefits.

The research study presented in this chapter describes the case of a Polish temporary work agency which recruits males for the positions of warehouse sorting workers in German courier companies. Over the nearly two years between November 2019 and September 2021, the agency recruited 964 workers, a relatively large group. The results of the study indicate that applicants were mainly young males under the age of 35. Employee turnover is high – workdays in courier companies averaged 73, with the shortest time of employment recorded for the youngest group aged 18–24. Young workers were also the least inclined to take on jobs in the same place, likely thanks to their better job prospects.

Issues related to casual work represent a vast research area. The considerations presented here are based on one case study. The conclusions of this chapter open the way for further in-depth research. Future work could be supplemented by other case studies and comparisons of other temporary work agencies. Another area that is ripe for investigation is employment changes over longer periods of time. A valuable contribution to this field of study could be made by comparisons of casual work in particular EU countries. Exploring the opinions of casual workers themselves along with their motives to take on such employment would also be a revealing and fruitful area of research.

References

Bartelsman, E.J., Gautier, P.A., & Wind, J.D. (2016). Employment protection, technology choice, and worker allocation. *International Economic Review, 57*(3), 787–826.

Bassanini, A., Nunziata, L., & Venn, D. (2009). Job protection legislation and productivity growth in OECD countries. *Economic Policy, 24*(58), 349–402.

Beauregard, T.A., & Henry, L.C. (2009.) Making the link between work–Life balance practices and organizational performance. *Human Resource Management Review, 19*(1), 9–22.

Bone, J. (2006). The longest day: 'Flexible' contracts, performance-related pay and risk shifting in the UK direct selling sector. *Work, Employment & Society, 20*(1), 109–127.

Brenner, Ch. (2004). Labor in the network society: Lessons from silicon valley. In M. Castells (Eds.), *The network society. A cross-cultural perspective* (pp. 174–197). Cheltenham: Edward Elgar Publishing.

Cappellari, L., Dell'Aringa, C., & Leonardi, M. (2012). Temporary employment, job flows and productivity: A tale of two reforms. *Economic Journal, 122*(562), F188–F215.

Cetrulo, A., Cirillo, V., & Guarascio, D. (2019). Weaker jobs, weaker innovation. Exploring the effects of temporary employment on new products. *Applied Economics, 51*(59), 6350–6375.

Degryse, C. (2016). *Digitalisation of the economy and its impact on labour markets.* Brussels: ETUI aisbl.

de Lange, M., Gesthuizen, M., & Wolbers, M.H. (2014). Consequences of flexible employment at labour market entry for early career development in the Netherlands. *Economic and Industrial Democracy, 35*(3), 413–434.

de Stefano, V. (2016). Casual work beyond casual work in the EU: The underground casualisation of the European workforce – And what to do about it. *European Labour Law Journal,* 7(3), 421–441.

Dockès, E. (2019). New trade union strategies for new forms of employment. *European Labour Law Journal, 10*(3), 219–228. doi:10.1177/2031952519870061.

Eurofound. (2007). Casual worker. Available at: https://www.eurofound.europa.eu/observatories/eurwork/industrial-relations-dictionary/casual-worker (accessed 10 August 2021).

Eurofound. (2015). *New forms of employment.* Luxembourg: Publications Office of the European Union. Available at: https://www.eurofound.europa.eu/publications/report/2015/new-forms-of-employment (accessed 10 August 2021).

Eurofound. (2017). Casual work. Available at: https://www.eurofound.europa.eu/observatories/eurwork/industrial-relations-dictionary/casual-work (accessed 15 September 2021).

Eurofound. (2019). Casual work: Characteristics and implications, New forms of employment series. Luxembourg: Publications Office of the European Union. Available at: https://www.eurofound.europa.eu/sites/default/files/ef_publication/field_ef_document/ef18044en.pdf (accessed 10 August 2021).

Eurofound. (2020). Labour market change: Trends and policy approaches towards flexibilisation, Challenges and prospects in the EU series. Luxembourg: Publications Office of the European Union. Available at: https://www.eurofound.europa.eu/publications/flagship-report/2020/labour-market-change-trends-and-policy-approaches-towards-flexibilisation (accessed 10 August 2021).

European Parliament. (2000). A typical work in the EU. Working Paper, Social Affairs Series, SOCI 106. Luxembourg.

European Parliament. (2016). Precarious employment in Europe: Patterns, trends and policy strategy. Available at: https://www.europarl.europa.eu/RegData/etudes/

STUD/2016/587285/IPOL_STU(2016)587285_EN.pdf (accessed 15 September 2021).

Grinza, E., & Quatraro, F. (2019). Workers' replacements and firms' innovation dynamics: New evidence from Italian matched longitudinal data. *Research Policy, 48*(9), 103804.

Kalleberg, A.L. (2011). *Good jobs, bad jobs: The rise of polarized and precarious employment systems in the United States, 1970s-2000s*. New York: Russell Sage Foundation.

Leslie, L.M., Park, T.Y., & Mehng, S. (2012). Flexible work practices: A source of career premiums or penalties? *Academy of Management Journal, 55*(6), 1407–1428.

Małkowska, A., Urbaniec, M., & Kosała, M. (2021). The impact of digital transformation on European countries: Insights from a comparative analysis. *Equilibrium. Quarterly Journal of Economics and Economic Policy, 16*(2), 325–355.

Ortega, B., & Marchante, A.J. (2010). Temporary contracts and labour productivity in Spain: A sectoral analysis. *Journal of Productivity Analysis, 34*(3), 199–212.

Piątkowski, M. (2020). Expectations and challenges in the labour market in the context of industrial revolution 4.0. The agglomeration method-based analysis for Poland and other EU member states. *Sustainability, 12*, 5437. doi:10.3390/su12135437.

Reljic, J., Cetrulo, A., Cirillo, V., & Coveri, A. (2021). Non-standard work and innovation: Evidence from European industries. *Laboratory of Economics and Management Working Paper Series, 6*, Available at: http://www.lem.sssup.it/WPLem/files/2021-06.pdf (accessed 25 August 2021).

Svensson, S. (2011). Flexible working conditions and decreasing levels of trust. *Employee Relations, 34*(2), 126–137.

Ter Hoeven, C.L., & Van Zoonen, W. (2015). Flexible work designs and employee well-being: Examining the effects of resources and demands. *New Technology, Work and Employment, 30*(3), 237–255.

Tremblay, D.G. (2008). From casual work to economic security; the paradoxical case of self-employment. *Social Indicators Research, 88*(1), 115–130.

Ustawa z dnia 24 czerwca 2021 r. o zmianie ustawy – Kodeks cywilny. Dz.U.2021 poz. 1509 (The Act of 24 June 2021 on Amendments to the Act – the Civil Code (Dz.U.2021/Journal of Laws/ point 1509).

Yearbook of Labour Statistics (2019). Warsaw: Central Statistical Office.

Wang, P., Lawler, J.J., & Shi, K. (2011). Implementing family-friendly employment practices in banking industry: Evidences from some African and Asian countries. *Journal of Occupational and Organizational Psychology, 84*(3), 493–517.

Whittle, A., & Mueller, F. (2009). 'I could be dead for two weeks and my boss would never know': Telework and the politics of representation. *New Technology, Work and Employment, 24*(2), 131–143.

14 Remote work in the digital economy

Michał Głuszak and Agnieszka Małkowska

Introduction

Remote working (RM) has become increasingly common in recent years, thanks primarily to the incredible technological advances in information and communication technology (ICT), globalisation and increased competitiveness in the economy and, in the last two years, the COVID-19 pandemic (Urbaniec, Małkowska, & Włodarkiewicz-Klimek, 2022). Remote working is one of the most widespread flexible working arrangements in the world today. Its development is clearly conditioned by the digital transformation, which has opened up new opportunities for business by breaking down geographical barriers to information, teamwork and employee-co-worker-manager-employer interactions. The development and availability of mobile technologies, mainly smartphones and tablets, and the reach of internet networks mean that work can be done anytime and anywhere.

A generic definition of remote working describes it as organisational work done outside the normal organisational boundaries of space and time (Olson, 1983). Business practice has developed various forms of work that can be regarded as remote working. The differentiation has been enriched and clarified by scientific publications further defining and systematising these forms. However, there is no uniform approach in either the terminology or conceptualisation of remote working models. Depending on their needs, the authors highlight different features that they consider important for this concept, and the definitions they provide are not always consistent (Mokhtarian, 1991). The various terms for remote working include distributed work, flexible work arrangement, telecommuting, telework, ICT-based work, eWork, virtual teams, mobile virtual work and work from home (Allen, Golden, & Shockley, 2005; Savić, 2020). The literature distinguishes four main dimensions used in definitions of remote working (Garrett & Danziger, 2007):

- the location of the work (e.g. home-based and non-home-based locations; flexiworker, fixed-site teleworker, mobile teleworker);
- the use of ICT technology (remote working makes ICTs essential to the work performed);

DOI: 10.4324/9781003254638-18

- the temporal distribution of the work in relation to its location (e.g. full time, part-time flexi-time workers);
- the formal arrangements between the employee and employer (e.g. regular employees, self-employed, contract workers).

The traditional and most commonly used synonyms for remote working are "*telework*" and "*telecommuting*" (Madsen, 2011). The term *telecommuting* reflects the essence of the matter, which is the replacement of physical commuting to the workplace (commuting) with remote access (thanks to ICT tools). Indeed, the initial push into telecommuting were a response to transport, urban and environmental problems (Nilles, 1975, 1988). The more commonly used term in Europe, *teleworking,* is defined by the EU as

> a form of organising and/or performing work, using information technology, in the context of an employment contract/ relationship, where work, which could also be performed at the employer's premises, is carried out away from those premises on a regular basis.
>
> (ETUC, 2002)

The entirely voluntary nature of telework for both employee and employer is also important from a regulatory point of view. Research on teleworking has developed robustly since the 1970s, and although emerging new nomenclature and definitions signal the diversity of forms of remote work, teleworking (telecommuting) seems to be the most universal term, applicable to working from home as well as from other locations.

A central feature of remote working is that it is done at a distance, off-site, and the location need not be limited to a single place. Morgan (2004) lists five typical telework locations:

- home-based telework – work is done mainly in the employee's own home rather than at an office;
- telecentres – typically local facilities that provide workspace for people who want to work away from a central location, thus reducing commuting costs, but do not want to work from home;
- functional relocation – business functions (and processes) are concentrated and performed at a distance, from anywhere using remote access to systems;
- telecottages – also local facilities created for local communities to facilitate access to work and technology, aimed at supporting and enabling personal interaction between workers who are not necessarily working full-time;
- mobile telework – the employee is not located in one place but moves, for example, between the premises of clients or employers.

Of the above, *working-from-home* (WFH) has attracted the most attention from researchers. Before the breakthrough year 2020, contributing to the move to toward home-based work were a better work-life balance, higher productivity and reduced absenteeism, and increased access to employees with special requirements or constraints (Baker, Avery, & Crawford, 2007). Working from home has an impact on the employee's personal life, the work performed and the organisation providing the work. How this impact will develop cannot be clearly predicted in advance, as the circumstances and conditions underlying the decision to work remotely, as well as the way in which it is implemented and managed, will all come to beard.

It is generally assumed that flexible arrangements that allow employees to work from home some of the time have a positive impact on their personal and family life. On an individual level, increased job satisfaction (Wheatley, 2012) and well-being are among the positive effects (Anderson, Kaplan, & Vega, 2015). However, research findings are often mixed, probably because the home working model analysed – full-time or part-time (Gajendran & Harrison, 2007), the expected duration of telework (Bailey & Kurland, 2002), but also the ability to control the boundaries between work and home by employee (Basile & Beauregard, 2016) – can all skew results. For example, flexibility in the scheduling of work and family obligations and time saved thanks to the lack of a daily commute are expected to contribute to the mitigation of work-family conflicts (Lautsch, Kossek, & Eaton, 2009). But there is also evidence (Eddleston & Mulki, 2017) that work-family integration increases mutual family-work conflicts. Moreover, working from home full-time causes some to overwork and leads them to neglect their family roles. The positive impact of remote working on work performance is expected mainly in terms of increased productivity as a result of longer working hours and modification of the working environment leading to reduced distractions. Working from home may also reduce the turnover intentions and work stress (Gajendran & Harrison, 2007). From an organisational perspective, remote working can lead to increased organisational commitment (Martin, & MacDonnel, 2012) and trust (Taboroši, Strukan, Poštin, Konjikušić, & Nikoloć 2020), but also worsen the quality of both workplace relationships (with co-workers and supervisors), especially under high-intensity arrangements (Gajendran & Harrison, 2007) and knowledge transfer within the organisation (Taskin & Bridoux, 2010). An interesting topic, identified in research even before 2020, is the role of remote working as a solution to ensuring business continuity in emergency circumstances (weather events, epidemics) (Allen et al., 2015).

Despite the range of potential benefits of work-from-home options, support from public policy and the progressing opportunities created by technology, this form of working tended to be exclusive until 2020 and used more widely in only a handful of professions and workplaces. Although the number of employees working at least occasionally remotely has increased since the 1970s, this form of work has not been widespread. As Figure 14.1 illustrates, the scale has also varied across the countries of the EU.

Countries where working from home was practically non-existent until 2019 include Bulgaria (98.9% of employees had never worked from home) and Romania (98.6%). In addition, the highest percentage of inexperience in

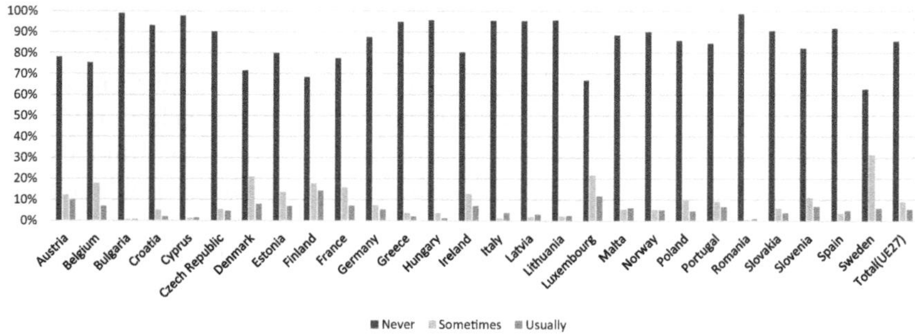

Figure 14.1 The prevalence of working from home in EU countries in 2019 by the structure of employees with experience working from home (in %)

Source: the authors' own research based on Eurostat (2019).

working from home was recorded in Central and Eastern European countries (Lithuania, Hungary, Latvia, Croatia, Slovakia and Czech Republic) and some Southern European countries (Cyprus, Italy, Greece and Spain). In contrast, a relatively high proportion of homeworkers (those who sometimes or often worked from home) was noted in Northern and Western Europe (Sweden, Luxembourg, Finland, Denmark, Belgium and France). One reason for this variation is the unique nature of the countries' economies and labour markets, and the degree of digital transformation and technological readiness to implement remote working (Chakravorti & Chaturvedi, 2020; Małkowska, Urbaniec, & Kosała, 2021).

Of course, the real catalyst for working from home proved to be the COVID-19 pandemic, which on an unprecedented scale radically reduced the ability to work from offices. Social distancing, forced isolation and lockdowns confined people around the world to their homes. Working from home was suddenly no longer a voluntary choice and privilege for professionals, but a necessity for everyone – employees, managers and employers. Moreover, it is predicted that even once the epidemic crisis is over, working from home will become a permanent feature of the labour market (Senz, 2020). Figure 14.2 shows the magnitude of remote working in European countries in 2020, stimulated by the COVID-19 pandemic.

The scale of work from home done in EU Countries in 2019 (Figure 14.1) and 2020 (Figure 14.2) shows that a huge progression has taken place. In countries that were already prepared through previous experience (Netherlands, Belgium, Finland, Ireland and Luxembourg), between 50% and 60% of employees worked from home. However, countries with a relative lack of experience with remote working, including Bulgaria and Romania, also recorded a significant increase. The largest increases in the share of home-based workers in 2020 (Figure 14.2) compared to 2019 (Figure 14.1) were found in

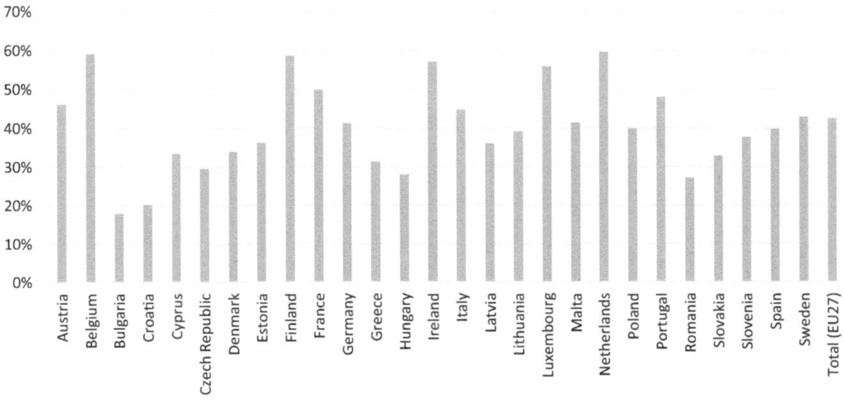

Figure 14.2 The prevalence of working from home in EU countries in 2020 during the COVID-19 pandemic

Source: the authors' own research based on Eurofound (2020)

Norway (49% increase), Italy (40%), Ireland (37%) and Lithuania (35%). The smallest increases in home-based workers were found in Denmark (5%) and Sweden (6%). Across the EU27, the average increase in the proportion of homeworkers was 28%.

The progress made in this field raises the question of how the remote working formula works. The digital economy and technological innovation have laid the current foundations for the development of flexible forms of work, including remote working, but specific pandemic conditions have accelerated these processes (Urbaniec, Małkowska, & Włodarkiewicz-Klimek, 2022). The emergency situation that has pushed companies and employees to move work from the office to the home justifies a new look at the benefits and challenges of remote working. Our research was conducted from the perspective of the company and its representatives in management. It assesses the benefits and challenges for the organisation in implementing remote working in the age of the digital economy, and in particular during the COVID-19 pandemic.

Research methodology

The research results are based on a survey conducted within the "Regional Initiative of Excellence" Programme funded by the Polish Ministry of Education and Science, involving 146 respondents, all of whom were managers of Polish medium-sized enterprises (50–250 employees). The respondents' characteristics are listed in Table 14.1. The survey was conducted in October 2020. The scope of the survey questions was broad and remote working was one of the topics addressed in the survey.

Table 14.1 Characteristics and structure of respondents

Criteria	*Respondents (No.)*	*Respondents (%)*
Position in the company		
CEOs/board members	17	11,64%
Director	61	41,78%
Manager	68	46,58%
Economic sector		
Industry and agriculture	80	54,79%
Services and commerce	66	45,21%
Operational scope		
Local and regional market	28	19,18%
National market	65	44,52%
International market	53	36,30%

Source: the authors' own research.

Among the respondents, the majority were managers (47%), the second largest group was made up of directors (42%) and the smallest of CEOs and board members (12%). They represented a variety of industries, of which 45% fell into the general category of industry and agriculture and 55% into trade and services. The spatial scope of their operations includes local and regional markets (19%), the national market (45%) and international markets (36%).

The companies had varying degrees of previous experience with remote working (pre-COVID-19) and diverse proportions of those working from home during the pandemic. Thus, 45% of respondents rated the level of remote working before the pandemic in their company as low and 55% of respondents as moderate. There were no companies in this pool that had much experience with remote working before 2020. Considering the share of employees working remotely in total employment at the time of the survey, 36% of respondents were employed by a company where up to 20% of employees worked from home, 39% of respondents represented companies where between 21% and 40% of employees were working remotely and 25% of respondents were from companies with more than 40% of their employees working remotely.

The research mainly focused on the benefits and challenges for the company and management, as well as measures to support remote working. This was motivated by the fact that previous research on the benefits and challenges of remote working mainly focused on employees and considered individual, family and work perspectives, while the companies' perspective has been studied comparatively rarely.

The questions on the benefits and challenges of remote working during COVID-19 were closed-ended. Respondents were asked to rate on a 5-point Likert scale which outcomes of working from home had occurred in their company. The benefits covered factors related to company and staff development. Barriers and challenges concerned technical, organisational and social fields aspects. The data analysis was exploratory. The results are presented in the next section.

Research findings

Benefits of remote working

The results of the survey show a high degree of optimism in assessing the impact of working from home on the company. This is quite surprising, given the social trauma and shock of the pandemic, the uncertainty about how it will unfold and the limited experience and readiness of companies to work in crisis conditions. In principle, all the potential benefits mentioned in the survey were assessed positively by the vast majority of respondents, who showed a high level of consensus. This may indicate both adaptation to new conditions, but also a clear added value generated by radical and enforced change. The percentage structure of the responses is shown in Figure 14.3.

All respondents agreed with the statement that remote working contributes to the building of a flexible organisation. Almost all respondents also confirmed that the key benefits of introducing remote working included training for employees in the use of modern technologies, diversification of products and services, cooperation with external entities for innovation and moving part of the company's activities online. The least important of the

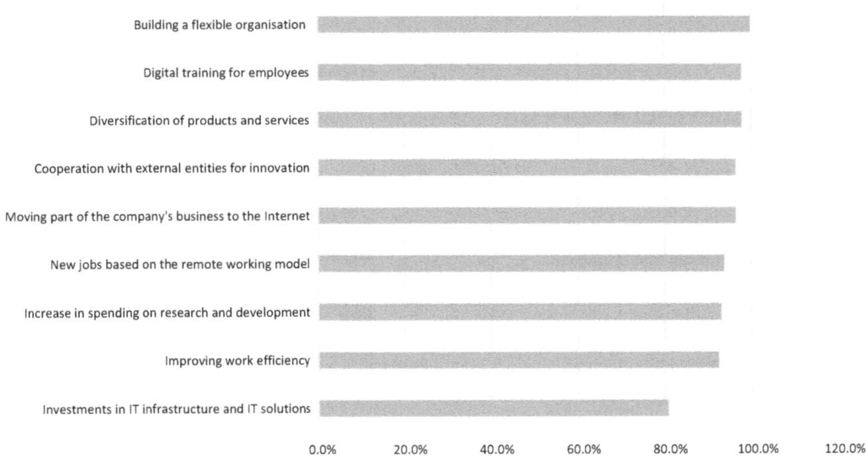

Figure 14.3 Pandemic-driven remote working benefits (in %)
Source: the authors' own research.

benefits was investments in IT infrastructure and solutions enabling remote working, though 80% nonetheless saw the benefit of doing so.

In addition to evaluating the benefits, respondents were asked to assess whether their company:

- supports employees in remote working on an ongoing basis (support);
- introduces new tools for remote work (new tools);
- monitors the effects of remote working (monitoring).

The responses were more diverse than in the case of benefit assessment (Figure 14.4). This differentiation deepened when the structure of the responses across the separate groups of companies was analysed:

- companies with little experience with remote working before COVID-19 versus those with medium experience;
- the three groups of companies according to the percentage of the total workforce working from home.

While implementing business measures to effectively support flexible forms of work is in itself a benefit for the company, it is above all a key condition for the effective management of remote working (Haines, St-Onge, & Archambault, 2002). These support measures were implemented to the greatest extent by companies that had more experience with remote working, and those where a sizable portion of the workforce (21–40%) worked from home. Remote working management factors were used least by those with the lowest proportion of employees working from home.

Challenges of remote working

As with respondents' attitudes toward the benefits associated with working remotely during the COVID-19 pandemic, their assessment of barriers was similarly positive (Figure 14.5).

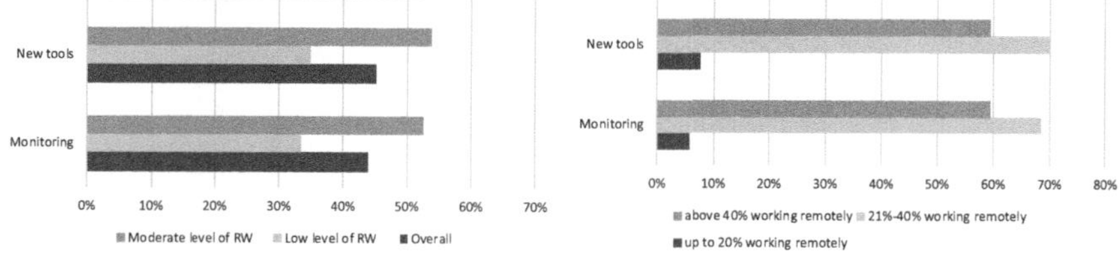

Figure 14.4 Employee support, implementation of remote working tools and monitoring of work effects in companies according to experience with remote working before and during the pandemic

Source: the authors' own research.

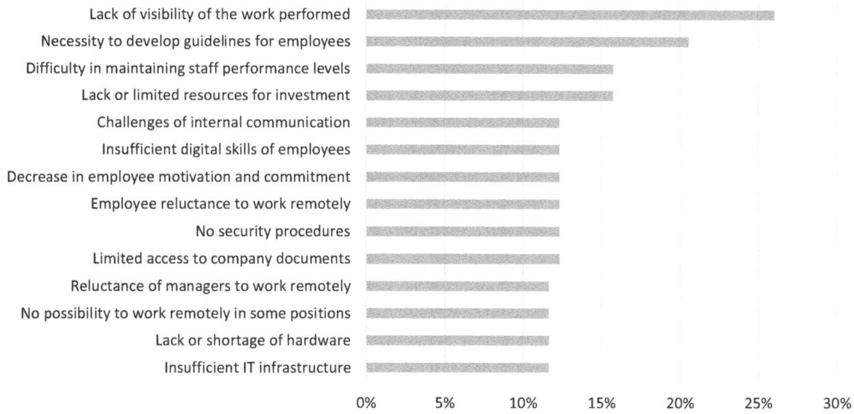

Figure 14.5 Pandemic-driven remote working challenges (in %)
Source: the authors' own research.

Only 11–26% of respondents consider any of the remote work challenges listed in the survey to be significant from a company perspective. The most frequently cited problem was the lack of visibility into the work performed and its progress (26% of responses). The inability to easily verify the quality and progress of an employee's work goes hand-in-hand with the third challenge identified in the survey – difficulty in maintaining staff performance levels (16%). The organisational unreadiness of companies for remote working was confirmed by respondents indicating the need to develop guidelines for employees (21% of responses).

Analysing the structure of responses in separate groups of respondents (according to the intensity of experience with remote work before and during the pandemic), the highest percentage of responses (and the most problems with remote work) was found among representatives of companies with little experience with remote work before the pandemic and with the highest (above 40%) share of employees working from home. Thus, 30% of respondents from companies with low levels of remote work before COVID-19 and 54% of respondents from companies with the highest levels of remote work consider the development of guidelines for employees to be the most important challenge for companies. Additionally, 49% of the latter group see the problems arising from a lack of sufficient resources to invest. Technical issues (IT infrastructure and hardware) were not a major challenge with any of the respondent groups surveyed.

Conclusions and practical implications

Our survey results and other studies conducted among Polish employees and employers indicate considerable optimism in assessments of the benefits and challenges of remote working and the prospects for the future. The attitude of respondents towards working from home and the perception of benefits is undoubtedly conditioned by the approach and solutions supporting remote work a company takes. Experiences in this regard are generally positive. More than 60% of the managers interviewed said that their company supports its employees in remote working on an ongoing basis, while more than 50% stated that the company has implemented new IT tools to enable remote working and monitors its performance (Figure 14.4). Dolot (2020) drew similar conclusions in a survey report on remote working during the COVID-19 pandemic. The support received by employees includes tasks performed, communication, feedback and well-being (Dolot, 2020). And while despite this fundamentally positive picture employees face difficulties and fears, 55% of Polish respondents indicated that part of their tasks can already be performed remotely, and 77% of employees point to the hybrid work model – combining elements of remote work with work in the office or at the client's premises – as the ideal formula. Only 14% of respondents would like to return to work as it had been done before the pandemic (PwC, 2021). Technological development and its impact on the labour market, including the rise of flexible work arrangements, is seen by most active workers as presenting more opportunities than threats (PwC, 2021).

In a survey commissioned by the Employers of Poland Organisation (Remote Work, 2021) on a sample of 1512 Polish employees and employers, 22% of respondents rated only the positive impact of remote working on the company in the COVID-19 period. 38% felt that the impact was both positive and negative. The most frequently cited gains for companies included the implementation of new solutions to facilitate work, the acquisition of new skills by employees, the expansion of the company's activities to include new forms of communication with customers, the provision of training for employees and the retrofitting of workstations with equipment to enable remote working. The two main drawbacks associated with remote working were the lack of remote working opportunities for some positions and a decrease in employee efficiency (Remote Work, 2021). The results of this study partly overlap with the findings presented in the previous section and partly complement them.

All indications suggest that remote and hybrid working will become a permanent part of the working environment in the digital economy. Even the end of the COVID-19 pandemic will not reverse this trend. This assertion is also supported by rapid technological transformation – a fundamental driving force behind flexible forms of work. Therefore, employers and managers should look at remote working not as a temporary and transient solution, but a sustainable trend that requires relevant preparation from both companies and employees. Further research should focus on sensitive issues such as infrastructure and conditions for remote and hybrid working, technology and cybersecurity, internal legal and organisational measures, alternative monitoring and motivation systems, personnel management and support. Undoubtedly, having appropriate regulations produced at the state level, defining the principles and conditions of remote working, will be crucial for companies implementing flexible forms of work.

References

Allen, T.D., Golden, T.D., & Shockley, K.M. (2015). How effective is telecommuting? Assessing the status of our scientific findings. *Psychological Science in the Public Interest, 16*(2), 40–68. doi:10.1177/1529100615593273

Anderson, A.J., Kaplan, S.A., & Vega, R.P. (2015). The impact of telework on emotional experience: When, and for whom, does telework improve daily affective well-being? *European Journal of Work and Organizational Psychology, 24*(6), 882–897, doi:10.1080/1359432X.2014.966086

Bailey, D.E., & Kurland, N.B. (2002). A review of telework research: Findings, new directions, and lessons for the study of modern work. *Journal of Organizational Behavior, 23*(4), 383–400.

Baker, E., Avery, G.C., & Crawford, J. (2007). Satisfaction and perceived productivity when professionals work from home. *Research and Practice in Human Resource Management, 15*(1), 37–62.

Basile, K.A., & Beauregard, T.A. (2016). Strategies for successful telework: How effective employees manage work/home boundaries. *Strategic HR Review, 15*(3), 106–111. doi:10.1108/SHR-03-2016-0024

Chakravorti, B., & Chaturvedi, R.S. (2020). Which countries were (and weren't) ready for remote work? Harvard Business Review. Available at: https://hbr.org/2020/04/which-countries-were-and-werent-ready-for-remote-work (accessed 30 July 2021)

Dolot, A. (2020). The influence of COVID-19 pandemic on the remote work-an employee perspective. *e-Mentor, 1*(1), 35–43.

Eddleston, K.A., & Mulki, J. (2017). Toward understanding remote workers' management of work-family boundaries: The complexity of workplace embeddedness. *Group & Organization Management, 42*(3), 346–387.

ETUC (2020). Framework agreement on telework. Brussels: European Trade Union Confederation. Available at: https://www.etuc.org/en/framework-agreement-telework (accessed 30 August 2021).

Eurofound (2020). Living, working and COVID-19 dataset. Dublin: European Foundation for the Improvement of Living and Working Conditions. Available at: http://eurofound.link/covid19data (accessed 16 August 2021).

Eurostat (2019). Employed persons working from home as a percentage of the total employment (%) [lfsa_ehomp]. Available at: https://appsso.eurostat.ec.europa.eu/nui/show.do?dataset=lfsa_ehomp (accessed 30 August 2021).

Gajendran, R.S., & Harrison, D.A. (2007). The good, the bad, and the unknown about telecommuting: Meta-analysis of psychological mediators and individual consequences. *Journal of Applied Psychology, 92*(6), 1524–1541.

Garrett, R.K., & Danziger, J.N. (2007). Which telework? Defining and testing a taxonomy of technology-mediated work at a distance. *Social Science Computer Review, 25*(1), 27–47.

Haines, V.Y., St-Onge, S., & Archambault, M. (2002). Environmental and person antecedents of telecommuting outcomes. *Journal of End User Computing, 14*(3), 32–50.

Lautsch, B.A., Kossek, E.E., & Eaton, S.C. (2009). Supervisory approaches and paradoxes in managing telecommuting implementation. *Human Relations, 62*, 795–827.

Madsen, S.R. (2011). The benefits, challenges, and implication of teleworking: A literature review. *Journal of Culture and Religion, 1*(1), 148–158.

Małkowska, A., Urbaniec, M., & Kosała, M. (2021). The impact of digital transformation on European countries: Insights from a comparative analysis. Equilibrium. *Quarterly Journal of Economics and Economic Policy, 16*(2), 325–355.

Mokhtarian, P.L. (1991). Defining telecommuting. *Transportation Research Record, 1305*, 273–281.

Morgan, R.E. (2004). Teleworking: An assessment of the benefits and challenges. *European Business Review, 16*(4), 344–357.

Nilles, J. (1975). Telecommunications and organizational decentralization. *IEEE Transactions on Communications, 23*, 1142–1147.

Nilles, J.M. (1988). Traffic reduction by telecommuting: A status review and selected bibliography. *Transportation Research Part A: General, 22*(4), 301–317.

Olson, M.H. (1983). Remote office work: Changing work patterns in space and time. *Communications of the ACM, 26*(3), 182–187. doi:10.1145/358061.358068

PwC (2021). Upskilling Hopes & Fears 2021. Available at: https://www.pwc.pl/pl/publikacje/przyszlosc-rynku-pracy-polska-perspektywa-badanie-2021.html (accessed 4 August 2021).

Remote work (2021). Praca zdalna 2.0 – rozwiązanie na czas pandemii czy trwała zmiana? Księga rekomendacji oraz ekspertyzy. Pracodawcy Rzeczypospolitej Polskiej. Available at: https://pracodawcyrp.pl/upload/files/2021/03/praca-zdalna-2-0-rekomendacje-i-ekspertyzy-v2.pdf (accessed 4 August 2021).

Savić, D. (2020). COVID-19 and work from home: Digital transformation of the workforce. *Grey Journal (TGJ), 16*(2), 101–104.

Senz, K. (2020). How much will remote work continue after the pandemic? *Harvard Business School Working Knowledge*. Available at: https://hbswk.hbs.edu/item/how-much-will-remote-work-continue-after-the-pandemic (accessed 22 March 2021).

Taboroši, S., Strukan, E., Poštin, J., Konjikušić, M., & Nikoloć, M. (2020). Organizational commitment and trust at work by remote employees. *Journal of Engineering Management and Competitiveness (JEMC), 10*(1), 48–60.

Taskin, T., & Bridoux, F. (2010). Telework: A challenge to knowledge transfer in organizations. *The International Journal of Human Resource Management, 21*(13), 2503–2520.

Urbaniec, M., Małkowska, A., & Włodarkiewicz-Klimek, H. (2022). The impact of technological developments on remote working: Insights from the polish managers' perspective. *Sustainability, 14*(1), 552, 1–18.

Wheatley, D. (2012). Good to be home? Time use and satisfaction levels among home-based teleworkers. *New Technology, Work & Employment, 27*(3), 224–241.

15 Job sharing in the digital economy

Joanna Kudełko and Dariusz Żmija

Introduction

In the era of the digital economy a flexible system of employment is being used by an increasing number and variety of organisations. One of the flexible forms of employment is job sharing – dividing a full-time job between two or more people who work part-time and voluntarily assume responsibility for the performance of tasks related to the position (French, Rayner, Rees, & Rumbles, 2008; Watton, Stables, & Kempster, 2019). This form of work was introduced in the US at the end of the 1960s, and it is still very common (Kalson, 2017). Over time it was adopted in other countries, hence there are differences in how it is defined and the terminology used to describe it. However, the term "job sharing" seems to be the one that is most widely used.

Different definitions of job sharing refer to the degree of interdependence of partners and their (possible) joint responsibility; but despite those differences job sharing always indicates the concept of a full-time job split between people. Because job sharing is a complex idea, it is regarded as superior to other solutions, for example job splitting, i.e., performing the same work by two or more people who work independently. The cooperation entered into by job sharers concerns how the time spent working is divided, enabling them to perform duties effectively. Their activities are independent and they do not share responsibility with others.

Another form of work is split-level sharing, in which work is shared not only in terms of time but also function. Employees who work within the same position have different qualifications, complementing one another in the effective performance of tasks. Unlike with job splitting, here the time it takes to perform tasks is a key factor. Job sharing, in a narrow sense, is based on the cooperation of employees in the same position in accordance with an employment contract. Employees are jointly responsible for ensuring continuous work, full staffing and the performance of tasks. Work shared by two people is called job pairing, and by three people, job tripling (Skowron-Mielnik, 2008).

Legal solutions related to job sharing contracts vary from country to country. In some, people who share work conclude individual job contracts, and

DOI: 10.4324/9781003254638-19

they share the compensation and related benefits of a full-time job on the basis of proportionality (Eurofound, 2015). In other countries, job sharing is based on one contract covering two or more employees. However, job sharing should not be confused with short-term reductions in working hours for the purpose of splitting work between employees, a strategy frequently applied as an alternative to workplace liquidation (Messenger & Ghosheh, 2013).

In some EU countries job sharing is a commonly used form of employment, while in Poland it is not subject to any specific regulations. Job sharing is used in compliance with the general regulations of labour law. Standard part-time employment contracts are applied, and work is shared on the basis of informal employer-employee agreements. Job sharing is mainly offered to those people who do not want to or cannot work full time. Employers and employees come to an agreement with regard to workloads, work schedules or replacement rules.

In practice, two forms of job sharing are adopted. In the first, two or more part-time jobs are created at the request of employees or employers. In the second, a full-time job is transformed into a position shared by two or more employees. Employers and employees decide on workloads, work schedules or replacement rules. With regard to job sharing, some EU countries have enacted legislation or regulations under collective employment agreements which set forth rules for employer and employee obligations. These rules do not specify how this form of employment is to be designed or implemented, instead vesting it in the hands of employers and employees. At issue may be the choice of contract, working hours or work organisation schemes (Eurofound, 2015).

In job sharing, key strategies are based on employing people with complementary qualifications (Dubourg, Ahmling, & Bujas, 2006). An important role is therefore played by the selection of people who share work. It should be assured not only that those sharing the job have suitable skills and competences facilitating the performance of tasks, but also that the individuals are compatible. Employees should understand each other and have friendly relationships based on cooperation, making the process of task delegation smooth and effective. Working time can be divided in many ways, depending on personal preferences and the type of tasks performed (Hajn, 2003). Modern organisations use increasingly team-based structures to bring together employees with different knowledge and experience to solve complex problems (van de Brake, Walter, Rink, Essens, & van der Vegt, 2020). However, job sharing is not the right solution for all types of work or positions as it is based on the possibility of dividing tasks by time- and qualifications-related criteria.

An important characteristic of job sharing is employees' shared responsibility for performing specific tasks. If a colleagues are absent, they must be replaced. This commitment is regulated by law; otherwise it results from an informal agreement or the company's practices. As Dubourg et al. (2006) highlight, successful and effective job sharing is conditioned by effective and continuous communication.

The main reasons employers are open to job sharing include an intention to offer flexible forms of employment, retain a full-time position, retain skilled workers, improve their own image and ensure effective workflows (Eurofound, 2015). Job sharing can increase the employment of marginalised groups of employees, e.g., mothers on maternity leave, senior workers, persons who require special care, persons with disabilities or sick persons who cannot work full time, or individuals who are studying. Also, job sharing reduces labour costs as compared with standard part-time jobs, and also enhances employees' commitment and productivity. It can also be treated as a form of mentoring (Eurofound, 2018). Job sharing helps maintain work-life balance (Bukowska, Tyrańska, & Wiśniewska, 2021).

In addition, job sharing may increase costs associated with selection, training and job postings. Other concerns include lost opportunity costs related to a full-time position, possible conflicts between job sharing employees and the lack of supervision over the character and effects of work (Branine, 2004). If it is not implemented properly, the job-sharing can increase workloads or necessitate overtime work, and increase work-related stress (McDonald, Bradley, & Brown, 2009).

Job sharing can help solve challenges the labour market is facing in the era of the digital economy. Wheatley (2013) suggests it should be used to both counteract unemployment among youth and mitigate the effects of an aging workforce. Daniels (2011) believes that job sharing has a positive impact on business continuity and increases productivity.

Job sharing is used in particular European countries in varying degrees. For example, 22% employers in Slovenia have used job sharing in most cases, and job sharers make up 5% of all employees. In Czechia, neither employers nor employees have shown much interest in job sharing (less than 7% of employers) (Eurofound, 2020). Other studies indicate that 39% of employees and self-employed people in Czechia are acquainted with the idea of job sharing, 14% have had personal experience with it, and 5% have benefited from this form of employment (Kyzlinková, Pojer, & Veverková, 2018). Interest in job sharing is likewise minimal in Slovakia and Lithuania: in 2019, a mere 0.4% of employers in Slovakia used it, while only nine such contracts were concluded in Lithuania (Eurofound, 2020).

Slightly more interest in job sharing is recorded in Poland, though there too it remains little known or used. According to one survey, only 6% of enterprises used job sharing (Deloitte, 2011). According to another survey, 8% of businesses had used it, and another 5% were considered it a future option (Sadowska-Snarska, 2006). Job sharing remains a rarely used system even in the UK, where the idea of work sharing is quite common. 12% of firms in the UK have used the system, but only 0.5% of employees have shared work with others (Eurofound, 2020). Employers in Austria (22%), Belgium (23%), Netherlands (23%) and France (19%) have all shown stronger interest in job sharing (Robert Half International, 2014). Meanwhile, 17% of employers in Germany expressed interest in 2018. Lastly, 61% of employers in Bulgaria are acquainted with the concept, and while a full 29.5% have used the system in their companies (Eurofound, 2020).

The economic sectors where job sharing is used vary considerably as well. For example, it is most often used in Belgium in the education and care-taking sectors; in Latvia in education, the financial sector and retail trade; in Hungary in administration; and in the Netherlands in elementary education. In Ireland job sharing is more popular in the public sector (13%) than in private firms (8%), while in Latvia it is mainly used in public administration (approx. 40%) (Eurofound, 2020). 2008 data from Slovenia indicates that job sharing was used by large public sector companies on a larger scale than in private sector services, industrial companies and agriculture. In Czechia, job sharing has been used periodically by 15% of companies representing the public and industrial sectors, 11% of trading companies and 10% of service firms (Eurofound, 2015). In Poland, job sharing was most widely used in healthcare services, public administration, tourism and education (Sadowska-Snarska, 2006).

Job sharing opportunities are addressed to social groups with a variety of qualifications. For example, it has been used in Czechia for positions not requiring advanced specialised skills, such as assistants or receptionists (Eurofound, 2015). In the UK it is used in administrative, teaching and clerical work, predominantly by married, middle-aged women with children (Wheatley, 2013). In Poland, 24% of people aged 18–65 years have job sharing experience, and 22% would be willing to share work (Owczarek, 2018). Sadowska-Snarska (2006) indicated that job sharing in Poland is done mainly by manual workers (41.0%), specialists (38.0%) and managers (14.0%). In Hungary, job sharing is most widely used by students of further or higher education and young mothers returning to the labour market, and senior workers. In Latvia, job sharing is popular among people aged 20–24 years (39%), and least widely used by those aged 60 and above (14%) (Eurofound, 2020).

Research methodology

Our results are based on surveys conducted among Polish employees in the "Regional Excellence Initiatives" programme, financed by the Ministry of Education and Science. The survey was conducted from May to July 2020 on the basis of an online questionnaire and CAWI. Additional invitations for participants were posted on wynagrodzenia.pl and affiliated portals. There were a total of 3,599 responses, which were data-cleaned. Responses that took less than five minutes were removed and "outliers" were assessed for quality. The analysis ultimately included 3,493 respondents. The survey was based on both random and purposive sampling. It was completed by employees and self-employed working in various economic sectors (full-time male employees aged 18–64 years, and full-time female employees aged 18–59 years). The different age limits correspond to the retirement age by gender in Poland. The sample was representative in terms of the number of population in Polish voivodeships.

Most respondents had university degrees (nearly 80%), confirming their high qualifications. The majority of respondents held the position of specialist (36.8%), senior specialist (21.3%) or manager of a small (16.2%) or big team (7.2%). A small percentage of respondents represented finished lower education levels and worked manual jobs. The majority of respondents had worked for their companies for at least several years. The majority of respondents had length of service in their jobs of from one to five years (44.0%) and more than five years (41.4%). Longevity attests to candidates' advanced understanding of their company's operations, changes in their positions resulting from technological advancement, and the flexible forms of employment used. The employees surveyed represented a range of economic sectors, but predominantly industry (15.7%), IT (11.9%), trade (9.6%), construction (7.9%), business services (6.8%) and banking (5.5%). The least represented sectors included culture and arts (0.6%), agriculture (0.5%) and NGOs (0.4%). The structure of respondents' employment by sector or employment area was slightly different. Most employees represented IT (18.2%), finance, accounting and auditing (10.2%), production (8.8%), administration and management board offices (7.7%) and sales (7.0%). The smallest group of respondents worked in such sectors as industrial safety and environmental protection (0.9%), risk management (0.7%) and public relations (0.3%). The range of questions in the survey was broad, and job sharing was one of many areas analysed in the study. The results of the exploratory data analysis used are presented in the next chapter.

Results of the study

A survey of employees was conducted to determine how technological advances affect their work (Figure 15.1).

The most common change in the respondents' positions due to technological advances is increased productivity, which was indicated by 44.7%

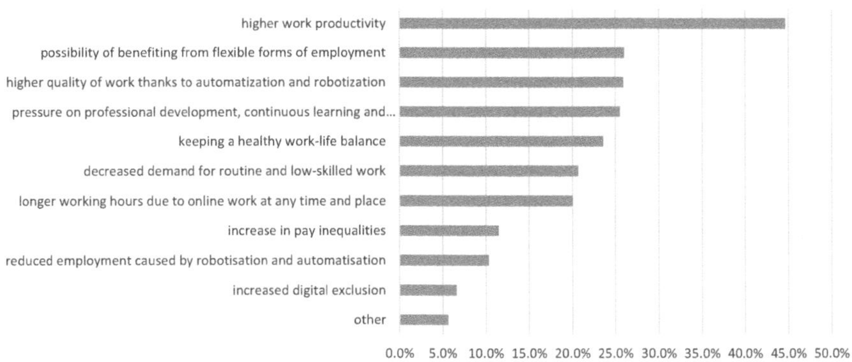

Figure 15.1 Technological advancement and changes in respondents' position
Source: the authors' own research.

of respondents. The results of the analysis show that 26.1% of respondents consider the possibility of sharing work in their positions. A relatively large number of such responses is likely to result from the type of position or department's respondents work in as well as the effects of the COVID-19 pandemic. 25.9% of respondents said automatisation and robotisation lead to higher quality work in their positions.

Such views correspond to general trends in the digital economy and the increasing dematerialisation of work processes, which are also observed in production and service companies, where manual work is increasingly being replaced by machines and robots using artificial intelligence and IT systems. These trends favour employees who have the ability to work in technologically advanced environments, while pushing aside workers without such skills. As 25.5% of respondents indicated, the need to use new technologies prompts professional development, continuous learning and retraining. 23.6% of respondents note that technological advancement enables them to maintain a healthy work-life balance, which is undoubtedly affected by a wide range of flexible forms of employments in the firms analysed. All of this leads to the conclusion that flexible forms of employment perform a key function in labour market changes in the contemporary digital economy (Małkowska, Urbaniec, & Kosała, 2021). To broaden the analysis and explore job sharing in greater detail, we investigated the flexible forms of employment offered by respondents' companies (Figure 15.2).

Flexible forms of employment mainly include unusual employment relationships (Puchalska, 2019). Respondents cited the following: remote work (62.8%), part-time work in the case of employment contracts (29.7%), civil law contracts (26.1%) and self-employment (21.5%). Job sharing is the rarest

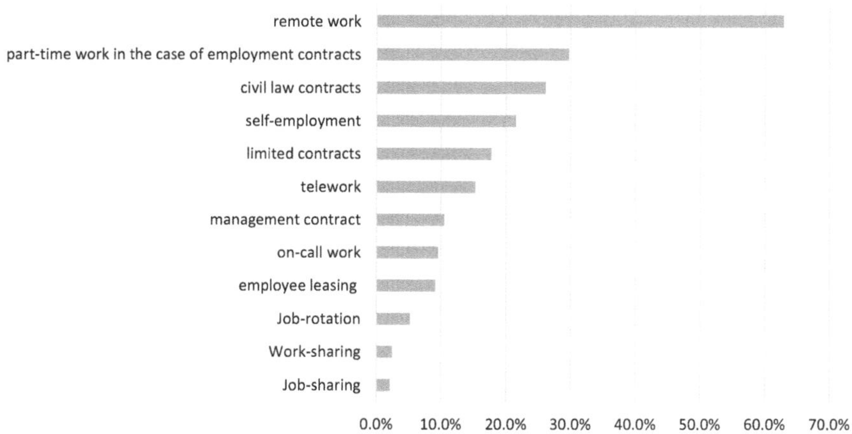

Figure 15.2 Flexible forms of employment offered in respondents' companies
Source: the authors' own research.

form of flexible employment offered by companies (2.1%) – only 72 out of 3,493 employees indicate this option. Table 15.1 presents the characteristics of those that did offer job sharing.

Table 15.1 The characteristics of companies offering job sharing

Town or city where company is based:	*Number of respondents*	*Share of respondents*
20 thousand or less	4	5.6%
21–100 thousand	11	15.3%
101–200 thousand	4	5.6%
201–500 thousand	14	19.4%
More than 500,000 inhabitants	39	54.1%
Company size (# of employees):		
1–5	1	1.4%
6–50	10	13.9%
51–250	19	26.4%
251–1,500	18	25.0%
More than 1,500	24	33.3%
Company's ownership status:		
Private with Polish majority shareholders	33	45.8%
Private with foreign majority shareholders	25	34.7%
State or self-government administration	3	4.2%
State treasury-owned	2	2.8%
Own business activity	2	2.8%
Other	6	8.3%
I don't know	1	1.4%
Company's sector:		
Industry	14	19.4%
IT	13	18.1%
Trade	6	8.3%
Banking	5	6.9%
Business services	4	5.6%
Science, education	4	5.6%
State administration	3	4.2%
Health care	3	4.2%
Insurance	3	4.2%
Construction	2	2.8%
Services	2	2.8%
Media, publishing, advertising, PR	2	2.8%
Energy and heating	1	1.4%
Logistics, transport, shipment	1	1.4%
NGOs	1	1.4%
Food production and processing	1	1.4%
Other	7	9.5%

Source: the authors' own research.

As Table 15.1 shows, job sharing was most frequently offered by companies based in large Polish cities, i.e., those with more than 500 thousand inhabitants (54.2%), and companies with more than 250 employees (58.3%) representing the private sector with Polish capital (45.8%) and foreign capital (34.7%). Job sharing was least frequently offered by public sector entities (state and self-government administration), state treasury-owned companies and self-employed persons. Companies offering job sharing belonged to the industrial sector (19.4%), IT (18.1%), trade (8.3%) and banking (6.9%). Individual cases of job sharing were recorded in such sectors as energy and heating, logistics, transport, shipping, NGOs and food production and processing.

Changes in position due to technological progress can also be negative (Figure 15.1). They include longer working hours resulting from remote work (at any time and any place) (20.0%), increased pay inequalities (11.5%), reduced employment due to robotisation and automatisation (10.3%) and increased digital exclusion (6.6%). Such effects also apply to flexible forms of employment including job sharing. For example, dividing work between two or more people can result in larger workloads than those described in employment contracts, the need to work overtime and it also leads to work-related stress and dispersed responsibility for tasks. Undoubtedly, job sharing increases pay inequalities as wages are lower than in the case of full-time jobs, and new technologies in the digital economy contribute to digital exclusion and, consequently, prevent certain social groups from taking up even part-time jobs.

Conclusions and practical implications

Job sharing can be useful in meeting many of the labour market challenges posed by the digital economy. Findings from a number of researchers indicate that this form of flexible employment is of relatively low importance to employers in Lithuania and Slovakia. In Czechia and Poland less than 10% of employers offered job sharing, while in some other countries the share was even 20% (Slovenia, Austria, Belgium, the Netherlands, France, Germany) and in the case of Bulgaria almost 30%. Job sharing is also used in various economic sectors – but to a larger extent in the public sector (education, administration, health) than in private companies (finance, commerce, services, tourism).

The results of our survey indicate that among the flexible forms of employment, job sharing was the least used by Polish employers (2.1%). The data confirms that there is little interest in job sharing in Poland. It is true that job sharing is not an appropriate form of work for all job types because the effective division of tasks is conditioned by factors related to time and employee qualifications. However, this obstacle is not of key significance in the light of the analysis of the economic sectors respondents worked in (industry, IT, trade, construction, business services, banking), the departments they represented (IT, finance, accounting, auditing, production, administration, sales) or their position in the hierarchy (specialist, senior specialist, manager). Moreover, job sharing offers flexi-time opportunities – part-time jobs and the possibility of adapting working hours to one's individual needs. At the same time, it decreases labour costs below those of standard part-time jobs, attracting greater commitment from employees and higher productivity.

Unlike in many European countries, job sharing in Poland was mainly offered by private sector entities, and rarely in the public sector. The highest number of companies offering job sharing was in the industrial sector, IT, trade and banking, while it was rarely used by entities in education, administration and health care. Given the shortage of workers in Poland and other countries (e.g. teachers and medical professions), job sharing should be more widely applied in the public sector, encouraging more people to take up work. Job sharing provides the flexibility needed by those who intend to enter the labour market and who want to maintain a work-life balance. In addition, job sharing can lead to conflicts between employees, while employers may find it difficult to supervise work, and job sharing may increase workload or result in the need for overtime, leading to increased stress. There is therefore a need for effective management of flexible forms of employment in organisations and for the right selection of people to share work.

References

Branine, M. (2004). Job sharing and equal opportunities under the new public management in local authorities. *International Journal of Public Sector Management, 17*(2), 136–152.

Bukowska, U., Tyrańska, M., & Wiśniewska, S. (2021). The workplace and work-life balance during the COVID-19 pandemic. *Annales Universitatis Mariae Curie-Skłodowska, sectio H–Oeconomia*, *55*(2), 19–32.

Daniels, L. (2011). *Job sharing at senior level: Making it work. The Job Share Project.* Available at: http://www.thejobshareproject.com/resources.html (accessed 30 August 2021).

Deloitte (2011). *Trendy HRM w Polsce.* Warszawa: Deloitte and Polskie Stowarzyszenie Zarządzania Kadrami.

Dubourg, L., Ahmling, J.A., & Bujas, L. (2006). Can job sharing work for nurse managers. *Australian Health Review, 30*(1), 17–24.

Eurofound (2015). *New forms of employment.* Luxembourg: Publications Office of the European Union.

Eurofound (2018). *Overview of new forms of employment – 2018 update.* Luxembourg: Publications Office of the European Union.

Eurofound (2020). *New forms of employment: 2020 update.* Luxembourg: New forms of employment series, Publications Office of the European Union.

French R., Rayner Ch., Rees G., & Rumbles S. (2008). *Organizational behaviour.* New York: John Wiley & Sons Ltd. West Sussex.

Hajn, Z. (2003). Elastyczność popytu na pracę w Polsce. Aspekty prawne. In E. Kryńska (Ed.), *Elastyczne formy zatrudnienia i organizacji pracy a popyt na pracę* (pp. 48–99). Warszawa: Instytut Pracy i Spraw Socjalnych (IPISS).

Kalson, A. (2017). Special job-sharing regulation-A promoter of flexible working. *Juridica International, 26*, 85.

Kyzlinková, R., Pojer, P., & Veverková, S. (2018). *New forms of employment in the Czech Republic*. Prague: RILSA.

Małkowska, A., Urbaniec, M., & Kosała, M. (2021). The impact of digital transformation on European countries: Insights from a comparative analysis. *Equilibrium. Quarterly Journal of Economics and Economic Policy, 16*(2), 325–355.

McDonald, P., Bradley, L., & Brown, K. (2009). Full-time is a given here: Part-time versus full time job quality. *British Journal of Management, 20*(2), 143–157.

Messenger, J.C., & Ghosheh, N. (Eds.) (2013). *Work sharing during the great recession: New developments and beyond*. Geveva: International Labour Organization (ILO).

Owczarek, D. (Ed.) (2018). *Nowe formy pracy w Polsce*. Warszawa: Instytut Spraw Publicznych.

Puchalska, K. (2019). Flexible forms of employment in Poland on the example of working phone. *Humanities and Social Sciences, 26*(3), 93–100.

Robert Half Talent Solutions (2014). *Job sharing: Deutschland in Europa Schlusslicht*. Available at: https://www.roberthalf.de/presse/jobsharing-deutschland-europa-schlusslicht (accessed 30 August 2021).

Sadowska-Snarska, C. (2006). *Elastyczne formy pracy jako instrument godzenie zawodowego z rodzinnym*. Białystok: Wyższa Szkoła Ekonomiczna.

Skowron-Mielnik, B. (2008). Job sharing – nowe możliwości organizowania pracy. *Zeszyty Naukowe Zarządzanie Zasobami Ludzkimi, 5*, 37–52.

van de Brake, H.J., Walter, F., Rink, F.A., Essens, P.J., & van der Vegt, G. S. (2020). Multiple team membership and job performance: The role of employees' information-sharing networks. *Journal of Occupational and Organizational Psychology, 93*(4), 967–987.

Watton, E., Stables, S., & Kempster, S. (2019). How job sharing can lead to more women achieving senior leadership roles in higher education: A UK study. *Social Sciences, 8*(7), 209.

Wheatley (2013). *Is it good to share? Debating patterns in availability and use of job share*. Discussion Papers in Economics, Nottingham Trent University.

16 Interim management in the digital economy

Maria Urbaniec

Introduction

The development of flexible work organisation is considered an important process, associated with economic and technological changes, globalisation, global competition and numerous other phenomena. Thus, the question is not whether to organise work flexibly or inflexibly, but how flexibly and where to apply different forms, maintaining a compromise between the flexibility of labour demand and the security of employment for workers. One form of flexible employment is interim management. It is a respond to a need for flexible employment of temporary managers in a dynamically changing labour market (Eurofound, 2020; Şenturan, 2018).

Interim management emerged in the 1970s in the Netherlands as a way to avoid very restrictive labour laws that required employers to pay large severance packages to dismissed employees (Davis, 2005; Dźwigoł, 2020). Confident of their value in the labour market, managers agreed to work for higher wages for a predetermined period of time or for the duration of a specific task, giving up the protection offered by labour law. This was beneficial for both parties: the employer, despite higher unit rates, did not have to pay severance and was guaranteed the result for which it hired the interim manager (IM). The interim manager, in turn, received higher remuneration for his advanced competence and participation in the risk and success of the employer. Interim management is reflected when experienced managers deliver results, products and knowledge transfer to the companies at the agreed time. It is the fastest, cheapest and most effective way to develop and respond to changes in the business environment.

The Institute of Interim Management in the UK defines interim management as "the provision of effective business solutions by an independent, board or near-board level manager or executive, over a finite time span. Such complex solutions may include change, transformation and turnaround management, business improvement, crisis management and strategy development" (IIM, 2020, p. 4). Accordingly, interim managers are highly specialised experts who are expected to solve a specific management problem or technical challenge (Eurofound, 2020). Host companies often use interim

DOI: 10.4324/9781003254638-20

managers in times of crisis, restructuring or to strategically prepare for business growth, innovation or diversification. In this way, companies achieve a specific objective and the interim manager provides access to his or her expertise without engaging in long-term commitments (Skowron-Mielnik & Sobiecki, 2020). The interim manager's main responsibility is to develop proposals for changes expected by the company, and then to implement them effectively in order to achieve the project results. The last task is to transfer knowledge, and above all to teach the successor how to properly maintain a solution that has been implemented under the manager's guidance.

The interim management market is highly developed in countries including the Netherlands, UK and Germany. In the UK alone, the IM market size is estimated at £1.5 billion (SIM, 2015). The development of the European market for interim managers is illustrated by the latest report "The 2021 European Survey", compiled by the International Network of interim Manager Associations (INIMA, 2021). This survey was conducted by interim managers in ten European countries among 750 practicing professionals. The results show that European interim managers worked in more than 35 different industries, with the top three being mechanical engineering, automotive and industrial manufacturing. The interim managers' main functional specialisations were general management, operations, human resources, finance and sales.

The most experienced interim managers were from Switzerland (11 years), the UK (ten years) and Liechtenstein (nine years). The youngest respondents were representatives of interim manager associations from Austria (49 years old), Poland (49 years old) and Spain (53 years old). Interim managers are change agents by nature, so change management and process optimisation are common tasks they perform. The average duration of temporary work in Europe was 11.4 months (INIMA, 2021). While long contracts of more than two years (often part-time) were popular in Italy, short contracts of less than three (3) months were popular in the UK (14%), France (12%) and Poland (10%). The range of daily rates was very wide, from €300 to over €2,000, reflecting the diversity of national economies, national labour markets, client sizes and sectors. European interim managers carry out assignments across the full range of companies, from start-ups with a few employees to large corporations. In Spain and Italy, more than half of the assignments were for companies with fewer than 100 employees.

According to the latest Interim Management Poland 2021 market research report, nine out of ten interim management projects carried out in recent months were not prompted by the COVID-19 crisis, but to the "everyday" implementation of new solutions, carrying out optimisation and increasing efficiency. Additionally, a comparison of the 2020 and 2019 survey results shows that there has been an increase of nearly 40% in the number of managers pursuing the interim career path (SIM, 2021).

In Germany, Norway and the UK, this form of employment is most often used by companies in the energy, oil and gas, road construction, information and communication technology, manufacturing and banking sectors

(Papmehl, 2019). The main motives companies have for using interim management are restructuring during crises (including internal reorganisation of positions), strategic planning of development (including international expansion) and introducing various types of innovation or diversification (new services or products) (Goffin, 2019; SIM, 2015).

A significant advantage of an interim manager over a full-time manager is that no employment relationship is established, so the company does not bear the burden of hiring a full-time employee (e.g. costs of adaptation, training, social package). An interim manager is hired for a specific period of time and for a specific project, thus helping to effectively manage cost planning and budgeting. The features of an interim project are: a defined duration, a defined and measurable business product, a defined and measurable business outcome, an appropriate set of product development activities (Goffin, 2019).

The employment of external managerial staff differs from the provision of consultancy services in that the interim manager has some authority to give instructions (on the basis of assigned tasks) and is also subordinated to the instructions of supervisors. Therefore, compared to external consultants, interim managers are integrated into the staff of the host company, although usually not to the same extent as other employees. In none of the European Union Member States is there any specific regulation specifying the framework of this form of employment. In Poland, the managerial contract corresponding to temporary management is usually concluded in the form of a civil law contract with a self-employed person. Nevertheless, the drive to make work organisation more flexible, taking into account the interests of both employee and employer, is having a significant impact on the development of this form of employment. The use of interim management leads to both tangible benefits and certain challenges.

Therefore, this chapter aims to analyse the impact of the digital economy on interim management as a profession. The following research questions were formulated: (1) What are the benefits and challenges of interim management in the digital economy? (2) What is the impact of digital economy on interim managers? In answering these questions, next sections introduce the research methodology and demonstrate the results of qualitative research conducted among interim managers in Poland. This aspect of the research identifies the impact of technological progress on the profession of interim manager, including the benefits and barriers. The final section concludes the chapter with a look at the practical implications.

Research methodology

Sampling

The objective of the study is to identify the motives, benefits and current challenges and prospects for development interim management in the era of digital transformation. The study is based on purposive sampling, where sampling is driven by the relevance of the case (Flick, 2009, p. 121). The sampling includes: (1) certified interim managers, cooperating with the Polish Interim Managers Association (SIM), (2) other experienced interim managers, (3) managers who have previous experience as interim managers. Overall, the research on interim management remains underdeveloped. As the object of this study involves new and multidimensional issues and thus needs to be explored incrementally (Denzin & Lincoln, 2005), it is based on a qualitative interpretative approach and a series of interviews with Polish interim managers. This approach (focusing on one specific target group of respondents) was used to provide contextualised, rich detail and dense description that can lead to theoretical insights.

The study made it possible to contact interim managers in Poland who have practical experience. It is worth adding that the number of interim managers in Poland has increased significantly in recent years (Eurofound, 2020; SIM, 2021). Poland has a stable and rapidly developing economy, a growing labour shortage and the demand for top-level business management know-how, especially among SMEs. These circumstances were viewed as likely to provide an interesting and relatively broad area of operation for experienced freelance interim managers (Dźwigoł, 2020).

The sampling strategy was based on several selection criteria, including that the managers be established with at least one year of work experience. In total, ten interim managers were selected to participate in the study (Table 16.1). Most of the interim managers had experience gained in Poland and abroad.

As this is an exploratory study, and in strictly theoretical terms, the selection of respondents ensures the diversity of manifestations of the phenomena to be examined (Babbie, 2013) in a given geographical context. In practical terms, this guided the aim of the study towards providing data collected among managers with experience in Poland as well as abroad.

Data collection

The study was conducted using a qualitative method with the technique of individual in-depth interviews (IDI) either by telephone or online (depending on the preference of the respondents). The selected interim managers were first explored online to collect available secondary data. The interim managers' websites were analysed along with relevant media publications, thus allowing for further triangulation of data. In the second phase of the research, potential respondents were contacted directly (in March and April 2021). The interview protocol consisted of open-ended questions and included themes drawn from analysis of the literature. The interview topics were provided to the respondents gradually as follow-up questions and according to the direction the interview took. In applied research, it is largely the respondent who leads the conversation (Cope, 2011). This meant the interviews were necessarily loosely structured. The interviews began with

Table 16.1 Characteristics of the study respondents

Interim Manger No.	Age (years)	Area of expertise	Years of professional experience
1	40–49	Human resource	12
2	50–59	Operational management, Business Development	4
3	50–59	Change management, post-merger integration	10
4	50–59	Finance, accounting,	11
5	More than 60	Human resource	8
6	40–49	Change management, reorganisation, human resources, crisis management, strategic management	5
7	50–59	Customer relationship management, brand and product awareness, company restructuring	20
8	More than 60	Operational and cultural transformation, organisational change, leadership and management	13
9	40–49	Management of small and medium-sized enterprises, crisis management, company restructuring	8
10	50–59	Change management	4

Source: the authors' own research.

very general questions and then moved on to more narrowly focused questions. The questions covered the following broad topic areas, including: (1) respondents' motives for choosing to become an interim manager; (2) the benefits and challenges of being an active interim manager; and (3) the impact of technological developments on the interim management.

While interim managers engage in an extensive range of activities, the focus of this study was to explore the impact of technological advances on their activities. It also provided insight into the changes resulting from current technological advances on labour relations. Each of the interviews ranged from 45 to 60 minutes and was recorded for content analysis. The interviews were conducted in an online format. All respondents were assured anonymity.

Data analysis

Each interview was first transcribed and carefully read with an attempt to recall the history and details of the relationship. This allowed for textual analysis (Denzin & Lincoln, 2005). Secondary data was used to support the evidence the respondents provided. During this phase, respondents were sometimes contacted again to clarify or elaborate on certain facts or themes and to control for interpretive bias. This inter-case reflective analysis and interpretation process was carried out for all transcripts separately. Open coding was applied to each case transcript. The data analysis process was carried out with MaxQDA software (Rädiker & Morgenstern-Einenkel, 2021).

This was followed by a cross-case analysis, comparing similarities and differences between cases for each research theme, looking for common aspects of experiences (patterns) and aggregating themes from different relationships. This led to the development of further categories, reflecting significant experiences and meanings related to the research phenomenon (Smith & Eatough, 2006) and resulting in the identification of additional themes. The analysis process used Yin's (2018) replication logic for two purposes: to capture the rich descriptive context of interim managers and to enhance the results of the analysis. The next stage of data analysis was interpretation; the interaction between the respondents' testimonies and the researcher's writing process. The final stage was analytical discussion and reading the literature with a view to providing theoretical explanations of the themes at a higher level of abstraction.

Research findings

The findings are presented according to the three key research areas: (1) motives for becoming an interim manager, (2) benefits and challenges of being an interim manager and (3) the impact of technological developments on this profession.

Motives for choosing to become an interim manager

According to the interim managers, an important inspiration for the development of this profession in Poland was the development of the British and German markets for this form of employment. For many years, the use of temporary projects in cooperation with experienced managers has been developing strongly in both countries. Nowadays, companies are more and more willing to use project- and task-based work, changing the opportunities on the labour market. There are many managers who have professional experience in corporations and want to work more independently, on their own account and have the ability to choose business projects. Table 16.2 shows the broad spectrum of motives interim managers have for entering the profession, which can be divided into individually-driven, organisation-driven and system-driven.

Respondents also indicated that there remains a lack understanding on the Polish market about what interim managers do in their profession? This is reflected in the following statements:

Table 16.2 Respondents' motives for becoming an interim manager

Main motives	Specific motives	Illustrative statements from respondents
Individually-driven	Independence and sense of empowerment	• *It is greater independence, self-reliance and I think a very important element, such as actually sharing knowledge with other companies, the possibility of influencing their development, changes (IM 1)*
	Predispositions	• *It simply turned out that I have such a psychological structure that I am more effective in difficult conditions (...), where projects carry a very high risk of failure (IM 9*
	Individual aspirations	• *Firstly, I have my own business, and secondly, I earn my living (...). This business gives me freedom to choose (IM 7)*
	Previous management experience	• *It is certainly not a path for everyone (...), it involves many aspects and is very specific, such as the baggage of experiences from different organisations, but also the ability to share these experiences and knowledge (IM 1)* • *There are many interim managers specialised in general management (former CEOs, directors of companies) and this is their profession as interim managers (IM 5)*
Organisation-driven	Attractive remuneration	• *I would venture to say that to feel comfortable in this profession, you need to be financially stable, and only then can you do it more for pleasure. Maybe I am exaggerating, because you can earn quite a lot of money (IM 5)*
	Project-based work	• *Ability to work on projects, tasks, objectives, results, specifics (IM 1)*
System-driven	Certified qualification	• *There is a certification programme. A qualifications framework is currently being introduced into the interim management profession, so there will also be a formal professional qualification (IM 1)*
	International career	• *Most of the projects I did were with foreign capital companies, where the decision-maker at some stage was a foreigner, so I always worked in full comfort (...). In the West, the role of the interim managers is very well known in business, it is very common and interim managers number in the thousands in countries such as Germany, Holland, France, Great Britain above all, but also in Spain and Italy (IM 5)*

Source: the authors' own research.

- *"This is due to the constant misunderstanding (...) of what interim management is and to what extent it can be applied in a company"* (IM 2);
- *"I have the impression that often companies or owners who commission work to an interim manager do not know whether they are hiring an interim or a consultant. (...) For me, the most important thing is that if I come and work with a company, I have to give it a specific, measurable result and meet its expectations"* (IM 7).

To conclude, interim managers are highly task-oriented individuals, but they are also aware that they need to be leaders that can engage people in a project. The motives outlined indicate that interim managers are experienced experts with advanced skills. Those interviewed work under a variety of legal contracts, including civil law contracts, freelance contracts, management contracts and, although rarely, fixed-term contracts.

The benefits of interim management

A cross-analysis of the material allowed the identification of the advantages of working as an interim manager (Table 16.3). Some respondents said that the responsibility of an interim manager is not only to ensure the transfer of knowledge to the organisation, but also to implement this knowledge in a variety of situations. Companies use interim management services when, for example, a member of management has a maternity or paternity leave, or during the recruitment process for a new high-level manager, which in the largest companies can take months. The main benefits of working as an interim manager are freedom of choice, being able to choose when and where you work, being involved in the transfer of knowledge, empowerment and satisfaction with work results (Table 16.3).

Interim management, as a flexible form of employment, enables companies to work with highly qualified specialists in various fields and also provides the opportunity to achieve a balance between personal and professional life. Employing an interim manager allows companies to evaluate the effectiveness of activities using and combining criteria such as time, cost and quality. Interim managers complete tasks in a short period of time, and do high-quality work at relatively low cost.

The challenges interim managers face

Admittedly, the disadvantages or challenges interim managers face are as multifaceted (Table 16.4) as the advantages. Nevertheless, the respondents clearly indicate that the lack of job security, lack of legal protection and salary stability are not a significant problem for them. In fact, the lack of social security is inherent to the choice of this profession, as evidenced by the following statement: "*I wouldn't call it an inconvenience, it's just a difference that you have to be aware of and you have to come to terms with internally somehow*" (IM 2). Some respondents stressed that challenges often depend on the industry they work in.

Table 16.3 The benefits of being an interim manager

Main benefits	Specific benefits	Illustrative statements from respondents
Individually-driven	Freedom of choice	• *The ability to shape what you want to do yourself and to choose what you do not want to do and with whom (IM 6)*
	Empowerment	• *The problem, with which the company has been struggling for a long time, is solved faster; so first of all the time and second the way to solve it (IM 2)* • *I have more freedom, often more influence (IM 4)*
	Work satisfaction	• *Interim managers derive a lot of joy from the effects of their work, and the fact they can actually influence a company's development. I think this is great satisfaction (IM 1)* • *Such a sense of responsibility from beginning to end, that I am responsible for a certain part and I like that. I like project work (IM 10)*
	Professional experience	• *It is the interim's experience that allows him very quickly to gather the information he knows he needs to do the job. It is a completely different learning process for the company, it is much faster, we just know what is important in terms of what the client wants (IM 6)*
	Professional fulfilment	• *It is professionally fulfilling because if you have the right knowledge and experience, and experienced interim managers undoubtedly do (IM 5)*
	Continuous learning	• *It gave me a broader perspective (IM 7)* • *By gaining experience in these different contexts and struggling with different problems (…), we also know, what qualifications or competences we do not have enough of and therefore we fill in these gaps (IM 9)*
	Soft skills	• *Trust is crucial in the work of interims, and even, in my opinion, in the work of any manager – it is the trust of both the owner and his colleagues (IM 7)*
Organisation-driven	Time and place of work	• *The fact that there is a very defined horizon in which the activities are done, so you can plan them quite precisely, you know when the end is (IM 4)* • *The feeling of freedom regarding time and place of work is positive (IM 5)*
	Knowledge transfer	• *The interim introduces the transfer of knowledge—that is, we build competences or we leave these competences in the company because after three or six months, when we leave the company, this knowledge should remain, the employees should continue to manage themselves by implementing a certain scheme of activities – this is another benefit for the client (IM 6)*
	Productivity	• *When an interim is hired to do a certain task, he declares that he will do it within a certain time and simply has to do it. Certainty and time are two aspects on the benefit side (IM 2)*
	Diversity of projects	• *Above all, diversity, as working as an interim manager allows you to navigate through different types of projects, different types of tasks and different types of business partners and clients (IM 6)*
	Financial benefits	• *The positives are mainly financial, because it is above standard, at least for Poland (IM 7)*

Table 16.3 Continued

Main benefits	Specific benefits	Illustrative statements from respondents
System-driven	Systemic support	• *I think the market is becoming a bit more professional, there are organisations such as the Association of Interim Managers, which brings this environment together and offers managers concrete support and professional training (IM 1)*
	Profession development	• *The breakthrough moment was the creation of the interim manager methodology in collaboration with the British Association of Interim Managers and the creation of concrete tools that really helped companies to become more confident, to see how to implement this formula at home (IM 1)*

Source: the authors' own research.

The challenges in the interim management are partly consistent with other studies. For instance, a study by Skowron-Mielnik and Sobiecki (2020) found the following typical barriers to IM employment: (1) power to take decisions – the need for additional legal safeguards to prevent possible damage to the organisation; (2) immediate threat to one's position – as outsiders IMs can replace the company's permanent managers who consequently may be unwilling to cooperate with them, fearing for their own jobs; (3) lower morale – lower morale can be observed along with resistance from the team; (4) duration of IM project – concerns about IM having the right skills and limited time to know the business inside out; (5) experience – doubts about whether it is possible to find an IM with the right skills for the business. In addition, the interim manager's entry into the company and getting to know the employees in a short period of time is another challenge in this profession.

The impact of technological developments on interim management

When analysing the impact of technological progress on the activities of the interim management profession, it is clear that the majority of respondents have experience with new digitalisation tools or are in the process of developing their skills in this area. As the analysis of the interviews shows, practically all industries are directly or indirectly dependent on technological progress, and the benefits associated with this can be measurable for companies through well-executed projects. The impact of technological progress on the activities of interim managers can be observed in terms of both the interim manager's personal development and the effects on the companies in which the managers carry out their projects. The effects that determine the development of the interim management profession in the digital economy are demonstrated in Table 16.5.

Table 16.4 Challenges facing interim managers in their profession

Main challenges	Specific challenges	Illustrative respondent statements
Individually-driven	Risk tolerance	• *There are different situations, certainly this ability to take risks, to manage risks is a very important challenge (IM 6)*
	Time pressure	• *The pace of work is faster, the responsibility is greater. I am responsible for my actions as an external actor, as a company and not as an employee (IM 2)*
	Professional instability	• *This is a certain category of unstable career formula, because here it is difficult to have a guarantee that immediately after the completion of one project there will be another one waiting, so this is a derivative of the market, which in Poland is still in an initial phase of development (IM 1)*
	Interpersonal skills	• *There is a great need for self-motivation and inner discipline. If you do not have that (...) it is difficult to organise yourself (IM 10)*
	Psychosocial abilities	• *We have to have not only the expertise, the skills, the tools, but also these psycho-physical abilities, to unravel as quickly as possible what they are telling us and to find out if it is a root cause, if it is really a symptom, only and exclusively (IM 8)*
Organisation-driven	High mobility	• *The disadvantage is that you have to be mobile (IM 5)* • *Interim managers are mobile because they rarely have projects at their place of residence, and for them this is really of little importance (IM 1)*
	Lack of business confidence	• *There is a lot of distrust (...) and as a result, the profession of a consultant has been corrupted; consultants are now treated as fraudsters by a part of Polish business (IM 3)*
	Measurable effects	• *What really matters is the completion of the task, so if it turns out that I misjudged the duration of the task at the beginning, it is my risk and my consequences (IM 2)*
	Competition within the company	• *It also happens that there is a hidden rivalry between the managers of the company, the owner of the company and the interim manager, even though the owner himself has hired him. Sometimes it is a kind of proving to oneself who is right, it takes time, energy and unfortunately slows down the project (IM 2).*
System-driven	Lack of knowledge of the job specifics	• *Very often when negotiating my projects I am compared to an employee (...) and here we have a certain dissonance (IM 2)* • *Often, when you say that you are an interim manager, it does not tell the other party much. What is it and what is the nature of the work? Unfortunately, it is very often equated with a replacement job, or a temporary contract, which is a bit misleading and devalues the profession (IM 4)*
	Lack of financial stability	• *There is already a pool of people who earn at the level of the European market, but there are also absolutely a lot of people who work for these relatively low wages and not all companies understand this need for interims (IM 1)* • *I keep saying that this is not a job for young people. Firstly because they do not have enough experience, and secondly because it does not provide financial stability (IM 5)*
	Lack of social security	• *The downside is that there is no accumulation of retirement capital, while most people entering this labour market simply do not care about it (IM 4)*
	Underdeveloped Polish IM market	• *In Poland, the market of companies that specialise in project sourcing for interim managers is still very small (IM 1)* • *As far as the challenges are concerned, it is definitely the specificity of the Polish market where the interim manager is just building his place, (...) he is just breaking through. And this is a challenge for people who 100% decide to enter the profession (IM 6)*

Source: the authors' own research.

Table 16.5 Impact of technological developments on interim management

Main effects	Specific effects	Illustrative statements from respondents
Individually-driven	Lifelong learning	• *I learn in such a way that the solutions are available. I am open to them and in my humble opinion you just have to follow what is happening and use proven tools, look at what other companies use, what customers use and adapt (IM 7)*
	The need to improve digital skills	• *I am actively searching all the time, I need to practice, I even happened to do some consulting projects for free, where I just had access to added, to tools, where I had to build some data models, just to do it on my own, because if you do not do it, if you do not practice these competences, you very quickly stop being able to use what technological solutions offer (IM 9)*
	Use of social networks	• *For us, as interim managers, it is quite important because through this media you can sometimes gain knowledge about what solutions are currently being used or what projects are being carried out by different companies (IM 7)*
Organisation-driven	Increase in efficiency	• *Digitalisation gives a lot of such tools and a real influence of the manager on the efficiency of the organisation. (...) Thanks to digitalisation we now have systems that can measure phenomena in the organisation with a regularity that was not possible in the past, and this in turn gives us the possibility to see, for example, where the reasons for some irregularities lie (IM 9)*
	Business demand	• *There has also been quite a big demand from clients for support precisely in transformation projects, digital transformation, because companies need to change, implement different kinds of solutions, improve, etc. (IM 1)*
	Quality of work	• *When I started, every single thing was in paper form. Now it is really about exchanging files through the cloud, it is about confirming or signing documents electronically already (...) and it is definitely more convenient and faster (IM 4)* • *Just the fact that most documents can already be sent electronically, that you do not have to print it out, that you can communicate, but you can see each other. It has changed the nature of work so much (IM 7)*
System-driven	Demand for interim managers	• *In the digital age there is now an increased need for interim managers (IM 3)* • *That is, to what is called analytics translator, i.e. translating these technical-information-art issues into the language of business and into the language of practical implementations, this is what interim managers will do if they want to survive in this profession of course (IM 8)*
	Impact of the pandemic	• *Digitalisation enforced by pandemics has strongly developed a whole range of skills and competences precisely in terms of communication and project management, management of distributed teams (IM 1)*
	Societal changes	• *Technological progress is forcing changes in our daily activities – we shop differently, make payments differently, do many things differently (IM 6)*

Source: the authors' own research.

In addition to the benefits resulting from the impact of technological progress, respondents also point out particular risks and constraints, including:

- limited interpersonal relationships: *It is hard to imagine working today, let alone tomorrow, without far-reaching digitalisation, but these are all tools. This leads to a complete alienation of workers, because workers need human contact, they need advice, they need someone to tell them things and talk to them about them. This cannot be done with a digital system, even with artificial intelligence* (IM 5);
- less effective communication through virtual tools: *It is certainly more difficult from the point of view of, for example, transferring certain information to the client, because it's a bit like transferring on the level of a shared screen; it's completely different from having personal contact, sitting in a conference room, making diagrams on a flipchart* (IM 1);
- low awareness of data security: *Here we get into the area of ensuring data security, which is key, and I don't mean RODO, but ensuring the data security of trade secrets, production secrets, technology secrets, business secrets. And this is a huge challenge, because at the moment in Poland again there is little original technical thought and few really rich companies, so this issue is relatively unknown* (IM 5).

The compilation of these benefits and limitations shows the key factors that may determine not only the decision to engage in an interim management collaboration but also the nature and effectiveness of such a relationship. To conclude, the results of this qualitative study reduce the existing gap in research on the state and development of interim management in the digital economy in Poland. The empirical data are intended to deepen this research. The available material, albeit mainly based on limited research populations, seems to indirectly indicate the role that the factors discussed here may play in ensuring that the needs of organisations are effectively met through the use of interim management solutions.

Conclusions and practical implications

Changes occurring on the market have increased the demand for highly qualified project leaders, including interim managers. The increase in industrial production in Poland and beyond, despite the pandemic, indicates that investments are being made in various ventures. This increases the demand for managers who have not only substantive competencies in finance, logistics and production organisation, but also the ability to communicate effectively with teams and build organisational culture. Experienced, creative, responsible and committed interim managers are sorely needed, particularly for managing digital transformation projects, which are often very unique. Analyses show that the use of interim management for temporary employment of highly qualified and experienced top managers may in many business situations be strategically more advantageous and financially more profitable than the use of other flexible forms of employment.

The Polish interim management market is a relatively new phenomenon. This study formulated two research questions: (1) what are the benefits and challenges for interim management in the digital economy? and (2) what is the impact of the digital economy on interim managers? Employing an empirical-inductive approach, this study considered a wide range of benefits and challenges of this flexible form of employment, which can be categorised into individually-driven, organisation-driven and system-driven.

These factors help to answer the general question: is it better to hire an employee on a traditional employment contract or an expert in a flexible form of employment? For this purpose, the advantages and disadvantages of both must be analysed, for both the employer and interim managers. This form of flexible employment can be used in companies of all sizes and in a variety of conditions. It can be applied in almost any workplace and will bring tangible benefits to both parties in the employment relationship.

From the perspective of European markets, interim management has evolved over the last few decades. It now focuses on projects executed in areas that are perceived as the most challenging tasks companies must solve: strategy, sales and digital transformation of the business model. Referring to the experience of previous years, it can be said that interim management is a formula whose popularity increases in times of economic crisis. This is also confirmed by examples from Western countries, where the market for interim management services is well-developed. In the face of globalisation, which has been brought about mainly by the development of information technology and telecommunications, entrepreneurs are forced to make decisions on which the existence of their companies often depends.

It is increasingly observed that employers apply a policy of reducing fixed costs, which are primarily employee costs. Companies are increasingly interested in looking for cheaper forms of employment, which may come in the form of flexible forms of employment. Flexibility influences the growth of mobility and the activity of employees on the labour market while increasing the competitiveness of companies applying such forms of employment. Flexible forms of employment are still a novelty on the labour market, as many of them are not covered by legal regulations.

References

Babbie, E.R. (2013). *The practice of social research* (13th ed.). Belmont, CA: Wadsworth Publishing.

Cope, J. (2011). Entrepreneurial learning from failure: An interpretative phenomenological analysis. *Journal of Business Venturing, 26*(6), 604–623.

Davis, J.B. (2005). Interim management: A new approach to trouble shooting. *Training Journal, June*, 46–49.

Denzin, N.K., & Lincoln, Y.S. (2005). Introduction: The discipline and practice of qualitative research. In N.K. Denzin & Y.S. Lincoln (Eds.), *Handbook of qualitative research* (3rd ed., pp. 1–32). Thousand Oaks, CA: Sage.

Dźwigoł, H. (2020). Interim management as a new approach to the company management. *Review of Business and Economics Studies, 1*(1), 20–26.

Eurofound. (2020). *New forms of employment: 2020 update.* Luxembourg: Publications Office of the European Union.

Flick, U. (2009). *An introduction to qualitative research* (4th ed.). Thousand Oaks, CA: Sage Publications Ltd.

Goffin, H. (2019). Interim management–das moderne Managementformat: Markt, Chancen, Risiken und reale Projekte. In P. Buchenau (Ed.), *Chefsache Interim Management* (pp. 25–49). Wiesbaden: Springer Gabler.

IIM. (2020). *IIM guide to Interim Management.* Surrey: Institute of Interim Management (IIM). Available at: https://www.iim.org.uk/wp-content/uploads/2020/10/IIM-Guide_to-Interim-Management_Oct20.pdf (accessed 20 August 2021).

INIMA. (2021). *The 2021 European survey.* International Network of Interim Manager Associations. Available at: https://www.inima.management/s/inima-europe-r5.pdf (accessed 5 September 2021).

Papmehl, A. (2019). Restrukturierung und Sanierung: Hinweise aus Interim Management-Perspektive. In A. Papmehl & H. Teichmanis (Eds.), *Deutsches Arbeitsrecht für ausländische Investoren (German labour law for foreign investors)* (pp. 113–123). Wiesbaden: Springer Gabler.

Rädiker, S., & Morgenstern-Einenkel, A. (2021). *Working in teams with MAXQDA. Organization, division of labor, and implementation in seven phases.* Berlin: MAXQDA Press.

Şenturan, Ş. (2018). Interim Management key points for success. *Knowledge International Journal, 28*(1), 69–72.

SIM. (2015). *Interim Management – Innovative solution in age and business management. Interim Management Methodology.* Warszawa: Polish Interim Managers Association (SIM).

SIM. (2021). *Interim Management w Polsce: Raport z badania realizowanego w 2020 roku.* Warszawa: Polish Interim Managers Association (SIM).

Skowron-Mielnik, B., & Sobiecki, G. (2020). Effectiveness factors in Interim Management projects-research concept. *Scientific Papers of Silesian University of Technology, 149*(1), 575–593.

Smith, J.A., & Eatough, V. (2006). Interpretative phenomenological analysis. In G.M. Breakwell, S. Hammond, C. Fife-Schaw, & J.A. Smith (Eds.), *Research methods in psychology* (pp. 322–341). Thousand Oaks, CA: Sage Publications.

Yin, R.K. (2018). *Case study research and applications: Design and methods* (6th ed.). London: SAGE Publications.

17 Zero-hours contracts in the United Kingdom

Iwona Kubica and Richard Pettinger

Introduction

Over the past 20 years, flexible working of all kinds has come very much to the fore. This has been driven by a variety of forces, including demographic shifts, labour market, regulations, macroeconomic and technological changes (ILO, 2021). The latter enables many jobs and occupations to be carried out anywhere that there is a computer, internet and IT link, and so it has become increasingly common for people to work remotely or from home. This trend accelerated during the 2020 economic crisis and the attendant changes in working patterns and locations brought on by the COVID-19 pandemic (ONS, 2021). The pandemic has also affected business activities.

Non-standard forms of employment, also referred to as flexible or diverse forms of work, atypical working or casual contracts (ILO, 2021; Datta, Giupponi, & Machin, 2019; Reljic, Cetrulo, Cirillo, & Coveri, 2021; Sanders, 2017) is an umbrella term encompassing a wide range of jobs. These terms differentiate a standard employment contract from other employment arrangements (OECD, 2019), often with no guaranteed working hours (so-called *zero-hour contracts*). The latter is not a legal term (Koumenta & Williams, 2018), but it's defined as "an agreement between two parties that one may be asked to perform work for another but there is no minimum set contracted hours" (CIPD, 2013, p. 3). Given the wide range of non-standard forms of employment, there is no "one-size-fits-all" approach to employment rights, as the person working under the contract can be an employee, a worker or a self-employed person (Adams & Prassl, 2018). To be called an "employee," a number of criteria must be considered (Cabinet Office, 2019):

- significant integration into the structure of the employer's organisation,
- clothing, equipment and/or other materials needed to carry out the work are provided by the employer,
- exclusivity must be determined (that is, if the person is allowed to work for others),
- the mode of payment and how the person is to be treated for tax and national insurance (NI) purposes must be decided,
- benefits and sick pay are provided.

DOI: 10.4324/9781003254638-21

In contrast, "workers" are individuals engaged on a contract for service basis (typically zero-hours contract workers). Such a contract states what pay the individual will get if they do work, and what will happen when they turn down work. According to ILO, flexible forms include *temporary employment; part-time and on-call work; temporary agency work and other multiparty employment relationships; as well as disguised employment and dependent self-employment.* Workers are entitled to certain basic employment rights, including paid annual leave, national minimum wage and discrimination protection, but the spectrum is smaller than what is offered with employment rights (Adams & Prassl, 2018; Cabinet Office, 2019; CIPD, 2013).

The specific form of these contractual arrangements varies among countries and legal frameworks, but a common feature of non-standard forms of employment is a reduction in job security, greater hour variability and featuring prominently on digital platforms (Farina, Green, & McVicar 2021; ILO, 2021). The United Kingdom regulates only one aspect of zero-hours contracts (UK Employment Rights Act, 1996) – prohibiting exclusivity clause, i.e. preventing an employee from working for another (more than one) employer (Cabinet Office, 2019). Several recent studies have shown that zero-hours jobs typically offer 30% to 50% lower wages than other jobs in the United Kingdom (Clarke & Cominetti, 2019; Farina et al., 2021). They also raise concerns about social protection in general, and pension protection in particular (OECD, 2019). However, the number of workers falling into the "non-standard employment arrangement" category has risen substantially in recent years (Figure 17.1).

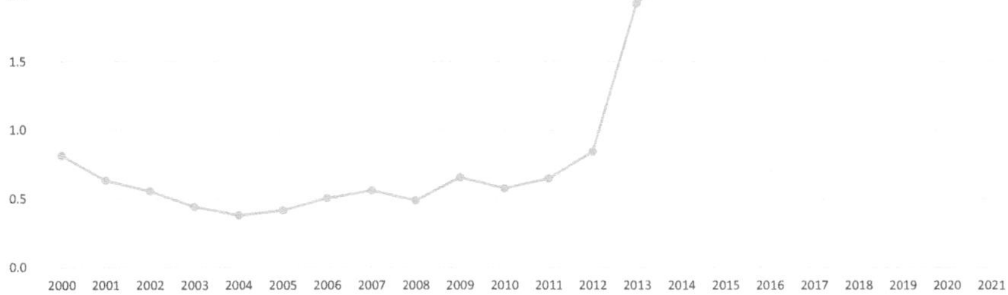

Figure 17.1 Percentage of people in employment on a zero-hours contract in the United Kingdom

Source: own elaboration based on ONS (2021).

According to ONS (2021), people on flexible contracts are more likely than other workers to be young, part-time (25.2 hours a week on average), women from a BME background (TUC, 2021) or in full-time education. The type of workers that might use zero-hours contracts includes casual hours (students who work only during holidays), cleaners, bank workers, care workers, administrative workers, delivery drivers, hospitality workers (CIPD, 2013; MIRS, 2021). Hence, non-standard workers are far from being a homogenous group, and often remain in this type of contract for a long time (Katz & Krueger, 2019; OECD, 2019).

This chapter takes stock of all the different non-standard patterns of work that fall under the description of a zero-hours contract in the United Kingdom. It looks at the gig economy, portfolio occupations and careers, flexible hours and attendance patterns, and payment by results while working in remote locations, from both positive and negative points of view. It also covers the need for organisational, supervisory and management relationships, and the patterns and expertise of supervision required to make them effective. Finally, it proposes the development of management practices and also addresses staff engagement issues that are required if these patterns of work are to be made enduring, viable and valuable to all stakeholders.

Research methodology

The study is based on a data set collected in the context of the non-standard working patterns, with a special focus on contracts, where employees have no guarantee of hours worked monthly. While the diversity in working patterns has allowed more workers to integrate into the labour market, it has also posed challenges in terms of working conditions and companies' performance, and has also led to changes in labour markets, economics and societies (ILO, 2021; Małkowska, Urbaniec, & Kosała, 2021). As mentioned above, employment status is important as it determines the individual's employment rights and is regulated by countries independently (OECD, 2019). In the United Kingdom, England and Wales, Scotland, and Northern Ireland each has separate legal jurisdictions and systems. Statutory employment protection legislation is common for Great Britain, but there are some subtle differences between Wales and the United Kingdom or the Isle of Man. Hence we focus on non-standard forms of employment in the United Kingdom as well as how they are both regulated and practiced (Adams & Prassl, 2018; Cabinet Office, 2019).

The analysis is based on the examination of secondary data, including from the public databases of the Office for National Statistics (ONS, 2021), as well as reports (TUC, 2021) and guidelines (Adams & Prassl, 2018) highlighting the most significant changes in the 21st century on the UK labour market.

In the United Kingdom, zero-hours contracts were regulated in 2015 by the Exclusivity Terms in Zero hours Contracts (Redress) Regulations made under the UK Employment Rights Act 1996. A year later, Matthew Taylor was commissioned as Chief Executive of the Royal Society of Arts to conduct a review of modern employment practices (Cabinet Office, 2019). Published in July 2017, his report included 53 recommendations, but only a few were directly relevant to zero-hours contract workers. Followed by further consultations, the Government published the "Good work plan" (HM Government, 2018) agreeing to:

- Extend the right to a written statement (contract) to all "workers" and consult on what information to include;
- Ask the Low Pay Commission (LPC) to consider the impacts of the introduction of a higher National Minimum Wage rate (NMW) for hours that are not guaranteed as part of the contract (zero-hours contract);
- Extend from two weeks to one month the relevant break in service as the basis for the continuous service qualifying period;
- Provide a right to workers on zero-hours contracts to "request a stable contract from the employer after six months if their hours, pattern of work and/or work activities indicate there is an ongoing relationship between the workers and the employer" (Cabinet Office, 2019, p. 32) or guarantee a stable contract after one year if the abovementioned conditions are met and the employer cannot justify withholding a stable contract on objective grounds and provide protection against dismissal and detriment to zero-hours contract workers who assert their statutory rights in respect of any of the above;
- Monitor the impact of corporate governance reforms, as companies beyond a certain size should report on how many requests they have received/agreed to from zero-hours contract workers for fixed hours.

It goes without saying that fair and decent work should be available to all, but digital economy and wider societal trends impact how, when and where people work. Both employers and workers/employees should be educated about employment rights for all and made aware of the benefits and drawbacks of various flexible forms of employment.

Research findings

It is essential for companies and organisations of all sizes to be able to hire and contract people for a variety of jobs and occupations at very short notice (implying, at the same time, that people can also be laid off at very short notice if there are further crises and lockdowns). Flexible and zero-hours work patterns and gig economy approaches have allowed great advances and developments in these forms of working.

Jobs and occupations

In practice, people often find they need to move or take multiple positions to afford the lifestyle they want. People are increasingly used to having to change careers many times throughout their lifetime, so the gig economy and gig economies can be viewed as a reflection of this occurring on a large scale. In this context, and also in practice, a wide variety of positions, jobs, opportunities and activities fall within the definition of gig working, flexible working and zero-hours contracts and contracting. For example:

- driving jobs, attached to all categories of vehicles and deliveries. The opportunities that these kinds of jobs provide have increased during the Covid-19 pandemic, as customers have had to rely far more on the delivery of goods and services, rather than going out and buying what they need and want;
- technology development, including coding, software and app development, again recognising that people's needs and wants have changed during the pandemic. This has led to entrepreneurial opportunities as well as gaining project work for larger and well-established organisations;
- delivering online teaching and learning. Over the course of the pandemic, those in full time school, high school, further and higher education have had more challenges than many, and this has, in turn, created opportunities for people to develop their own specific approaches to every aspect of education. School and home tutoring, micro qualifications, special interest courses, executive development and some core technology qualifications can all now be found online, and they deliver these services and opportunities in ways that communities, markets and locations demand. Alongside this, the delivery of general interest courses has also expanded (creative writing, cookery, fitness, yoga and pilates, to name a few);
- care working for all at-risk and vulnerable groups. Many local authorities that would normally deliver these services have found themselves unable to cope with the sheer volume of demand, and this has led to clients in these groups seeking alternative provisions.

As the opportunities for flexible and quick response work has grown, many people in regularised jobs and occupations have also taken up gig and zero-hours working as second or subsidiary jobs. Again, these opportunities have been opened up by technology, and by the ever-greater growth in demand for this kind of work that is occurring in all sectors and locations. While many of these opportunities and activities were there before the pandemic, the proliferation has taken place because of the developments in technology connectivity and assurance, mobile technology and platforms such as WhatsApp, Zoom and Teams. Presenting these opportunities is also far easier because of the use of social and digital media marketing and other activities, and because the movement restrictions brought on by the pandemic, people are now used to searching for them online.

From an organisational point of view, this means that organisations can target their resources much more effectively, so that they pay only for the work that is required, when it is required. Employers also have a wider range of applicants to choose from at short notice. Those who work as gig workers, zero-hours, freelancers or as temporary staff do not go through extensive, expensive and exhaustive recruitment and selection processes: they are hired as the result of a brief meeting or phone/zoom call, or as the result of email or SMS exchanges. The work can be commissioned much more quickly (in many cases instantly) and payment methods and schedules agreed on an individual basis. This also means the costs of premises can be reduced.

Economic and financial considerations also contribute to the development of the gig economies. Employers who cannot afford to hire full-time employees hire part-time or temporary ones to shore up staff at busier times or for specific projects. This process is constantly evolving and developing; those who work zero hours and as contractors are now starting to take on tasks that were historically core organisational activities, including:

- some core human resource management activities (e.g. payroll, problem solving, managing and commissioning training and development);
- technology development, especially software development and its management;
- customer services management: while large organisations tend to hire specialist firms in this area, smaller companies now find themselves taking on local specialists who work for them when required;
- marketing activities, especially the hiring of gig economy and zero hours workers to manage and direct social and digital media marketing activities;
- local delivery services, e.g. for people who cannot easily get out to buy and consume products and services as they did before, and which historically would have been done by the particular organisations directly.

Moreover, employers need to plan for changes to the world of work, including the gig economy, when the crisis has ended. This will mean (in fact, means already) that companies are going to have to take active steps to manage the relationships between themselves and their freelancers, so that enduring, productive and profitable relationships continue. No company wants to find itself unable to build on its strengths and opportunities and the growth and development available because of staff and expertise shortages.

Portfolio occupations and careers

Handy (1993) defined, developed and popularised the "portfolio" concept. His identified the 'portfolio career' when he realised that individuals would be required to develop portable skillsets to meet the needs of a fast-moving future workplace and working environment. His prediction foresaw everything with which we are now familiar: gig economies, zero hours, hours to suit and non-standard hours, flexible working patterns and a proliferation of locations of work and locations where work can be done, as well as addressing the key social and wider concerns around work-life balance.

New patterns of work and gig economies provide people opportunities to build 'portfolio careers'. A portfolio career comprises a variety of roles rather than one job at a single organisation. Portfolio occupations and careers combine multiple paid roles and activities, integrated by the individual to deliver the required volumes of work and income, and integrated into their own desired quality of life and work-life balance.

Zero-hours contracts have many advantages. In principle there are advantages to employees in that they work the hours they choose, and they can spread these hours out over the whole of the day/week/month so as to fit in with the other life and social choices that exist for everyone around their work. Organisations take the view that they can call on people at any time to ask them to work more hours now in return for time off during quieter periods. This also suits many people in their roles as workers, enabling them to have many different jobs and occupations at the same time, knowing that none of these are full-time (Woodcock, 2020). When everything is positive, this benefits:

- employers, in that they effectively get an extensive trial of staff working in these ways, allowing them to see who is best and most reliable in terms of a work ethic and in the ability to deliver the results sought and demanded. Employers can then expand working relationships with individuals they find to be a good operational and cultural fit;
- employers, in that they are able to further maximise and optimise the use of their premises. In many cases employers have been able to shut off and either sell or reallocate premises because of the amount of work that is now being done remotely or by gig workers;
- individuals, in that they too get the opportunity to work for a variety of different employers and contractors, to see who is the best fit in terms of rewards, culture, relationships and working environment. Again, so long as the work and rewards are suitable, individuals can then develop greater and more substantial relations with those with whom they enjoy productive, profitable and positive working relations;
- individuals, in that they get to choose where they work from, and when. In many cases, those on zero hours or other flexible working bases do need to attend the organisation as and when demanded. In other cases, individuals choose to work from home, business centres, hotels, cafes and other convenient locations.

Flexible hours and attendance patterns

In addition to the above, flexible hours and attendance patterns are driven by:

- organisations maximising and optimising the use of their premises in relation to employee attendance;

- staff working to hours that suit them, enabling them to balance work with other priorities (child care, care for elderly relatives);
- concentration on delivering results rather than attendance and visibility;
- the nature of work, e.g., many administrative tasks require results delivered by deadlines, but where and how these tasks are completed is immaterial.

This has led to many organisations offering work from home and remote work as normal practice. A key advantage is that staff then do not have to travel to work but can start as soon or as late as they choose, or work out of normal hours – subject only to the delivery of the right volumes of work, to the required quality and standard, and to deadlines (Petriglieri, Ashford, & Wrzesniewski, 2018). Flexible working has also led to zero-hours working, especially on a daily basis. If full flexibility is allowed, this can mean that people will work no hours on some days, and up to 20 hours on others. For some organisations and individuals, this may be a logistical problem; for others, it is exactly what is needed. So long as the targets are met, how the employees themselves decide how their work is delivered; the work processes are not directly supervised by the organisation.

Piecework and payments by results

Piecework and pay-by-results occupations often involve working from home, with the individual getting paid upon receipt and acceptance of the products and services delivered by the organisation. There is no recognition of the length of time or commitment required to produce the items (though it is common to factor in a part of the payment for the hours worked). Such occupations include garment production, computer programming, 'creative' activities such as painting and sculpture. In these sectors there is a history and tradition of working in these ways, and so those who go into these occupations know and understand the organisational and occupational parameters and choose to work within them. In many cases, effective use of IT and the opportunities afforded by the technology driven environment have enabled those who work in these industries to enlarge their reach and activities.

Hybrid organisations and work patterns

Hybrid organisations are those that do not require traditional, established and assured patterns of attendance and occupation. Hybrid organisations were defined by Hemingway and Breu (2003) as having a very strong social orientation, as well as requiring sustainability and viability. This proposition was developed by Pettinger (2020) to include organisations based on there being an integrated place of work and remote working activities. Hybrid organisations were always considered to be those that had task-oriented culture (Handy, 1994), focused on company behaviour (Deal & Kennedy 1982) and matrix structures (Pettinger, 2002). In such workplaces, where and how work is done is not as important as the results achieved. This also applies to Porter's (1980) cost leadership and competitive advantage strategies.

Growing out of the COVID-19 pandemic, hybrid organisations with mixed patterns of work have developed because of the availability of communications and information technology, and the linkages that have enabled people to work from places other than their organisation's premises (e.g., home, hotel business suites, business centres, cafes and restaurants). This has led to fundamental shifts in hours and patterns of work, occupational content, and context, and working and occupational (and social) relations. It is also leading organisations to re-evaluate their needs, wants and demands for physical premises, what those premises are to be used for, their size, location and scale.

Hybrid organisations, in turn, become very amenable to employing people on flexible, gig work, contracted and zero-hours contracts. Those who choose these forms gain full flexibility (Petriglieri et al., 2018). Subject to the organisation's ability to call up staff to work at determined and agreed forewarnings and patterns of notice, work is carried out to maximum commercial advantage for the organisation, and maximum convenience to the staff involved.

Hybrid organisations and flexible and zero-hours working patterns enable contractor-client relationships to be built. Staff are not on payroll, but are summoned on the basis that they are self-employed and will work as contractors whenever there is work to be done. This pattern of zero hours is not new: companies and organisations have always employed specialists on an 'as and when demanded' basis. What is new is the broadening out of this approach to include what are described as unskilled and semi-skilled occupations, e.g., Amazon employs some warehouse staff on this basis, as do many bars and restaurants in urban environments.

Gig economies

Major by-products of zero hours and flexible working practices have come to be described as 'gig economies'. The plural 'gig economies' is more useful and accurate than the singular 'the gig economy' because gig workers are likely only to be able to work in their given locality, and to be as flexible and responsive as they choose to be there. However, location also includes virtual locations; and while virtual locations do give an overtly global reach, gig and zero-hours workers will most likely choose those with whom they are more or less familiar if possible.

In gig economies, temporary and flexible jobs are commonplace and give full flexibility to both the companies that hire gig and zero hours workers, and to the workers, who then choose to work the hours and places and for the clients and contractors that they choose. In gig economies, large numbers of people work in part-time or temporary positions or as independent contractors. They work from locations other than standard and established company and organisation premises; and as above, these premises include the home, business centres, cars, cafes and other more or less suitable and convenient premises.

In many cases the outputs of flexible and gig working and gig economies are wide ranging, widely available and often cheaper, more efficient and more readily available services, such as transport (Uber), accommodation (Airbnb), food delivery (JustEat), courier services (Randox and other specialist deliveries) and a range of other delivery services (contractors who work for DPD and Amazon).

However, the overall effectiveness of gig economies and gig working will ultimately depend on universal and assured IT and internet connectivity, and the consequent ability to call up any and all services at short notice. People who don't use technological services and the internet may be excluded from the opportunities and benefits of gig economies and gig working. Gig economies need to have their own definable critical masses to support gig and flexible workers from a social and economic point of view. Cities tend to have the most varied and widely developed opportunities for gig and zero-hour contract workers (Datta et al., 2019). Smaller and more rural gig economies require a greater willingness to be flexible for gig and zero-hours workers: the opportunities are still there, but those who work in these ways may have to accept a much wider variety of gig, zero-hours and flexible work if they are to make these ways of working economically and financially viable.

Contextual factors

Despite their numerous benefits, numerous contextual factors and caveats must be recognised and addressed when considering these ways of working and gig economies. These patterns of work remove other social patterns of work and life structures that people are accustomed to. They also remove well-understood career and occupational development pathways that are still socially as well as occupationally a part of mainstream business activity. For some workers, the flexibility of working in these ways is disruptive to the work-life balance, sleep patterns and activities of daily life. Flexibility in gig economies often means that workers have to make themselves available any time gigs come up, regardless of their other needs; and they must always be looking around for new opportunities.

In effect, therefore, flexible, zero hours and other non-standard workers in gig economies and activities are more like entrepreneurs than traditional workers. While this may mean greater freedom of choice for the individual worker, it also means that the security of a steady job is removed. Regular pay, benefits and rewards (intrinsic and extrinsic) are removed also. Socialising with colleagues, and forming and developing social as well as occupational patterns of behaviour, and daily routines that have characterised work for generations are being diluted. This therefore means that those who work in these ways have to be given the space to develop in their own ways.

Conclusions and practical implications

All departures from regular patterns of attendance affect the organisational culture and climate. They also affect the organisation's social strength and orientation. This is not to say that such changes are or need to be negative; but they do have to be acknowledged and recognised, as do the effects on the overall culture, structure and climate in terms of development, cohesion and inclusion. The results of this analysis show an evaluation of all the different non-standard work patterns that fall under the description of 'zero hours'.

The patterns of flexible working or zero hours identified include concepts such as the gig economy, portfolio occupations and careers, flexible working hours and patterns of attendance and payment for performance when working remotely, as well as organisational and managerial patterns and knowledge. These patterns demonstrate the nature and effectiveness of employment relationships, but also organisational identity and employee practices in the United Kingdom, from both a positive and negative perspective. The results of the analysis may contribute to the development of sustainable practices at the organisational level, employee engagement and organisational leadership:

- organisational relations – changing organisational relationships requires the use of ties and habits formed in the past. In many cases this means recognising and acknowledging that what has brought the organisation this far is no longer either effective or suitable (in occupational or human terms).

  From a behavioural point of view, adjusting to and dealing with this shortcoming is difficult. Hybrid working and flexible and zero hours and gig-based patterns of work are driving a social as well as commercial and industrial revolution and evolution (Pettinger, 2020). This is being enhanced in many cases by the enforced physical separation from previously assured patterns of work and occupation: people are not even allowed to go into their organisation for any reason. They are directed to work from home or from COVID safe locations. When they do finally get back on the premises, they are going find that so much has changed.
- staff engagement – staff engagement is traditionally based on recognising organisations as both social and occupational entities. This, in turn, becomes a cornerstone of the strength and integrity of the organisation overall. People build friendships and social as well as occupational networks at work. Zero hours working, flexible working, portfolio careers and the gig economy all change the workplace experience for those involved. The overall social patterns that exist in organisations are historically based on seeing people every day, knowing that they are in and around, and relating everything to the ability to see and meet with others whenever needed or wanted. Many of these interactions are as much social as occupational, and whatever the purpose of the interaction, there is a strong social underpinning in terms of norms, forms of address,

manners, appearances and demeanour. This is fundamentally changed in zero hours, flexible working and gig economy patterns of employment. People do not meet on a regularised and assured or assumed basis. If conversations take place by phone, or using digital platforms such as Zoom and Skype, then the human dynamic changes; and above all, the three-dimensional face-to-face situation is lost. Seeing body language, hearing inflexions of language and judging general demeanour are harder to do through virtual, camera-enabled connections than at face-to-face meetings.

This is compounded when there is a more or less universal opportunity for all staff to flexi-work or work zero hours or hours to suit. Everyone having their own patterns of work make it much less likely that they will meet with colleagues on a regular and (perceived and real) assured basis, and so the relationships and dynamics underpinning them change.

- leadership – none of this is to say that any of this is a bad thing; nor does it presume that regular attendance and full familiarity are good things. It does require a fundamental shift in leadership, management and entrepreneurial attitudes, approaches and expertise if hybrid organisations and flexible and zero hours working are to be effective and deliver the performance levels and outputs demanded. Patterns of leadership and the expertise that accompanies them (Vicary & Jones, 2017) have to be developed so that:

  - staff on zero hours and other flexible patterns of work are as fully integrated as everyone else;
  - staff on zero hours and other flexible patterns of work have their contribution recognised as thoroughly as everyone else;
  - staff on zero hours and other flexible patterns of work must be subject to the same standards of discipline, conduct, behaviour and performance as everyone else;
  - staff on zero hours and other flexible patterns of work must have the same rights to sickness leave, holiday pay, time off and away from work as everyone else.

  Leaders, executives, managers and supervisors must therefore learn how to evaluate and deliver in each of these areas on an equitable and transparent basis. Organisations need to benefit from the flexibility afforded by using the gig economy and flexible patterns of work, including zero hours, and use it to their best advantage. However, there has to be recognition that whenever those on zero hours or other patterns of work do work, they are making a full and critical contribution to the organisation (otherwise they should not be working at all).
- Changes and developments in leadership, managerial and supervisory expertise – the above key fundamental changes required in leadership, managerial and supervisory expertise must be made if zero hours and

flexible patterns of work are to be effective, mutually beneficial and profitable, and sustainable. This expertise has to shift to include the effective and sustainable management, engagement and commitment of people who are not always (or indeed ever) visible. A key managerial task has therefore to be going out to see and meet with people who work on a flexible and non-standard basis and getting to know them in the same ways a manager gets to know and understand those who work according to standard patterns.

The full range of staff management tasks and imperatives should also be considered:

- recruitment, selection and orientation/onboarding;
- integration of new staff;
- performance management and appraisal;
- discipline and sanctions;
- sickness, absence and non-attendance/non delivery of work;
- holiday pay;
- rewards and recognition;
- collective and individual development;
- career development.

All of these issues require a fundamental shift in the collective and individual understanding of the needs, wants and demands of the organisation, the work, and those who work on zero hours and other flexible/non-standard bases. It is also important to recognise that those working on permanent contracts within the gig economy are building their career portfolios; and this, in turn, requires a much broader understanding of what employee, organisation and staff development should strive to achieve (Senge, 1996).

References

Adams, A., & Prassl, J. (2018). *Zero-hours work in the United Kingdom*. Geneva: International Labour Organization.

Cabinet Office. (2019). Chief Minister's zero hours contracts committee. Report. Available at: https://www.gov.im/media/1366407/chief-ministers-zero-hours-contracts-committee-report-2019.pdf (accessed 24 August 2021).

CIPD (2013). Zero-hours contracts: Myth and reality. Research report, November 2013. London: Chartered Institute of Personnel and Development.

Clarke, S., & Cominetti, N. (2019). *Setting the record straight: How record employment has changed the UK*. London: Resolution Foundation.

Datta, N., Giupponi, G., & Machin, S. (2019). Zero-hours contracts and labour market policy. *Economic Policy, 34*(99), 369–427.

Deal, T.E., & Kennedy, A.A. (1982). *Corporate culture: The rites and rituals of corporate life*. New York: Perseus Book Publishing.

Farina, E., Green, C., & McVicar, D. (2021). Are estimates of non-standard employment wage penalties robust to different wage measures? The case of zero-hour contracts in the UK. *Industrial Relations, 60*(3), 370–399.

Hemingway, C.J., & Breu, K. (2003). From traditional to virtual organisation: implications for work unit boundaries. In *ECIS 2003 Proceedings* (pp. 778–787). Available at: http://aisel.aisnet.org/ecis2003/68 (accessed 24 October 2021).

Handy, C.B. (1993). *Understanding organisations*. Oxford: Oxford University Press.

Handy, C.B. (1994). *The empty raincoat*. London: Arrow Books.

HM Government (2018). Good work plan. Industrial Strategy. Available at: https://assets.publishing.service.gov.uk/government/uploads/system/uploads/attachment_data/file/766187/good-work-plan-printready.pdf (accessed 24 August 2021).

ILO (2021). *Non-standard forms of employment*. International Labour Organization: Geneva. Available at: https://www.ilo.org/global/topics/non-standard-employment/lang--en/index.htm (accessed 24 August 2021).

Katz, L.F., & Krueger, A.B. (2019). *The rise and nature of alternative work arrangements in the United States,* 1995–2015. *LR Review, 72*, 382–416.

Koumenta, M., & Williams, M. (2018). An anatomy of zero-hour contracts in the UK. *Industrial Relations Journal, 50*(1), 20–40.

Małkowska, A., Urbaniec, M., & Kosała, M. (2021). The impact of digital transformation on European countries: Insights from a comparative analysis. *Equilibrium. Quarterly Journal of Economics and Economic Policy, 16*(2), 325–355.

MIRS. (2021). *A guide to Zero Hour Contracts*. Douglas (Isle of Man): Manx Industrial Relations Service.

OECD. (2019). *Pensions at a Glance 2019*. OECD and G20 Indicators. Paris: OECD Publishing: Paris. https://doi.org/10.1787/b6d3dcfc-en

ONS (2021). *Labour market overview*. Office for National Statistics: London Available at: https://www.ons.gov.uk/employmentandlabourmarket/peopleinwork/employmentandemployeetypes/bulletins/uklabourmarket/august2021 (accessed 30 August 2021).

Petriglieri, G, Ashford, S.J, & Wrzesniewski, A. (2018). Thriving in the gig economy. *Harvard Business Review*, March – April, 140–143.

Pettinger, R (2002). *Mastering organisational behaviour*. London: Palgrave.

Pettinger, R. (2020). *The socio-economic foundations of sustainable business: Managing in the fourth industrial revolution*. Cham: Springer.

Porter, M.E. (1980). *Competitive strategy: Techniques for analyzing industries and competitors*. New York: Free Press.

Reljic, J., Cetrulo, A., Cirillo, V., & Coveri, A. (2021). Non-standard work and innovation: Evidence from European industries. *Economics of Innovation and New Technology*, 1–29. doi:10.1080/10438599.2021.1893139

Sanders, A. (2017). Fairness in the contract of employment. *Industrial Law Journal, 46*(4), 508–542.

Senge, P.M. (1996). *The fifth discipline*. New York: Currency.

The Exclusivity Terms in Zero hours Contracts (Redress) Regulations 2015. Available at: https://www.legislation.gov.uk/ukdsi/2015/9780111139950 (accessed 2 September 2021).

TUC (2021). *BME workers on zero-hours contracts. A joint report by the Trades Union Congress and Race on the Agenda*. Trades Union Congress: London. Available at: https://www.tuc.org.uk/sites/default/files/2021-06/RotAreport.pdf (accessed 30 August 2021).

UK Employment Rights Act 1996. Available at: https://www.legislation.gov.uk/ukpga/1996/18/contents (accessed 24 August 2021).

Woodcock, J. (2020). *The gig economy: A critical introduction*. Cambridge: Polity.

Vicary, A., & Jones, K. (2017). The implications of contractual terms of employment for women and leadership: An autoethnographic study in UK higher education. *Administrative Sciences,* 7(2), 20.

18 Profile of digital workers in Spain

Víctor F. Climent

Introduction

As a result of the impact of the SARS-CoV-2 pandemic (COVID-19) entering every dimension of people's lives, quantitative studies have been carried out in most European countries to investigate changes caused by the lockdowns imposed by governments on society and the economy. Survey 3316,[1] carried out by the CIS (Sociological Research Centre, Spain), gathered data on a nationally representative sample of the population with at least 162 items on digital behaviour in the labour market, among other aspects of life (CIS, 2021). The survey focused primarily on teleworking. Data were collected from the 8th to 17th of March 2021, coinciding with the end of the third wave of infections, the peak of which had occurred at the end of January, with 600 deaths reported daily. Due to the lockdowns decreed in Spain, most employees, but especially teachers, administrative, managerial and managerial support staff, were required to switch to online work and telework. For the purposes of this study, telework involves the use of the internet, digital tools like email and/or digital platforms, and the necessary skills enabling the worker to perform their skills from home.

There is no universally accepted definition of teleworking. However, our review of the literature suggests that a definition can be outlined based on various characteristics that distinguish teleworking from traditional ways of working. These include the use of ICT (Information and Communication Technologies) (Gray, Hodson, & Gordon, 1993), autonomy at work (Olsen, 1988) or locations involving intra- and extra-organisational communication (Gillespie, Richardson, & Cornford, 1995). Belzunegui-Eraso and Erro-Garcés (2020) also highlight the use of computers and telematic technologies to perform tasks and provide services remotely. In this study, we pay particular attention to the use and availability of ICTs as government-imposed lockdowns have forced workers to establish a workplace at home. As a result, the location is supposed to be fixed for those workers who came under the mandate. The variables included in the 3316 survey conducted by the CIS effectively capture the heterogeneous use of the internet connections and the uneven availability of digital equipment for work in citizens' homes. These

DOI: 10.4324/9781003254638-22

variables also enable us to assess the productivity of survey workers, given the digital nature of the tasks they had to perform remotely due to the lockdown.

Even though the digital transformation is considered to be extended to every aspect of everyday life, in the Spanish labour market several problems have been widely highlighted. These are considered to strengthen the negative impact of economic crises such as the 2008 financial bankruptcy or the COVID-19 pandemic. Under the hypothesis that the uses and availability of ICT is not homogeneously extended and distributed among all strata of society, beneath the lack of heterogeneity lie structural imbalances that can shed light on the different profiles of digital workers in the Spanish labour market.

The common axis of the empirical analysis and the wider academic debate place the origin of the broader set of the structural problems in the Spanish labour market in the historical imbalances observed in the industrial evolution and development. Among the most important debates, the reproduction of pre-democratic power structures is particularly noteworthy (Etxezarreta, 1991; Fernández Cuesta & Fernández Prieto, 1999; Nadal, 1975). The same applies to the expansion of Spanish industry in the semi-periphery, where the capacity to retain the value obtained in the production chain is less than in the central places of the global economy. (Díaz-Mora & García López, 2016; Martínez Peinado, 2011; Martínez Peinado & Carió Céspedes, 2014).

These imbalances placed Spain in a well-known scenario in the aftermath of the 2008 financial crisis. The country's labour market reform focused mainly on flexibilisation measures (Lorente Campos, Pitxer, & Sánchez, 2013; Lorente Campos, & Guamán Hernández, 2018) rather than on modernising industry or creating space for more productivity and added value in the digital economy. As a result of a major structural reform that does contribute to economic development with the creation of value, a real reduction in technological gaps and integration with digital production methods, on the one hand, the COVID-19 pandemic has left many Spanish workers unemployed and facing structural imbalances and precariousness, on the other. However, the pandemic lockdowns are an additional factor that may help to identify some of the structural imbalances that have again exacerbated the short- and medium-term effects of a crisis. In analytical terms, the lockdown is an opportunity to determine both the actual availability of digital resources for workers, and other socioeconomic aspects, such as workers' digital skills and their areas of application as well as the possibility of digitising work in line with the dynamics of production in the Spanish economy. In other words, the force that shifted Spain towards digital work has reduced some of the socio-structural mismatches that workers experienced.

Empirical research on inequality is often grounded in class structure (Carabaña, 2021; Wright, 1978, 2000, 2009, 2019). The present study analyses the effects of the "forced" introduction of teleworking during the pandemic and its differential causality within the social structure. However, the analysis of social class, one of the most important issues in sociology as a field of knowledge, is constantly being revised in order to capture the transformations imposed by the dynamics of social change. In a generalised way, sociology focuses on explaining the system of social class and status that encompasses the widest range of positions consistent with the social structure. Defining a system that represents social positions and the distribution of individuals within such a system is essential to the analysis of inequality, social mobility and other structural dynamics resulting from social conflict.

Thus, from the 1970s until today, the theoretical framework for the analysis of social structure has revolved around a fluid definition of social class. The conception of social class and social status that is common today goes beyond the typical rigid classification of the Fordist period, when social status was objectified through the possession or non-possession of productive assets or occupations the individual performed. Today, the analysis is more oriented towards a reflexive understanding – the individual can construct his or her own social class identity by comparing his or her position with others in a social context. At the same time, the analysis emphasises participation in the cultural dynamics that contribute to the emergence of social class and status identities such as insecure, poor, working class, etc. and their merging in a differentiated social space. The expansion of the global economy and the growth of international divisions give greater prominence to this definition of social class, which better matches the growing complexity of digital and global work.

The questionnaire for the 3,316 survey includes a question about self-perceived status, which respondents answered spontaneously. We will study this independent variable as subjective social status, but that does not mean that social status cannot be calculated using objective variables such as occupation, resulting in a five-category classification according to the scheme proposed by Erikson, Goldthorpe, Portocarero (EGP), and Krokstad, Ringdal and Westin (2002), which is more useful for analysing social structures of the Fordist period. In our case, subjective social status will be used to capture reflexive dynamics as well as occupation, but not reclassified according to the EGP schema.

The aim of this chapter is therefore to conduct an empirical analysis of the challenges and opportunities for Spanish digital workers based on the CIS survey. The variables included in the survey make it possible to check the workers' point of view on the digital reality imposed by the pandemic, where social segments do not have access to the same level of technology and the opportunities to create and maintain added value through the digital jobs are not the same for all social classes.

This study addresses three detailed objectives. First, trends in teleworking during lockdown will be analysed, as teleworking is spread in different ways and to varying degrees in the work structure. These dynamics point not only to technological mismatches in the base (pre-COVID) positions of workers in the organisation but also to other socio-structural inequalities that also condition the broader development and strategic role of the digitalisation of work at the global level. Second, employee opinions on the quality of teleworking will be clustered, as the level of technology and digital skills were also found to be heterogeneous within the workforce structure. Compared to other EU27 economies, there is an emphasis on moving beyond existing deviation of investment and the use of resources and technological competencies for activities that are not productive. This trend points to a mismatch between digital behaviours and digital work dynamics that affect digital demands in the labour market. Third, the study examines the relationship between prior digital habits across social classes and combined work-digital patterns resulting from lockdowns. For this analysis, the definition of subjective social status (SSS) (Diemer, Mistry, Wadsworth, López, & Reimers, 2013, p. 79) is used. Due to the analytical depth required to discuss this topic, this chapter does not include a systematic approach to socio-historical inequalities in Spanish industry. Nevertheless, some specific and recent socio-economic trends in this context will be briefly analysed.

Research methodology

The study focuses on an empirical analysis of the impact of the digital economy on flexible forms of employment exemplified by teleworking during the COVID-19 pandemic in Spain. The empirical approach was based on a survey[2] conducted by the CIS that is publicly available (CIS, 2021). The questionnaire covers employees' opinions about teleworking and its impact on four dimensions: companies, workers, family and society. In addition, employees were asked about teleworking, its introduction as a result of the pandemic, and other non-productive internet and digital resources uses related to leisure consumption and e-commerce. The study also measures the definition of subjective social status (SSS), as well as the positions of workers in the labour market structure. As noted above, SSS is usually measured by a person's perception of his or her social class, while traditional socio-economic status (SSE) takes into account other variables focused on resource control. As the number of items that were introduced to measure the impact of digital work and telework on people's lives is relatively large (92 questions in total), the dimensions were reduced through factor analysis, where each item was treated as a dummy variable to enable quantitative analysis (Yip & Tsang, 2007). Each of the four dimensions – companies, workers, society and family – is measured in terms of positive and negative impacts. This study examines only the effects of digital work on employees. The factors' scores will be analysed as dependent variables that can be predicted by social strata, digital background, occupations and education level. This analysis will provide insights into the order of importance of the independent variables in the predictive model. Based on this, the impact of prior experience in the digitised domestic environment and social class are used to identify digital gaps in the context of social structure.

Once the number of variables has been averaged, the multivariate analysis will include Chi-square automatic interaction detection (CHAID) to determine whether, on the one hand, the availability of an internet connection and, on the other hand, the necessary hardware equipment at home to perform remote tasks can predict perceptions of the quality of work during the lockdown. This analysis will contribute to the discussion on the mismatch in the use of technology and digital work. Finally, an automatic linear modelling analysis will be conducted to measure employees' perceived benefits of teleworking according to subjective social status, occupation, education and teleworking experience.

Research findings

Measuring the use of telework and trends in the digital economy during the COVID-19 pandemic in Spain

According to the CIS study, 46.3% of workers did telework during the lockdown in Spain. However, most of the workers who teleworked during the pandemic had been working from home before it. Depending on the position in the organisation, the ratio of new teleworkers ranges from 29.8% (Directors and CEOs) to 74.8% (other occupations: qualified farmers, craft workers and qualified operators) (Table 18.1).

One's digital work background is strongly dependent on the individual's occupation (Table 18.2). However, the rate of telework increased sharply during lockdown for every position on the labour market. Nevertheless, directors and CEOs experienced a smaller increase due to the higher rates of participation in telework tasks compared to the pre-pandemic period.

For the EU-27, Samek Lodovici et al. (2021, p. 26) highlight that in 2020 "… workers starting to work from home have been registered in those countries where teleworking was already well-developed before the pandemic (…), and in those that were most affected by the outbreak of the pandemic (…)". They also note that, in the EU-27 in 2020, the rate of "new" teleworkers reached 46% (of the total number of teleworkers), while in Spain in 2021 the figure rose to 55,2%, according to the CIS survey.

The tasks most frequently performed by teleworkers in Spain were administrative and technical support at work or participation in work meetings, including interaction through digital platforms (Table 18.3). In general, the higher the position in the organisation or the more technical the telework or digital work, the less the rate of teleworking increased during the lockdown. As did the findings in the analysis carried out by Samek Lodovici et al. (2021), these findings confirm that the high rate of digitalisation and teleworking in some jobs before the pandemic is associated with a broader use of teleworking in other jobs during the lockdowns.

Thus there is a concentration of digital tasks in terms of participating in work meetings and responding to customer and user inquiries that cover all non-administrative positions. For administrative workers, this type of task is the main focus of digitalisation, while in other professions greater digitisation

Table 18.1 Cross tabulation for occupation categories and teleworking prior to the COVID-19 pandemic

		Occupation						
		Professionals, scientists & intellectuals	*Professionals, scientists & intellectuals*	*Mid-level technicians*	*Support administrative staff*	*Workers of services & trade-salesman*	*Other occupations*	*Total*
Carrying out teleworking activities t before March 13, 2021	Yes, it was a regular or frequent way of working	37 30.6%	46 18.9%	42 19.0%	6 7.1%	10 20.4%	4 22.2%	145 19.7%
	Yes, it was an occasional way of working	48 39.7%	65 26.77%	53 24.0%	11 12.9%	12 24.5%	5 27.8%	194 26.3%
	No, I began to telework due to the pandemic	36 29.8%	132 54.3%	126 57.0%	68 80.0%	27 55.1%	9 50.0%	398 54.0%
Total		121 100.0%	243 100.0%	221 100.0%	85 100.0%	49 100.0%	18 100.0%	737 100.0

Source: the author's own research based on CIS (2021).
Carrying out teleworking activities before March 13, 2021.
[a] Occupation crosstabulation

Table 18.2 Chi Square value for the cross tabulation of occupation and teleworking before the COVID-19 pandemic

	Value	*df*	*Asymp. Sig(2-sided)*
Pearson Chi-Square	53,159[a]	10	,000
Likelihood ratio	55,805	10	,000
Linear-by-linear Association	**6,246**	1	,012
N of valid cases	737		

Source: the author's own research based on CIS (2021).
[a] Two cells (11,1%) have expected count less than 5. The minimum expected count is 3.54.

is observed more uniformly across all categories. As a result, the new "teleworkers force," which according to the CIS survey represented 55.2% of the total "pre-pandemic" teleworker workforce and 14.8% of the total workforce, was entirely devoted to performing any type of job duties from home. These data do not include those workers who teleworked regularly, frequently or occasionally did telework (Table 18.3).

A comparison of Tables 18.1 and 18.4 shows that the occupations that experienced a greater increase in teleworking during the pandemic are those that perceived less importance of the internet and ICTs after it. While these are occupations in work environments that are less vulnerable to digitalisation (qualified farmers, craft workers and qualified operators), the lockdowns meant actual teleworking experience for a large group of workers in these positions. Nonetheless, administrative workers, who are generally more exposed to digitalisation and remote working, are more suspicious of the post-lockdowns impact of the internet and ICTs than directors, CEOs, mid-level technicians and professionals, intellectuals and academics.

These results indicate that the propensity to telework is concentrated in higher positions in the organisational structure or in technical and professional jobs. Even if the type of task makes remote work more appropriate, the willingness to do it decreases in an organisation's operational core.

This analysis highlights a crucial dilemma De Benito-Canastedo brought to light (2017). It arises due to the low internet usage in the labour environment, while almost every company has an internet connection. In this regard, point to intergenerational digital subjectivity as a factor explaining the poor relevance of digital resources for older generations and the scarcity of mediators in the industry context who could increase digitisation-readiness by creating spaces of shared digital interests for workers of all ages.

Perceived quality of telework performance: the availability of digital technology

According to the CIS survey, more than 70% of teleworkers in Spain believe that teleworking has made it easier to maintain the quality of their work

Table 18.3 Cross-tabulation on teleworking tasks performed during the lockdown by occupation

		Occupation				
		Directors & CEO	*Professionals, scientists & intellectuals Column N %*	*Mid-level technicians Column N %*	*Support administrative staff Column N %*	*Workers of services & trade-salesman Column N %*
Respond queries from clients, users, patients or students by phone, email or web	Yes	94.5%	87.9%	83.2%	70.2%	88.5%
	No	5.5%	12.1%	16.8%	29.8%	11.5%
Perform administrative tasks, solve technical problems, carry' out studies or other usual procedures by accessing	Yes	96.2%	85.9%	95.2%	95.4%	53.5%
	No	3.8%	14.1%	4.8%	4.6%	16.2%
Interact through digital platforms with employer companies, suppliers, users, clients, etc.	Yes	89.5%	81.4%	82.7%	70,2%	85,6%
	No	10.5%	18.6%	17.3%	29.8%	14.4%
Participate in work meeting through digital platforms	YES	92.4%	95.8%	90.9%	72.0%	91.3%
	No	7.6%	4.2%	9.1%	28.0%	8.7%
Give classes or training activities	Yes	57.2%	66.6%	58.9%	36.8%	49.5%
	No	42.8%	33.4%	41.1%	63.2%	50.5%
Make organisational, coordination and management steps	Yes	88.3%	80.4%	72.6%	52.6%	71.0%
	No	11.7%	19.6%	27.4%	47.4%	29.0%

Source: the author's own research based on CIS (2021).

N = 3014; Sampling error = 0.05; Confidence Interval = 95.5%. For every combination of categories, Sigma < 0.05 for Chi Square test.

(see Table 18.4). However, it can be hypothesised that the general employee population, with the exception of directors and CEOs and a small share of other professionals, was not technologically prepared at the beginning of the pandemic to adapt to the teleworking requirements the lockdowns suddenly thrust upon them.

Table 18.4 Cross-tabulation of the importance of the internet and ICTs after the pandemic by occupation

		Occupation						
		Directors & CEOs	*Professionals, scientists & intellectual*	*Mid-level technicians*	*Support administrative staff*	*Workers of services & trade- salesman*	*Other occupations*	*Total*
Importance of the Internet and ICTs after the end of the pandemic	More important	122 64.6%	207 69.9%	233 66.0%	75 56.5%	98 49.7%	121 47.3%	856 60%
	Same importance	62 32.8%	82 27.7%	114 32.3%	55 41.7%	94 47.7%	125 48.8%	532 37%
	Less important	5 2.6%	7 2.4%	6 1.7%	2 1.5%	5 2.5%	10 3.9%	35 2.5%
Total		189 100.0%	296 100.0%	353 100.0%	132 100.0%	197 100.0%	256 100.0%	1423 100%

Source: the author's own research based on CIS (2021).
N = 3014; Sampling error = 0.05; Confidence Interval = 95.5%. For every combination of categories, Sigma < 0.05 for Chi Square test.

As a result, opinions about the extent to which job quality was maintained through teleworking may vary according to technical preparedness. To test this hypothesis, a hierarchical segmentation was used, with several predictors used to divide the population into groups according to a homogeneous opinion about perceived job quality. Two items measuring the level of technical preparedness were introduced as predictor variables: first, whether the respondent had had to purchase increased internet bandwidth since the COVID-19 pandemic had begun, and second, whether they had had to purchase a computer or computer equipment?

The algorithm CHAID (Chi-squared Automatic Interaction Detection) splits the sample into different groups when one of the predictor's categories collapses in a separated node a casuistry of categories of the dependent variable that is significantly different from the casuistry of other or others (Escobar Mercado, 1998, 2017; Ortiz, Rúa Vieites, & Bilbao Calabuig, 2017). In this study, this occurs when those who have purchased computers or computing equipment have a significantly different opinion about the quality of telework than those who have not had to buy any equipment.

As Figure 18.1 shows, the CHAID algorithm rejected the inclusion of the *hiring increased internet bandwidth* as a predictor of the level of job performance quality as *hiring or not of increased internet bandwidth* does not differentiate opinions with respect to the quality of job performance during lockdowns. However, the *purchase or lack of purchase of a computer or computer equipment* results in a varying casuistry of opinions with regard to the quality of job performance and duties.

According to Eurostat (2021), the level of household internet access in the EU-27 reached 91% in 2020, while in Spain it hit 95%. However, the figures invert when it comes to availability of computers in households: 83% of homes in the EU-27, and 78% in Spain.

The CIS survey confirms the general trend captured by Eurostat: the internet is used in Spain more for entertainment, commerce, household, banking, communication or training/teaching than it is in other countries in Europe.

Internet availability in Spain is almost fully covered. However, as Eurostat data show, Spanish households on average have less hardware equipment to effectively meet the telework or digital needs than do other countries of the EU-27. The CIS survey estimates that 23.7% of employees were forced to purchase computers or computer equipment to comply with digital work procedures during the COVID-19 pandemic.

Table 18.5 shows the distribution of investment in technology for teleworking during the lockdown. Between 19.6% (directors and CEOs) and 42.3% (professionals, researchers and intellectuals) of employees were asked to use their own equipment to telework during the pandemic. In addition, the majority of teleworkers did not receive any compensation for using the internet.

The companies were neither prepared nor willing to supplement or pay for the necessary computer equipment during the lockdown, forcing an average of 23.7% of teleworkers to purchase equipment for remote work. These

Node 0			
	Category	%	N
■	Agree	70,8	1824
■	Disagree	17,4	448
■	Doubts	11,8	303
	Total	100,0	2575

Have you acquired a computer or computer equipment since COVID-19 started?

Adj. P-value=0,041, Chi-square=8,601, df=2

No, <missing>

Node 1			
	Category	%	N
■	Agree	69,8	1370
■	Disagree	17,5	343
■	Doubts	12,8	251
	Total	76,3	1964

Yes

Node 2			
	Category	%	N
■	Agree	74,3	454
■	Disagree	17,4	105
■	Doubts	8,5	52
	Total	23,7	611

Figure 18.1 Segmentation tree for predicting opinions about the quality of job performance during teleworking enforced by the pandemic

Source: the author's own research based on CIS (2021).

trends are also confirmed by the general Eurostat data, pointing to superior internet coverage but poor technological capabilities. The CIS data analysis also reveals wider use of home and mobile internet access for entertainment, domestic duties, commerce than for remote work, which is much less developed due to the weak demand for digitalisation in industry, as well as the low willingness of companies to internalise the costs of technology.

The structural background of imbalance has been analysed as a cause of the current problems facing the Spanish economy. Industry is on the periphery or semi-periphery of the global division of labour, where the results of the digitalisation of the economy bring a lower level of value added. The current debate also points to these inequalities as an explanation for the comparative bias toward non-work uses of the internet.

However, recent research has highlighted an additional problem with technological gaps between generations, social classes and gender (Ovelar Beltrán, Benito Gómez, & Romo Uriarte, 2009; Rodicio-García, Ríos de Deus, Mosquera-González, & Penado Abilleira, 2020). In addition to the

Table 18.5 Share of employers and employees required to purchase technology during lockdowns

		Occupation					
		Directs & CEOs Column N%	*Professionals, scientists & intellectuals Column N%*	*Mid-level technicians Column N%*	*Support administrative staff Column N%*	*Workers of services & traded salesman Column N%*	*Other occupations Column N%*
Your employer had already equipped you. with a laptop prior to the pandemic	YES	65.3%	40.4%	46.0%	20.9%	57.1%	49.1%
	No	34.7%	59.6%	54.0%	79.1%	42.9%	50.9%
Your employer gave you a laptop that you did not have before the pandemic	YES	23.6%	22.4%	25.7%	36.6%	28.4%	23.4%
	NO	76.4%	77.6%	74.3%	63.4%	71.6%	76.6%
Your employer asked you to use your own computer until He/She provided you with a laptop	YES	16.9%	23.9%	24.5%	27.4%	24.5%	14.8%
	NO	83.1%	76.1%	75.5%	72.6%	75.5%	85.2%
Your employer asked you to use your own laptop during the confinement	YES	19.6%	42.3%	33.5%	38.6%	25.1%	39.9%
	NO	80.4%	57.7%	66.5%	61.4%	74.9%	60.1%
The cost of Internet connectivity was paid by you.	YES	89.8%	92.3%	88.8%	97.3%	95.5%	100.0%
	NO	10.2%	7.7%	11.2%	2.7%	4.5%	0.0%
You had to hire extra internet capacity and your employer compensated you for the cost	YES	3.8%	3.1%	2.3%	2.4%	0.0%	11.6%
	NO	96.2%	96.9%	97.7%	97.6%	100.0%	88.4%
Yom. employer organised technical support to implement telework effectively for employees	YES	68.6%	62.6%	67.9%	82.2%	57.4%	100.0%
	NO	31.4%	37.4%	32.1%	17.8%	42.6%	0.0%

Source: the author's own research based on CIS (2021).

more than likely link between historical imbalances and technological gaps, the latter are considered to be a socio-structural problem that decreases the ability to modernise and overcome economic crisis in a digitalised work environment and global world.

In Spain, public policies for the development of digital skills, especially for the promotion of training activities, were stepped up, not only as a result of the SARS-CoV-2 crisis, but also through several initiatives at national, regional and local levels. An example of this public policy is the implementation of a collaborative framework between the State Employment Service, the State Foundation for Employment Training and large technology companies to disseminate and access free digital competency training courses.

Most of these measures, carried out in a coordinated manner by labour market agents and the government, in addition to other measures that have been developed mainly for the labour reforms, such as the regulation of platform economies, are aimed at reducing the digital divide that has been identified between different social classes, genders and age groups. Those responsible for these efforts have recognised the digital gap as a major barrier to the labour market's complete modernisation, enshrining it as an exclusive goal of public policies for the development and implementation of digital culture.

However, from an academic and research perspective, it is apparent that, as with other labour market reforms that have been introduced since the late 1990s, the motivations underlying the introduction of public policies on digitisation generally and systematically ignore a set of specific imbalances in Spanish industry. In general, the documents announcing the benefits of public measures and policies directed at work and digital skills training are reduced to the very opportunity associated with the expansion of the digital economy for workers and industry. Correcting these imbalances has been presented as a prerequisite in the few studies that highlight its benefits in terms of return on investment, both at the individual and public administration levels. This research approach is rooted in the broad heritage of the social sciences, which have been particularly critical of the systematic omission from the public policy narrative of any reference to the internal and structural imbalances of the Spanish economy (Etxezarreta, 1991; Solá, 2014).

Subjective social status: traditional vs. new teleworkers

The CIS survey includes questions designed to measure the perceived impact of telework on various dimensions of life in the context of the lockdown legislation passed in response to COVID-19 pandemic. A positive or a negative opinion about telework can be determined by several factors. However, a mainly structuralist perspective should focus on the positions of workers in the social structure to explain the importance of telework as a social phenomenon and, in particular, as a type of social relations governing the dynamics of production, social and labour inclusion.

While factor analysis was conducted to reduce the positive and negative dimensions of teleworking in different areas of people's lives, the number of factors extracted is still too large. As a result, the focus is on the positive meanings that workers themselves attribute to teleworking as a social and productive relationship. Another factor to consider when choosing positive meanings is that they are more reliable. It is well known that answering negative scale items requires extra effort from respondents who "(...) have to reverse their thinking when saying that they agree or disagree (...)" (Hartley, 2014, p. 84).

To look at the positive meanings associated with telework from a structuralist perspective that reveal the pattern underlying the digital gaps, a set of "socio-structural" independent variables such as *subjective social status*, *occupation* and *education* were introduced. *Telework experience gained prior to the COVID-19 pandemic* was also included, as the socio-structural variables should influence both current and prior familiarity with teleworking. To proceed to the analysis aimed at addressing the gaps between social strata, Automatic Linear Modelling was conducted, which "(...) accelerates the data analysis process through several automatic mechanisms (...)" (Yung, 2013, p. 27), compared to traditional regression analysis, which involves procedures for categorical variables.

Predictably, only three of the six categories of the importance of telework are attributable to the positions that workers occupy in the social structure as subjective social status. Figure 18.2 shows the effects of independent variables on the importance of teleworking. For the upper classes, teleworking is an uncomfortable way to protect themselves from the COVID-19 pandemic, boosting productivity but not increasing autonomy or threatening jobs.

The middle and working classes believe that teleworking does not necessarily increase productivity but does threaten jobs by not protecting workers from infections. The working and poor classes are in between the upper and middle classes. They believe that teleworking increases autonomy, threatens jobs and boosts productivity. However, this stratum is far from considering telework an inconvenient inferential protection mechanism.

The experience of teleworking also has a significant impact on the perceived importance of increasing productivity. The middle and working classes do not believe that remote work increases productivity, while the upper classes and poor-working classes believe it does. Occupation also has a constant effect on perceived importance, and a particularly pronounced one as an inconvenient mechanism for maintaining safety during the COVID-19 pandemic. Mid-level technicians and other occupations (qualified farmers, craft workers and qualified operators) rejected this point of view, while directors, CEOs, professionals, academics, intellectuals, administrative supportive staff, service workers and sellers all agreed with it. The analysis clearly differentiates the three teleworking importance profiles according to position in the social structure, demonstrating that social strata exist as a set of "watertight compartments" with different internal logics regarding telework (Figure 18.2).

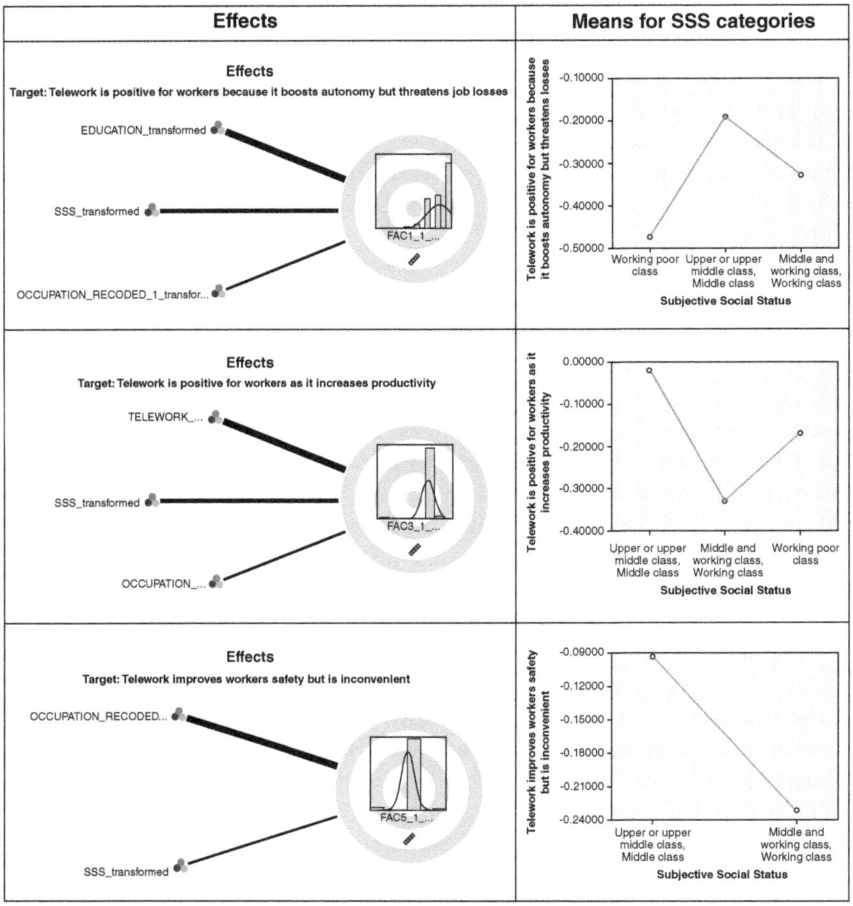

Figure 18.2 Effects of the independent variables on predictors of the importance of telework and the means of the factor corresponding to each SSS category

Source: the author's own research based on CIS (2021).

The perceived importance of telework as a social phenomenon is, like any other category, founded upon human beliefs and social knowledge. The Spanish labour market is a differentiated space where the relevance of work, professional success, welfare and labour relations are a productive field of symbols around job security. The middle classes as well as mid-level technicians make up the social stratum that is most likely to engage in teleworking. This stratum is also the most highly trained segment of the labour force with respect to labour market returns. Nonetheless, for this class, educational mismatch and even the *déclassement* – young people cannot achieve the same social status as their parents or get a return on their investment in education for social advancement – are typical and widely documented features of the Spanish labour market (Bogino Larrambebere, 2015, 2018, 2019).

Conclusions and practical implications

The Spanish labour market's historical instability and insecurity, analysed in this chapter in terms of Franco-era industrial imbalances, have contributed to the creation of a space of social conflict where any change is interpreted as a threat to any position in the labour market. The financial crisis of 2008 or the COVID-19 pandemic are not the only milestones that contributed to increased unemployment and precariousness. Since Spain's transition to democracy, more than 14 labour reforms have been introduced. Most of them were enacted during or after the economic crisis, implementing internal or external flexibility measures that led to precariousness and loss of labour rights. In order to avoid an increase in unemployment, the entire labour force, particularly the middle class with its wide range of occupations, have been continuously eroded due to the introduction and expansion of part-time and temporary contracts, without consolidating an alternative or general labour market environment that fully corresponds to welfare characteristics and development conditions.

Gaps in the industry have contributed to this scenario. As a result, the anxiety and fear observed among the middle class in the analysis must be understood in the context of a systematic process of erosion of working conditions, the lack of a political discourse aimed at the structural causes of unemployment, and working conditions becoming more precarious as a reflex action during periods of crises.

This study shows that perceptions of the quality of work during lockdowns was closely related to the scarcity of technological equipment, except for internet connectivity. Internet access in workplaces, despite its availability, is poor, which indicates a limited expansion of digital procedures for remote work. The perception of work quality during lockdowns increased significantly among employees who were forced to purchase a computer or computer accessories. This confirms that the pre-pandemic digital culture was limited. In addition, companies were not always willing to cover the costs of technological investments to provide employees with the proper environment to work remotely. The limited digital engagement of employers highlights the technological gaps that affect every labour market agent.

In general terms, the COVID-19 lockdowns forced employees, particularly those in administrative support positions, to work from home. This group of workers has a less positive view of the future importance of teleworking after the COVID-19 pandemic and highlights the non-digital work environments for a wide range of workers in core areas of business.

Beyond the COVID-19 pandemic, the development of telework is associated with several gaps, which stands it in contrast to the general trend in digitalised labour market. On the one hand, a wide range of workers perceive digitalisation and remote work environments as a threat due to the potential for job losses. The fear of job loss stems from a systematic political discourse pointing to regulatory rigidity as the cause of Spain's high unemployment rate. On the other hand, companies show little commitment to investing in workplace digitalisation. At the same time, the low level of digitalisation has more to do with poor usability rather than connectivity, which is offered by almost every company.

The CIS data has helped deepen the study of workplace digitalisation. However, the analytical framework for a better understanding of the causes should cover both local and internal industrial imbalances, as well as global trends like the international division of work.

Notes

1 The CIS numbers each of its studies for an identification: 3316 – Trend in the Digital Society During the COVID-19 Pandemic.

2 Probabilistic Sample: 3014 cases representing the Spanish population over 18 years of age, for a confidence level of 95.5% (two sigma) and P = Q, the real error is ± 1.8% for the whole sample, in the assumption of simple random sampling.

References

Belzunegui-Eraso, Á., & Erro-Garcés, A. (2020). Teleworking in the context of the Covid-19 crisis. *Sustainability, 12*(9), 1–18. doi:10.3390/su12093662

Bogino Larrambebere, V. (2015). La cuestión del desclasamiento social educativo. *Revista de la Asociación de Sociología de la Educación, 9*(1), 114–128.

Bogino-Larrambebere, V. (2018). La vivencia del desclasamiento. El caso de la cohorte de treintañeros con título superior en España. *Política y Sociedad, 55*(2), 491–512. doi:10.5209/POSO.58006

Bogino-Larrambebere, V. (2019). Los determinantes del desclasamiento social educativo. Un análisis sobre la cohorte de treintañeros con título superior en España. *Comunitania: International Journal of Social Work and Social Sciences, 17*(1), 9–33. doi:10.5944/comunitania.17.1.

Carabaña, J. (2021). Conmemorando a Erik Olin Wright. *RES, 2*(30), 1–5. doi:10.22325/fes/res.2021.40

CIS (2021). Data sheet. Available at: http://www.cis.es/cis/export/sites/default/-Archivos/Marginales/3300_3319/3316/Ft3316.pdf (accessed 16 August 2021).

De Benito-Castanedo, J. (2017). Bibliographic analysis of the digital divide and literacy in new technologies. *Revista electrónica Educare, 21*(2), 1–10. doi:10.15359/ree.21–2.9

Díaz-Mora, C., & García López, E. (2016). Explaining factors of transnational production networks in the EU: Core economies vs. eastern and southern peripheries. *Revista de economía mundial, 43*(1), 179–204.

Diemer, M., Mistry, R., Wadsworth, M., López, I., & Reimers, F. (2013). Best practices in conceptualizing and measuring social class in psychological research. *Analyses of Social Issues and Public Policy, 13*(1), 77–113. doi:10.1111/asap.12001

Escobar Mercado, M. (1998). Las aplicaciones del análisis de segmentación: El procedimiento Chaid. *EMPIRIA Revista de Metodología de las Ciencias Sociales, 1*(1), 13–49.

Escobar Mercado, M. (2017). *El análisis de segmentación: técnica y aplicaciones de los árboles de clasificación*. Madrid: CIS.

Etxezarreta, M. (1991). *La reestructuración del capitalismo en España: 1970–1990*. Barcelona: Icaria / Fuhem.

Eurostat (2021). *Database*. Available at: https://ec.europa.eu/eurostat/web/main/data/database (accessed 18 August 2021).

Fernández Cuesta, G., & Fernández Prieto, J.R. (1999). La distribución de la industria en España: pautas regionales y cambios recientes. *Ería, 49*(1), 129–158.

Gillespie, A., Richardson, R., & Cornford, J. (1995). *Review of teleworking in Britain: Implications for public policy. Report to the Par!iamentary Ofice of Science and Technology*. Newcastle: University of Newcastle Upon Tyne.

Gray, M., Hodson, N., & Gordon, G. (1993). *Teleworking explained*. Chichester: Wiley.

Hartley, J. (2014). Some thoughts on Likert-type scales. *International Journal of Clinical and Health Psychology, 14*(1), 83–86. doi:10.1016/S1697–2600(14)70040-7

Krokstad, S., Ringdal, K., & Westin, S. (2002). Classifying people by social class in population based health surveys: Two methods compared. *Norsk Epidemiologi, 12*(1), 19–25.

Lorente Campos, R., & Guamán Hernández, A. (2018). Expansión de la temporalidad y erosión de la relación de empleo estándar en España: ¿La irrupción de un nuevo paradigma de relación de empleo? *Cuadernos de Relaciones Laborales, 36*(1), 35–63. doi:10.5209/CRLA.59556

Lorente Campos, R., Pitxer, J.V., & Sánchez, A. (2013). Temporalidad y precariedad del trabajo asalariado: ¿el fin de la estabilidad laboral? In A. Guamán Hernández, & V. Corderi Gordillo (Eds), *Temporalida y precariedad del trabajo asalariado: ¿el fin de la estabilidad laboral?* (pp. 35–91). Albacete: Bomarzo.

Martínez Peinado, J. (2011). The theoretical structure core/periphery and the analysis of the global economic system : obsolete or necessary? *Revista de Economía Mundial, 29*, 27–57.

Martinez Peinado, J., & Cairó i Céspedes, G. (2014). The meaning of semiperiphery for global capitalism: Factor analysis testing. *Revista de Economía Mudial, 38*, 253–272.

Nadal, J. (1975). *El fracaso de la revolución industrial en España, 1814–1913*. Barcelona: Ariel.

Olsen, M. (1988). Organizational barriers to telework. In W. Korte, S. Robinson, & W. J. Steinle (Eds.), *Present situation and future development of a new form of work organization*. Amsterdam: North Holland, p. 253.

Ortiz, J. M., Rúa Vieites, A., & Bilbao Calabuig, P. (2017). Aplicaciones de los árboles de clasificación a la detección precoz de abandono en los estudios universitarios de administración y dirección de empresas. *Revista Electrónica de Comunicaciones y Trabajos de ASEPUMA, 18*, 177–201. doi:10.24309/recta.2017.18.2.05

Ovelar Beltrán, R., Benito Gómez, M., & Romo Uriarte, J. (2009). Nativos digitales y aprendizaje. Una aproximación a la evolución del concepto. *Revista de comunicación y nuevas tecnologías, 12*, 31–53.

Rodicio-García, M.L., Ríos de Deus, M.P., Mosquera-González, M.J., & Penado Abilleira, M. (2020). The digital divide in Spanish students in the face of the Covid-19 crisis. *Revista Internacional de Educación para la Justicia Social, 3e*(9), 103–125. doi:10.15366/riejs2020.9.3.006

Samek Lodovici, M., Ferrari, E., Paladino, E., Pesce, F., Frecassetti, P., Aram, E., & Hadjivassiliou, K. (2021). *The impact of teleworking and digital work on workers and society: Special focus on surveillance and monitoring, as well as on mental health of workers.* L-2929- Luxembourg: Policy Department for Economic, Scientific and Quality of Life Policies. EMPL committee. European Parliament. Available at: http://www.europarl.europa.eu/supporting-analyses (accessed 13 August 2021).

Wright, E.O. (1978). Race, class, and income inequality. *American Journal of Sociology, 83*(6), 1368–1397.

Wright, E.O. (2000). *Class counts. Comparative studies in class analysis.* Cambridge: Cambridge University Press.

Wright, E.O. (2009). Understanding class. Towards an integrated analytical approach. *New Left Review, 60,* 101–116.

Wright, E.O. (2019). *How to be an Anti-capitalist in the 21st Century.* London: Verso.

Yip, P.S., & Tsang, E.W. (2007). Interpreting dummy variables and their interaction effects in strategy research. *Strategic Organization, 5*(1), 13–30. doi:10.1177/1476127006073512

Yung, H. (2013). The case for being automatic: Introducing the automatic linear modeling (LINEAR) procedure in SPSS statistics. *General Linear Model Journal,* 27–37. Available at: http://www.glmj.org/archives/articles/Yang_v39n2.pdf (accessed 13 July 2021).

Index

Note: **Bold** page numbers refer to tables; *italic* page numbers refer to figures and page numbers followed by "n" denote endnotes.